North Dakota State University Libraries

GIFT FROM

Dr. John K. Cox
North Dakota State University
Department of History
2009

SOCIAL REVOLUTIONARIES AND SECRET AGENTS:

THE CARINTHIAN SLOVENE PARTISANS AND BRITAIN'S SPECIAL OPERATIONS EXECUTIVE

by

Thomas M. Barker

EAST EUROPEAN MONOGRAPHS, BOULDER
DISTRIBUTED BY COLUMBIA UNIVERSITY PRESS, NEW YORK

1990

EAST EUROPEAN MONOGRAPHS, NO. CCLXXVI

The publication of this work has been facilitated by a grant made by the State University of New York, Albany.

Copyright © 1990 by Thomas M. Barker
ISBN 0-88033-173-9
Library of Congress Card Catalog Number 89-81324

Printed in the United States of America

To my sister, Mary M. Barker-Duncan,
who thoroughly deserves to have this book dedicated to her.

Alfgar C.G. Hesketh-Prichard

Once a revolution has been unleashed on the premise that old injustices must be put right under a new social order, it acquires its own momentum and pays no need to the admonitions of moralists, historians, and political scientists. We stumbled from emergency to emergency, from chaos to chaos, from massacre to being massacred in a constantly ..... changing pattern..... One is the victim of unforeseen circumstances in which no quarter is expected or given, and lives of individual people are of absolutely secondary importance..... And it is an even more chilling thought that much of the cruelty was inspired by revolutionary idealism. We had sound ideological explanations for the brutality..... If one has a choice between evolution and revolution, one should choose evolution. But this choice is not always open to us.

Milovan Djilas, "Encounter"

This setting of respectable grouse-shooting City men and squires to the work of helping poachers led to strange confusion and many tears, and may seem a silly way of trying to win the war. In fact the silliness was only apparent. Its rationale, from SOE's point of view, was part of the whole idea. If you had to dabble in protest and upheaval – and how else were you going to promote resistance to established order? – then you had better get it done by persons who would limit the damage, and prefer, wherever possible, to help people like themselves.

Basil Davidson, *Special Operations Europe: Scenes from the Anti-Nazi War*

Contents

Preface and Acknowledgments xi

Part One: Carinthia's "Little War": What Happened and Why

Introduction 3
Chapter One. The Setting and Mechanisms of Nazi Rule 7
Chapter Two. 1942-1943: The Partisan Challenge 17
Chapter Three. 1944: The SOE as Protagonist 27
Chapter Four. The Last Winter: Blood on the Snow 43
Chapter Five. The Vernal Finale: Opera Buffa 55
Chapter Six. The Aftermath: A Legacy of Bitterness 67
Conclusions 77

Part Two: Documentary Appendixes

A. Memorandum on the Revolt in Slovenia,
   Peter Wilkinson 83
B. Report of Operations: Military Sub-Mission,
   Fourth Operational Zone, Jugoslav Army of
   National Liberation, 14 May to 7 December 1944
   Franklin A. Lindsay 118
C. Clowder Mission Records 141
D. Report on Slovenia, *Peter N.M. Moore* 146
E. Sub-Source's Impression of Partisan Activities
   in Slovenia [in German] 159
F. Memorandum: Slovene Claims to Carinthia, 1919–1945,
   William Deakin 164
G. Main 5 Corps Personal Directive of 6 May 1945,
   Charles F. Keightley 174

H. Number Six Special Force Staff Section (Clowder Mission) 178
   i. Notes on the Political Situation
      in Carinthia and Western Styria 178
   ii. Letter of Finlay Lockhead to
       Brigadier Anthony Cowgill 191
I. The Interrogation of Erwin Rösener 193
J. Conclusion and Security Implications,
   *Intelligence Branch, Ad. Hq. (Vienna),
   British Forces Austria, Army Div., Austria* 195
K. Report on Yugoslav Abductions 197

Notes 201

Supplementary Bibliography 231

Index 233

Illustrations

Maps

The Dismemberment of Yugoslavia, 1941
The Partition of Slovenia, 1941
The Deportation of Anti-Nazi Carinthian Slovenes, April 1942
Nazi Strongholds and Partisan Operational Sectors
   in Southeast Carinthia, Mid-1944
Sabotage Activity of the Eastern Carinthian Odred
The Pincers, Phase I
The Pincers, Phase II
The Advance of the Fifth Corps into Carinthia, 6-8 May 1945
The Military Situation in Carinthia, 15 May 1945
The Battle of Ferlach/Borvolje, Phase I
The Battle of Ferlach/Borovlje, Phase II
The SNLA's Invasion of Carinthia

Photographs

Frontispiece: Alfgar C.G. Hesketh-Prichard
Karel Prušnik-Gašper
Franc Pasterk-Lenart
Reich Labor Service Militiamen
Jelka With Her Own Four and Two Foster Children
The Staff of the Fifth Courier Relay Sector
Charles Villiers and Peter Wilkinson
Sgt-Major Hughes and Hesketh-Prichard Hitch a Ride
Hesketh-Prichard Gets a Partisan Haircut
Partisans During Skirmish with SS Police
Wilkinson's Party Crosses the Reich Border
Anton Okrogar-Nestl
Hesketh-Prichard and the Saualpe Partisans

Preface and Acknowledgments

The writer's interest in the Carinthian Slovenes goes back to the early spring of 1952 when, as a Fullbright exchange student in Austria, he was giving talks about life in the United States to secondary school pupils, among whom was an auditorium-full of apprentice, Slovene-speaking gunsmiths in Ferlach/Borovlje, "Windische", as he was told by his Germanophone local hosts. His interest in the partisans as such derives not only from intellectual dissatisfaction with an earlier account of their actions but from a trip to the hunting preserve of the Carinthian Slovene-owned cellulose factory of Miklauzhof/Miklavčevo near Eisenkappel/Železna Kapla in August 1986. His guide, Ing. Peter Kuchar – born on the same day in 1929, son of a partisan heroine ("Jelka"), and a quondam underage volunteer himself (like the author's American Civil War great grandfather) – had him clamber up a fifty foot high tree stand and arranged for a prime roebuck to saunter into the crosshairs of his 7mm Sauer-Weatherby. It was thus clear that fresh research could no longer be delayed.

A further factor in the genesis of this book was the quick realization, after a bit of work done in England pursuing a hunch, that a major part of the story had been repressed for three and a half decades and was only beginning to emerge. The fixation of British governmental circles upon secrecy even when security considerations no longer apply – fear of embarassing or, if they are dead, besmirching the memory of bureaucratic and political predecessors, seems to be a major factor – has now achieved world-wide notoriety. The fatuous machinations of the authoritarian-minded Thatcher government in the Peter Wright or Spycatcher affair, intended to cover up the story of an MI5 out of control during Harold Wilson's prime ministership, coincided with the author's research in the United Kingdom. The pending Official Secrets Act – following upon the damage done to British higher education in the name of managerial-financial efficiency – will result in yet further inhibition of the free flow of information so necessary to the workings of a democratic society.

In the present instance, this obsession, a bit difficult for North Americans to fathom, has resulted in the sequestration and/or destruction of historiographically crucial SOE records. (In contrast, one can rummage at will among the records of the OSS). However, enough evidence has survived in the Public Record Office – the vetting was erratic – or can be gleaned from published memoirs and the witness of participants to provide a fairly clear picture of Britain's role in Slovenia and Carinthia during the latter years of World War Two.

While the Slovene partisans had good reasons of their own for saying little about British "liaison officers" after 1945, some of the material in the following pages is likely to be a revelation for them and their conationals. Inter alia, the subject of the postwar massacres of their prisoners, if no longer entirely tabu, remains highly sensitive as it does for German Carinthians and certain, incorrigibly doctrinaire, anti-Communist Slovene émigrés and those who share their views. In all events, the writer has tried his best, despite a deep revulsion for Naziism and a natural sympathy for Carinthia's Slovenes, too long the victims of ethnic intolerance and discrimination, to render balanced judgments.

A word or two about the phrase "White Guard" (*Bela Garda*) also seems in order. The ex-collaborationists, their descendants, and sympathizers find it objectionable because of its Communist origin and derogatory connotations. Nevertheless, it is well rooted historically as an internationally accepted designation for the mish-mash of armed Slovene quislings who were active prior to Italy's surrender in September of 1943. (The latter label also infuriates people who found Fascism and Naziism less odious than Marxism and became, wittingly or unwittingly, Hitler's tools; as Vidkun Quisling did, they will vigorously deny that their commerce with evil was a betrayal of nationality and will insist that their stance was ineluctable under the given historical circumstances.) After Italy's defeat the White Guard was reconstituted as the *Slovensko domobranstvo*, but both the partisans and the Allies continued to use the old name until the end of the war. (See also note 162.)

Another terminological dilemma is the appellation "Nazi". The term is employed in its World War Two context of the German enemy as a whole as well as in the specific sense of the National Socialist German Workers Party (NSDAP). The label "Austria" is no less tricky. The country did not exist legally during the period 1938-1945 (although some nitpicking jurisconsults would dispute this) nor in the minds of a large proportion, probably a majority, of its inhabitants. On the other hand, from 1943 onward the Allies made clear their intention of resurrecting it, and certain contemporary documents refer to it as a tangible reality. That is why it is sometimes set it off in quotes in the text.

The material reproduced in the Documentary Appendixes has been made to ressemble the stencilled and stamped originals as far as possible. Only obvious typing errors have been corrected. The author's glosses are indicated by brackets.

If Peter Kuchar was the unintending father of the idea, the volume itself could not have been written without the generous help of others. Naturally no blame for its failings should attach to them, and it should be emphasized that they will not necessarily agree with everything in it. In all events the author wishes to express cordial thanks to: Bengt Åhslund; Ivo Banac; Mary Barker-Duncan; Dušan Biber, who prevented many an error; Thomas Brimelow; Peter Brouček; Jonathan Chadwick; Anthony Cowgill; William Deakin; Zmago Drole, map-maker; Christopher Duffy; Cornelia and Michael Eckett; Gary Elliot, wordsmith and Adirondacks backwoodsman par excellence; Raymond Emmett, who has provided some useful insights about Britain's upper crust; Ernest Fantle; Tone Ferenc; Christopher Fix; Claudia Fräss-Ehrfeld; Richard Grosser, who insisted upon word-processing; France Hočevar; Don Hunt, gunsmith par excellence; Robert Knight, whose public forthrightness is based upon the most meticulous kind of scholarly research; Matjaž and Vladimir Klemenčič; Svantevita Kolar; Franklin A. Lindsay; Fitzroy Maclean; John Keegan; Patrick Martin-Smith; Metod Milač; Peter N.M. Moore; Andreas Moritsch; Géza Perjés; John Rucigay, a Slovene-descended B-24 copilot rescued by the partisans; William Schwarz, SUNY Albany Computer Center; Willie Shaw, intellectual foilsman; Alan Sked; Edward J. Slattery; Edi Šelhaus; Ferdinand Trauttmansdorff; Peter Urbanc; Mark Wheeler, who has played an indispensable intermediary role; Peter Wilkinson, pescator; and Gerry Zahavi, colleague and computer consultant.

Great Britain's Public Record Office (Kew) with its superb, computerized delivery system and its singularly efficient and good-natured staff, provides an archival working atmosphere that hardly can be equalled. Permission to reprint certain materials, copyright to which is held by the Crown, is hereby gratefully acknowledged. Pictures six to ten, taken by Peter Wilkinson, have been reproduced with the permission of the Imperial War Museum. The author is likewise endebted to the personnel of the British Library, the libraries of the London School of Economics and Political Science and of London University's School of Slavonic and East European Studies, the London University computer service as well as the Interlibrary Loan Service of the University at Albany, State University of New York (Gwen Deiber and Sally Stevenson) as well as the *Seminar slovenskega jezika, literature in kulture* at the University of Ljubljana (Darinka Počaj-Rus and Franc Zadravec).

PART ONE

Carinthia's "Little War": What Happened and Why

Introduction

There are two reasons why the story of the Carinthian Slovene partisans deserves closer attention.[1] First, armed resistance to Nazi tyranny – itself the culmination of a century of discrimination and oppression – has taken on great symbolic importance for Carinthia's vestigial national minority.[2] This is hardly surprising since, in the last analysis, heroes and martyrs are essential to every human community with a collective consciousness.[3] The second justification is the availability of fresh materials, both secondary and primary.

Three monographs deserve special mention: Josef Rausch's *Der Partisanenkampf in Kärnten* [4]; Franci Strle's *Veliki finale na Koroškem* [5]; and August Walzl's *Kärnten 1945: Vom NS Regime zur Besatzungsherrschaft*.[6] The first book exploits fragmentary, if substantial Nazi-era documentation as well as nearly all relevant Yugoslav publications and focuses upon a minute portrayal of combat operations. While it far supersedes earlier treatments of the subject, one can easily interpret it as implying – something which Rausch may not have intended consciously and is certainly contrary to his data – that the guerrilla campaign in Carinthia was an alien, Yugoslav phenomenon. Strle provides copious, meticulously annotated information, but the ideological slant of his work is unmistakable. Sponsored by the veterans' association of the Fourteenth Shock Division of the Slovene National Liberation Army or SNLA (*SNOV = Slovenska Narodna Osvobodilna Vojska*) and codedicated "to all those who fell in the endeavor to secure justice for the Carinthian Slovenes", it has a strong patriotic flavor, uses affective teminology, and fails to examine (or does so only in passing) certain still highly delicate and controversial issues. Walzl's compendious tome concentrates heavily upon the the day-to-day ebb and flow of events within the framework of his poorly demonstrated, albeit correct thesis that the change from Nazi rule to British military government left Carinthia's basic social and economic order unaltered. Despite inadequate exploitation (including erroneous citation) of British primary sources and consequent grave misjudgments, the study is a very useful supplement to Rausch and Strle, at least for most domestic Carinthian topics.[7]

Published memoirs stand out among the second category of materials. Two are of overriding importance. The first is the remarkable autobiography of Karel Prušnik-Gašper (1910-1980), *Gamsi na plazu* (*Chamois Atop the Avalanche*), which has appeared in two Slovene and two German editions.[8] While the author, like Strle, reminisces rather selectively – on the last page of his book he does obliquely concede that on occasion the heat of battle caused him and his comrades to behave questionably –, his engrossing narrative is essential. It is insdispensable both for facts and for understanding the social roots, nationalist orientation, political ideology, and genuinely autocthonous character of Carinthia's "little war". Also useful for such purposes, especially as regards the strength of will required to endure almost inconceivable hardships in the thickly forested Karawanken mountains not to mention torture and death in Klagenfurt's Gestapo dungeons, are the recollections of Helena Kuchar.[9] A veritable "Mother Courage" whose partisan pseudonym was "Jelka" ("The Fir Tree"), her narrative is especially noteworthy because of its female perspective. It serves to remind historians of the integral role of women in the guerrilla struggle, whether as gun-toting warriors, political activists, couriers ("legal" or "illegal"), intelligence agents, or victuallers. Since so many military-age Carinthian Slovene males – including Jelka's husband – had been drafted into the Wehrmacht, the involvement of the other sex was both necessary and inevitable. Surely Jelka and others like her merit the appellation of *partizanka*, of which the fray's survivors are so justly proud.[10]

As far as unpublished sources are concerned, it is still too early, because of the fifty year time lapse rule, to sift files freely in the Carinthian Provincial Archives. (Walzl, who frequently employs the ambiguous citation *nach amtlichen Quellen*, and a few other native researchers are apparently not subject to this restriction.) Nor can one be certain how much has survived the vicissitudes of time and local politics. However, Great Britain is another matter. A rich fund of papers, particularly the reports of Allied representatives, that embraces not merely Carinthia but all Slovene-inhabited territory during World War Two is easily accessible in London's Public Record office (Kew). No less fortunate is the fact that Sir Peter Wilkinson, K.C.M.G., the professional soldier responsible for supplying the Carinthian Slovene partisans at a point in time when such aid almost certainly insured the survival of armed opposition to the Nazis, has become an historical researcher since his retirement from public life. He brings unusual, even unique credentials to his new métier. Detached from the crack Royal Fusiliers already in March of 1938 for a special, supersecret kind of duty, he rose to the rank of lieutenant colonel and, once the war was over, pursued a diplomatic career, serving as Britain's ambassador to both South Vietnam (1966-7) and Austria (1970-71). Wilkinson's superiors, who first sent their man to Prague and then to Warsaw where he experienced the outbreak of hostilities, clearly made a wise choice. An associate later described him as having "a mental stance..... two or three moves ahead of most people with whom he had to deal". His first achievment-together with a brother officer, the pallid, sharp-eyed, restless, and supremely gifted "Alfgar" (Alfred) Cecil Giles Hesketh-Prichard, M.C.-was to furnish the Czech resistance with the new-fangled explosives utilized to do in the heinous Reinhard Heydrich. Next, as part of a wide-ranging plot to infiltrate agents into Hitler's *Ostmark*, he and his compatriot, a volunteer warrior whom the partisans came to know under the pseudonym of "Major Cahusac", betook themselves to Apulia in now Allied-controlled southern Italy. On 3 December 1943 they hitched an airplane ride with the subsequently famed Brigadier Sir Fitzroy Maclean, flying in a USAAF Dakota from Lecce to Bosnia's Glamočko polje and thence making their way to Tito's command post in nearby Jajce. Having charmed the half-Slovene Yugoslav leader into allowing him to pursue his clandestine venture on Yugoslav soil, Wilkinson set out forthwith accompanied by Hesketh-Prichard, a wireless operator (Company Sergeant Major George Hughes), and courier-guides. Slipping past enemy garrisons, he and his companions trudged or rode an ox-cart northwestward first to Croatian partisan headquarters in Otočac and then to its Slovene counterpart at Črmošnjice in the "liberated zone" of Dolenjsko or Lower Carniola (coincidentally the operational zone of the SNLA's Seventh Corps).

   The Slovene general staff (*glavni štab*) officers, like the Croatians, claimed that they were totally ignorant of conditions in Carinthia, but the Englishmen could go and see for themselves. Joined by an itinerant member of Maclean's entirely independent mission to Yugoslavia ("No. 37" or "Macmis"), the tiny party trekked on to Cerkno (Circhino) in the guerrilla-ruled part of Primorje-the then still theoretically Italian Littoral. The town was the headquarters of the Ninth Corps which allegedly handled all links with Austria. While Hesketh-Prichard stayed behind in order to set up a base camp, an attempt was made (7-9 February 1944) to cross the Julian Alps into German-annexed Bohinj (Wochein). When couriers who were supposed to escort him into the Karawanken failed to appear, the "exhilarated" Wilkinson decided that it was time to turn about. What was he doing, he asked himself, "mucking about in the snow?" London "knew nothing of all these things". The project needed to be consolidated on Allied soil. Agents would have to be briefed for the task at hand. It was crucial to return by the March moon.

Leaving Hesketh-Prichard behind in Istria (27 Febuary) after an initial, abortive attempt to get away in a submarine, Wilkinson hiked back to Drvar in Bosnia, immediately (March 24) recrossed the Adriatic in a "dolled-up", Soviet-owned Dakota, and wrote a preliminary report. Thereafter, operating mainly from Italy, he ran his own "private army". The enterprise, one of many cabals in the world-wide subversion program of the belatedly famous Special Operations Executive, went under the official code name of the "Clowder Mission", a term devised by Wilkinson and Hesketh-Prichard when they first conceived their scheme to penetrate "Austria" in early August of 1943. Sir Peter's generous and patient responses to investigators' queries, along with the PRO holdings, make it possible to throw much new light upon the subject of this volume.[11]

Although Rausch seems to overstress the Yugoslav Slovene role, both the circumstances of Wilkinson's odyssey and other data do make it quite clear that the relationship between the Slovene heartland and marginal territories was decisive. Nazi power in Carinthia would hardly have been threatened without the appearance in Slovenia proper of both the ultimately Communist-dominated Liberation Front or OF (*Osvobodilna Fronta*) – founded in Ljubljana on 27 April l941 by a congeries of eighteen political and quasi-political bodies in order to combat the Italo-German invaders – and its offshoot, the SNLA. However, there should be no misunderstanding about the military character of the latter organization. Unlike the Yugoslav National Liberation Army or YNLA (*NOV = Narodna Osvobodilna [Oslobodilačka] Vojska Jugoslavije*) or, as of 1 March 1945, *Jugoslovenska Armija*) which arose to fight the Axis forces farther south, it never evolved into a genuine, properly equipped regular host, disposing of a stable rear and capable of engaging in sustained frontal action. (Slovene partisan unit designations derive from a more theoretical than real integration with the YNLA.) Its title, professional-sounding order of battle, and auxilliary services notwithstanding, the SNLA and even more so its adjunct of strictly local, defensive forces, the Slovene Partisan Detachments or POS (*Partizanski Odredi Slovenije*), remained an agglomeration of *guerrilleros* until VE day. Wilkinson, reflecting the professional soldier's characteristically harsh attitude toward militiamen, recalls the more or less autonomously operating partisans he encountered in Primorje and Istria as having been interested mainly in "keeping alive", at least at that stage of the war. In any case, despite fierce disciplinary procedures – in the words of another British observer "the Red Queen has nothing on a Partisan judge" –, there is no question but that the SNLA was often unruly and prone to follow the irregular warrior's age-old practice of rapine.[12]

1
The Setting and Mechanisms of Nazi Rule

The physical realm in which the events recounted in this book occurred transcended the relatively new borders of the 1919-1941 and post-1945 eras, encompassing, as in Habsburg times, the Meža valley (Mießtal) and Jezersko (Seeland). Nazi Carinthia must also be thought, as a practical matter, to have included the adjoining salient of Slovene or Lower Styria (*Štajersko*) which was centered upon the Logar and upper Savinja (Solčava) valleys and belonged to the *Reichsgau Steiermark*. In all events, attempts to disassociate regions so similar in topography, marked by centuries of common historical experience, and possessed of analogous, ethnically intermingled social structures must be regarded as intellectually counterproductive (even if they strike a resonant cord in a still ultra-xenophobic Carinthia). Conversely, while Gorenjsko or Upper Carniola also belonged to the *Reichsgau Kärnten* – as there was a Greater Germany, so too, after April of 1941, was there a "Greater Carinthia" –, what took place in the northwestern Sava valley should probably be treated within the parameters of a study about Slovenia altogether. This seems advisable despite the fact that Gorenjsko constituted the platform for mounting resistance to the Nazis in a zone that lay directly north of the interwar frontier and was a segment of what may be called the polliwog tail of Slovenophone Carinthia.

Because of its military historical importance the latter territory should be demarcated more precisely. Beginning in Arnoldstein/Podklošter near the entrance to Italy's strategically crucial Canale valley, it stretched due east to the north-south line of the road leading from the Drau/Drava river near Ferlach/Borovlje to the Loibl/Ljubelj pass and, on occasion, to the longitudinal parallel formed by the highway running from the Drau through Eisenkappel/Železna Kapla to the Seeberg/Jezersko pass. At the same time it bears mentioning that some Slovene-speakers lived – and still live – as far west as Hermagor/Šmorje some forty kilometers up the Gail/Zila river, a southwestern tributary of the Drau. Indeed, Wilkinson hoped to sneak some of his people into the area with the help of Italian partisans – the leftist "Brigata Garibaldi" – operating in the Carnic Alps. However, nothing came of the ploy. The Gail valley remained a backwater until the waning days of the war when, quite suddenly, it acquired major strategic prominence.[13]

In commencing with Hitler's conquest of a Serbian-led Yugoslavia one must be careful not to overlook earlier indications, however exiguous, of a negative Carinthian Slovene reaction to Naziism, namely, the decision of a few youths – especially from the ethnically homogenous border commune of Zell/Sele – to vote against the Anschluß with their feet, cross the Karawanken boundary, and thereby also avoid service in the Wehrmacht. In the second half of 1941, under completely changed circumstances, some of them entered the ranks of the nascent partisan movement. Others, apparently the majority, returned to their native Carinthian bailiwicks. Lurking in the woods and feasting on venison, they became known after the war as the "Green Cadres" – it seems unlikely that any of them were hiding there earlier[14] – and managed to hold out until they had a chance to associate themselves with guerrilla units being organized south of the old frontier. It may also be noted that a year earlier arms merchant Julius Hanau ("Caesar"), a British agent working from his Belgrade flat, had forged a sabotage network known as "TIGR" ("Trst, Istra, Gorica, Rijeka"). Individual Carinthian Slovenes and a few German Austrian leftists were part of it and succeeded in damaging rail lines in Styria and the Canale valley and in destroying a bridge near Villach/Beljak before they were found out and crushed by the Gestapo.[15]

To be sure, the initial Carinthian Slovene response to the Nazi takeover, like that of certain other, frightened, former Austrian citizens, was to dissimulate and feign cooperation, there being no other recourse for most of them. Although the minority's few existing rights were gradually abrogated, it sought to make the best of things even after Yugoslavia's downfall and the imposition of ever harsher measures. The turning point came on 14-15 April 1942 when 178 Slovene families were torn from their homes and later packed off to work camps in the Old Reich – a complex episode that is closely tied to the expulsion of perhaps 55,000 Slovenes from Upper Carniola and Lower Styria and cannot even be adumbrated here.

For present purposes, the euphemistically labeled *Aussiedlung* (*izselitev*) – another hundred odd families were uprooted later, some for having supported the partisans – can be said to have had a dual effect. On the one hand, although this was not the Nazis' primary objective (if at all), the action deprived the only incipient partisan movement of what would have been useful logistical and manpower resources. The vacant farms were handed over to ethnic Germans from the Canale valley and the South Tyrol; sold down the river by Hitler, they would soon have cause to regret having accepted their comparatively meager reparation. The opposite side of the coin was the indignation aroused among the somewhat impassive, clerically-oriented and led Slovenes, not to mention merely linguistic Slovenes and even some German Carinthians. Persecution created a psychological climate propitious over the long run to the incitement of political and military resistance.

The social matrix of the ensuing partisan warfare may be described next. The later immensely influential ideas of Mao Tse-Tung were as yet only slightly known in the West.[17] Nevertheless, the Yugoslav Communist leadership understood perfectly – not from imbibing the Chinese leader's doctrine but (probably) because so many of its members had had a previous experience of insurgency in Spain – the cardinal principle that guerrillas should be like fish in the water. A successful national liberation struggle demands strong political commitment based upon an awareness of social injustice. Thus one may well ask, what kind of people were the Carinthian Slovenes who were destined to become the object of urban, Yugoslav Slovene, revolutionary intellectuals' attention? Prušnik-Gašper's and Jelka's memoirs leave little doubt about the basically rural-proletarian character of the persons who formed the obdurate core of the local OF and partisan units. They were hard-scrabble, often self-taught mountain peasants, impoverished cottagers, petty horticulturists, beekeepers, seamstresses, housemaids, lumberjacks, herdsmen, and ill-paid employees of the few regional industrial enterprises based upon forest and mineral resources (especially in the Meža valley). Many, probably most, were victims of the economic dislocations of the first Austrian republic and the Great Depression, although standards of life had improved a bit as a result of the Nazi government's heavy capital investment just after the Anschluß.[18]

Prušnik-Gašper's choice of words, the cry "we fight for our time-honored rights" (*za staro pravdo*), is a clear echo of primeval boorish protest against seignorial exploitation. The spite this self-converted, pre-1938 Austrian Communist activist felt for the clerical-fascist counts of Thurn-Valsassina-Como-Vercelli, the traditional lords of Eisenkappel (in American parlance a "company town") who still inhabit the neighboring castle and wartime Nazi bulwark of Hagenegg, was exceeded only by his visceral hatred for the comital game wardens. Regarded by poor Slovenes as as kept servants of the ruling class and sometimes as ethnic renegades (*nemčurji* or "German-lovers") as well, they seem, on occasion, to have shot first and asked questions later in their relentless battle against real or presumed interlopers, illicit berry and mushroom pickers. Surely, the competition over the region's abundant synergetic resources was a bitter one. Hunting easily becomes an obsession, and men who have little or no opportunity to indulge their passion nurse a profound grievance, far worse than the normal envy of successful fellow nimrods. In any case, the Slovene partisans later had the satisfaction of returning the fire and of killing or indeed executing *Aufsichtsjäger* who had meanwhile become Gestapo toadies. Moreover, the guerrillas now often subsisted from game – occasionally in the form of jerky – theoretically reserved for the Thurns and other German masters.[19]

However, this intense hostility was not merely a manifestation of outrage over gross material inequality and deprivation. Many hill country Slovenes, people who had experienced little or no upward social mobility and were untouched by the process of embourgeoisement that could turn linguistic brothers or even blood kin into Nazis, somehow linked their grinding poverty, in a dynamic sociopsychological process, with their maternal speech and cultural heritage, with their folklore, song, and dance. The perception of belonging to an underclass and acute resentment of the denigration of their ethnic character – the still used Carinthian German sneer word for them is *Tschusch'n* – coalesced and created the preconditions, in the face of Nazi excesses and Communist agitprop, for resorting to a violent resolution of their predicament. Having heard little more than devotional homilies from their socially-blinkered, ecclesiastical champions – personally brave though the priests, an ersatz intelligentsia, were when push came to shove –, they were ripe for the materialist gospel of the OF's Marxist missionaries. Suppressing the temptation to belittle the Church in view of the positive response of a least some devout peasants and clerics, clandestine orators preached an alluring message of redemption. The Nazis would be overthrown, all Slovenes united into one state as part of a new, federative Yugoslavia, and social justice guaranteed, especially by expropriating "feudal" magnates like the Thurns or avaricious, parvenu capitalists such as the Leitgeb clan of Kühnsdorf/Sinča vas.[20]

Which of this cornucopia of objectives was most important to the Communist faithful who managed to establish their hegemony within the OF and the SNLA? Although human motivation is always an obscure and intricate phenomenon, it is likely that for some Party stalwarts, the paramount goals were not to unify the nation and wipe out the bourgeoisie. They sought rather to secure power and the perquisites of office for themselves (and would come in time to constitute Milovan Djilas's "new class"). Such, at any rate, was the considered opinion of a few perspicacious Allied liaison officers during the latter stage of the war. Slovene patriotism, however potent an historical factor, may well have been more a means than an end. In all events it served as an ace card in the Slovene heartland where the partisans carried on their fratricidal contest with archconservative Catholic elements organized militarily as the White Guard with the aid of the Italians and Germans.[21]

Quislings of this ilk could not be found among Carinthia's nationally conscious Slovene population. Whoever among the better situated had little use for Communism and hence was at least partly susceptible to incessant Nazi propaganda about the Marxist menace, held aloof (if he could), and bided his time, "caught between Scylla and Charybdis", as the author's Yugoslav Carinthian-born friend, Metod Milač, has so aptly put it. North of the Karawanken and from the peculiar vantage of a customarilly hard-pressed ethnic minority, the horrors of Naziism – Milač stresses that the Carinthian variety was the most repugnant of all – were tangible and the specter of Communism a little more remote. Roughly comparable conditions obtained in Lower Styria and Upper Carniola where, upon incorporation into the Greater German Reich, deportation and other forms of repression took on massive dimensions. Primorje, after several decades of denationalization efforts by its Italian rulers, was hardly inclined to collaborationism either. Only closer to Ljubljana, in Notranjsko and the Suha Krajina, was there widespread popular support for it: in this instance at any rate use of the term civil war is not inappropriate.

Carinthia's nationally-oriented Slovene-speakers were but a small fraction of the province's inhabitants. Their attitudes differed sharply from the rest of the population which may be considered next. The community as a whole – native German speakers plus the partly or fully assimilated Slovenophone element – continued to support the Nazi system or at least not to lift a finger against it even after the initial period of prosperity had passed and the strains of war were all too evident, indeed until it collapsed under the concerted assault of its external foes. Of the strength of German nationalism and National Socialism in Carinthia, the most loyal of the Führer's alpine fiefdoms, there can be no reasonable doubt. As Kurt von Schuschnig, who inherited his Slovene patronym from a Carinthian grandfather, is reputed to have remarked, "Put a barbed wire fence around it, and you will have built an internment camp for Nazis." Another of Carinthia's solid Nazi historical credentials is the fact that the city of Klagenfurt spawned, at least in a cultural and ideological sense, one of the principal artificers of the Holocaust. Contemporary Carinthians, understandably enough, prefer to forget Odilo Globocnik who, because he was thoroughly corrupt, was picked to set up the extermination camps in Poland, yet escaped justice by swallowing a cyanide pill just after his arrest by the British near Paternion in the upper Drau valley on 31 May 1945.

On the other hand, it would be incorrect and unjust to give the impression that no German Carinthians detested Hitler and his hatchetmen. Morally earnest Catholics, idealistic Socialists, and, above all, Germanophone Austrian Communists (the KPÖ) on occasion aided the partisans and paid a blood toll to the Gestapo. However, as was true of the *Ostmark* altogether, this opposition was in the last analysis weak and ineffective, and Prušnik-Gašper's frequent complaints seem justified, at least up to a point.[22] The fact of the matter is that, taken as a whole, German Carinthians and other "Austrians" did not "win their passage home", as Sir Charles Villiers ("Major Buxton"), another Wilkinson intimate and later chairman of British Steel, hoped they would and as they were expected to do according to the Moscow Declaration of 1 November 1943.[23] Although historians dare not overlook numerous individual instances of fortitude and martyrdom among the non-Nazi elites (as in the case of the German Resistance), one may say that relatively few Carinthians and "Austrians" were made of the same stern stuff as the nationally well-matured Danes and Norwegians, the SOE's chief success stories. Wilkinson conceded as much in reviewing the causes for the failure of the Clowder Mission.[24]

It is in this context that an essentially successful Nazi counterinsurgency effort must be viewed. Heinrich Himmler's repressive apparatus, with its characteristic linkage of party and civil offices, was firmly rooted in Carinthian soil. Its strength derived from the fervor of native Nazis and at the very least from the acquiescence of other German and bilingual Carinthians whose higher social status and unwillingness to become part of Yugoslavia made them deaf to the OF's political siren song. A purge of bureaucrats and school teachers not regarded as thoroughly committed to the New Order and their replacement, on a higher, albeit still intermediate level, with Reich Germans – much resented for their architypical *Bieffke* or Boche arrogance even by the local Nazis – made up for any potential *österreichische Schlamperei*.

While the nuances must be passed over in this study, it is necessary at least to outline the various armed formations at the beck and call of the Third Reich's trio of Alpine-Adriatic tetrarchs – two of whom were Carinthians. Although these forces could not eradicate the partisans or establish undisputed control of remote mountainous precincts, they unquestionably maintained both the tactical initiative and complete strategic supremacy in "Greater Carinthia", as well as in neighboring

Friulia, until early May of 1945. (The situation in the Littoral, Istria, and Carniola was not as clear-cut.)

At the start at any rate, the rural gendarmes, traditional tools of Europe's ruling strata for preserving their social control, bore the brunt of the struggle to to shield the Gau's economic infrastructure, communications, transportation facilities, and loyal population from partisan incursions. (However, there were occasional "live and let live" arrangements with the guerrillas, especially at the war's end.) One of the two main branches of the Orpo (*Ordnungspolizei*), the gendarmerie was seconded by the Schupo (*Schutzpolizei*) or municipal police as well as by town constables and a few, special paramilitary Orpo units. The Security Police or Sipo (*Sicherheitspolizei*), consisting of the Gestapo and the Kripo (*Kriminalpolizei*) and closely tied to the SD (*Sicherheitsdienst*), the NSDAP's intelligence arm, was a no less important element in the workings of totalitarian rule.

Thanks to its extensive web of casual stoolpigeons, regular informers, and artfully planted, sometimes Slovenophone "moles" – agents known as "G-men" (from *Gegner* or "enemies") –, the Germans remained excellently informed, even of the identities of individual partisans. The guerrillas had to be constantly on their guard against such decoys. Sent into the woods, the game wardens (who were especially dangerous), hired hands, herdsmen, self-proclaimed couriers and victuallers, not to mention bogus fellow irregulars, ran high risks and and faced immediate execution if unmasked. The partisans learned to rely on tried and true local inhabitants whenever they encountered suspiciously aimiable strangers. Nevertheless, the Nazi spies racked up one success after another virtually until the last day of the war.[25]

All such organs were satrapies within the gigantic police and military empire of the Reichsführer SS. Himmler's powerful, on-the-spot Carinthian henchman was the Westphalian-born, fanatically Nazi *Höhere SS und Polizeiführer* (HSSPF), Erwin Rösener. A gifted military leader but a sexually dissolute, perversely cruel killer who was characterized by his own wife as a modern-day *Landsknecht* and was executed in Ljubljana in 1946, he still represents for the Slovene nation the veritable incarnation of evil. As head of one of the larger SS administrative sectors (*Oberabschnitte*) – the region known as "Alpenland" which was coterminous with Defense Circuit (Wehrkreis) XVIII of the Wehrmacht's Replacement Army (*Ersatzheer*) – he exercised far reaching security coordinating and command functions in the quondam Austrian mountain provinces of Vorarlberg, Tyrol, Salzburg, Carinthia, and Styria (the latter two Gauen within their expanded, post-1941 borders). Upon Italy's surrender in September of 1943 he also assumed resposibility for central and southern Carniola, the defunct "Provincia di Lubiana". He concentrated his efforts there, working closely with the local quisling leaders, Ljubljana mayor Leon Rupnik (a former Imperial Austrian and Royal Yugoslav officer), and the city's bishop, Gregorij Rožman.[26]

Rösener's colleague in adjacent Friulia and Venezia Giulia – a British-employed, Italian-derived territorial concept embracing the provinces of Gorizia, Trieste, Istria (Pula), Canaro (Rijeka/Fiume), and Zadar (Zara) – was the Trieste-born Globocnik, of German stock despite his Slovene-sounding name. Having left Poland under a financial cloud in mid-1943, he set about exterminating captive partisans, anti-Fascist Italians, and the few remaining Jews he found in what the Nazis rechristened the "Adriatic Coastland" (*Adriatisches Küstenland*). His chief military task – in which he was assisted by the Wehrmacht, the ruthless ethnic German Karstwehr Brigade (*Karstjäger*), the reserve battalion of the Waffen SS Division "Prince Eugene", errant Serbian Chetniks, and Fascist militiamen – was to keep Slovene and Friulian guerrillas from joining forces, a not entirely real danger that also bothered certain Allied authorities, and government officials.

It may be noted that the employment of Rösener, Globocnik (who apparently indulged his associate's taste for Polish Jewesses), and other such omnipotent police commanders was a key feature of Nazi control of Europe altogether. In the immediate instance, moreover, a loose form of coordination was exercised by Globocnik's bosom friend, the native Carinthian *Gauleiter* and *Reichsstatthalter* Friedrich Rainer who also held the posts of civil administrator of Gorenjsko, Supreme Commissar of the Adriatic Coastland, and, at the war's end, Reich Defense Commissar for the vast territory stretching from the Piave to northern Dalmatia. Not as depraved as Rösener with whom he got on poorly and carried away by far-fetched, Imperial Austrian-flavored schemes for a postwar, multi-ethnic Alpine-Adriatic satellite domain that he tried to sell to Himmler, he too was extradited to Slovenia (1947), tried by a Yugoslav court-martial for war crimes, and hanged.

The most effective individual counterinsurgency tool at the disposal of HSSPF were the fearsome Police Regiments, militarily structured, highly mobile successors to the "barracks police" (*Landespolizei*) of the Weimar Republic. Normally led by Reich German police professionals but made up in part of non-German Nazi sympathisers and equipped with rifles, automatic weapons, mortars, light cannon, and armored vehicles, as many as thirty of them were scattered throughout the continent, although they tended to be concentrated in the rearward areas of the eastern front and in Yugoslavia. The dispatch of the Thirteenth SS Police Regiment from central Russia to the Klagenfurt basin in April of 1944 was a crucial factor in subsequent events. Led by Lieutenant Colonel Hans Fleckner (hanged along with Rainer), it soon proved its worth to the Nazi regime. Three brother regiments trained Rupnik's equally hard-bitten *domobranci* as the White Guard was known from late 1943 onward. The collaborationists resented their dependence upon the suddenly a bit more accomodating Germans, but they were given at least a modicum of autonomy and grew notably stronger in the last nine months of the war. Together with the SS hooligans and with occasional, albeit major help from the Wehrmacht, they were able to keep the SNLA at bay south of the Karawanken until the Nazis were forced to abandon Yugoslavia altogether.[27]

Among Rösener's and Rainer's other (strictly Carinthian) minions were the auxiliary policemen of the so-called *Freischar* and *Landwacht*. These were ununiformed, randomly armed older men, especially World War One veterans, who were supposed to perform various kinds of guard duty and intelligence-gathering. So were certain Nazi party organs, the SA and the General SS (especially in the Meža valley and on the Saualpe/Svinja). Considerably more useful than such superannuated troops – whom the partisans readily disarmed and often released – were the well-equipped, if largely untried, local contingents of the Replacement Army. They encompassed units such as the light mountain infantry (*Gebirgsjäger*) that were still in training or about to be sent to the front, plus border guards and second-line territorial riflemen (*Landesschützen*).[28]

The Nazi leaders also disposed of various odds and ends. They included bits and pieces of the Waffen SS such as the Klagenfurt cadet school (*Junkerschule*) and the Death's Head concentration camp guards whose assignment it was to "oversee" the moribund prisoners who were carving out a highway tunnel under the Loibl pass. Other miscellaneous armed bodies were customs patrolmen or border guards, factory security squads (*Werkschutz*) as well as the teenagers of the National Labor Service (*Reichsarbeitsdienst*) and the Hitler Youth. On one occasion at least a large troop of home guardsmen from Nazi "Greater Styria", *Wehrmänner* (*vermanšaft*) also apparently served in Carinthia. The role of the *Volkssturm* at the end of the war was evidently quite inconsequential.[29]

The dimensions of this variegated host are a matter of conjecture. However, with respect to the number of men who were young and good enough to have fought for Hitler elsewhere in Europe, the average probably approximated an understrength German field division, say some 10,000 soldiers. Although this may seem a negligible quantity in comparison with the overall magnitudes of World War Two, it was a respectable figure considering the relatively limited extent of the territory in question.

While the tactics of counterinsurgency will be treated further on, the static defenses erected in Carinthia may be more conveniently sketched here. They consisted of a well-conceived gridiron of strongholds, independent but interlocking barriers made up of concrete bunkers, pillboxes, minefields, barbed wire enclosures, and reinforced buildings. The American reader, accustomed to think in terms of wooden housing, should bear in mind the immemorial character of southeastern European architecture with its emphasis upon thick walls made of hard, largely noncombustible materials, timber being used mainly in outlying rural settings. Additional protection was afforded by warning devices, both optical and auditory. Thus it proved possible, if not to split up and hermetically seal off individual partisan groups, at least to greatly obstruct their movement. This scheme proved particularly effective along the banks of the Drau, serving to protect not only the huge hydroelectric works already in operation or still under construction but also to gravely hinder – though not to prevent – the partisan movement's extension into the center of the Klagenfurt basin.[30]

2

1942-1943: The Partisan Challenge

The Nazi bosses reached into their grab-bag of military resources piecemeal as OF activity increased and guerrilla strikes became more frequent. In late 1941 the Cankar Battalion (later a brigade) stationed in Gorenjsko sent a few patrols north of the old frontier. However, apart from causing the Nazis to recognize the existence of a security problem and to tighten their watch a bit, the situation remained stable for almost a year. The first of what were to be as many as 600 shootouts and firefights occurred only on 25 August 1942 when the First or Kranjc Battalion of the so-called "Second Styrian Group" of *Odredi*" was passing through Carinthia from Upper Carniola in order to rendezvous with fellow units. Ambushed by a small SS party, apparently a hunt-and-kill commando (*Jagdkommando*) of cadets from the Klagenfurt school, near the village of Robesch/Robež, two kilometers south of the Drau beneath the Little Obir, the partisans quickly riposted, slaying a half dozen or so of their adversaries, reportedly Dutchmen, at a cost of several Slovene dead. Though the guerrillas had no choice but to resume their march toward safer elevated terrain, news of their diminutive victory spread like wildfire, raising the dashed hopes of the many Carinthian Slovenes who were suffering a form of collective trauma because of the recent deportations of their co-nationals.[31]

While the Robesch skirmish was the first between organized formations in pre-1938 Carinthia, it did not signify the beginning of Yugoslav Slovene-directed opposition to Nazi tyranny per se. The scuffle had been preceded by a modest amount of still rather disjointed OF political mobilization. The fact that this work was not fully coordinated is due, in part at least, to a circumstance that bore heavily upon the future course of events. The Slovene resistance, both military and political, fell into two, at best only tenuously linked, occasionally overlapping sectors of the northern Karawanken and its piedmont. One–to use Prušnik-Gašper's endearing expression–was the "Wild West" (*divji zapad*), the merely seven to fifteen kilometer wide strip of territory heretofore delimited. The other, much deeper (at least 35 kilometers) eastern belt stretched, on a north-south axis, from the edge of the Jauntal/Podjuna well into the Meža valley and the northwestern salient of Slovene Styria.

As far as the Wild West was concerned, the Carniolans and their Carinthian Slovene comrades had plans as early as the spring of 1942 to create a full-fledged SNLA *odred* or "detachment". This was a peculiarly Yugoslav partisan unit of up to 1000 men but often much smaller, indeed as few as a 150 guerrillas, especially in Carinthia. Wilkinson described it as having, if by no means a totally passive, at least a geographically more or less static role in contrast to the larger, offensively oriented "shock brigade" (*udarna brigada*).[32] Be that as it may, the time was not yet ripe in "western" Carinthia for so ambitious a project. The political groundwork had to be laid first. This task fell to Matija Verdnik-Tomaž who slipped into the Rosental/Rož in September of 1942.[33]

Building upon the indignation over the *Aussiedlung* and the encouraging example of Robesch, Verdnik-Tomaž ultimately managed to recruit a dozen or so local Slovenes in the region from which his own parents stemmed. Backed by a company of the Upper Carniolan *Odred*, he thereupon instigated a spectacular assault upon Feistritz im Rosental/Bistrica na Rožu on 17-18 May 1943. After blowing up the power plant of the Jungfer generator factory–a small, if important cog in the machinery of Greater Germany's war effort–the Carniolans departed. News of the action was duly reported by the BBC. The so-called "Carinthian Platoon", joined by some fugitive Soviet POW's from Villach, became a company in its own right. Pushed hard by the now thoroughly alarmed Nazis, it suffered heavy losses and had to pull back to Gorenjsko where it was wiped out. Rainer appealed for reinforcements from elsewhere in the Reich but had to content himself with trying to stop furloughed Carinthian Slovene soldiers from going over to the partisans. In all events Verdnik-Tomaž's initial success had a positive effect upon his political endeavors. By the end of 1943 he had organized a network of 20 OF committees south of the Drau, even if contacts with the KPÖ came to nought after the Gestapo uncovered and smashed its cells.[34]

The military withdrawal from the Wild West proved only temporary. The situation changed for the better as the result of a stroke of luck south of the Karawanken, namely, Italy's withdrawal from the Axis. The SNLA, showing very quick reflexes and great skill in negotiating with its erstwhile foes, appropriated the equipment and weapons of six of the fourteen divisions stationed on Yugoslav soil, indeed even enlisted some Italian technical personnel.35 For a short while at any rate the partisans operating in the "Provincia di Lubiana" as well as in Istria and Primorje were flush with resources. Thus a nucleus of sorts for what would be called the Western Carinthian *Odred* was established in the liberated zone of Cerkno on 13 October. The far-fetched plan of the Slovene general staff (which probably seemed feasible in light of the partisans' momentary strength) was to strike at the communications hub of Carinthia. It was thought that an attack there, as well as similar actions in the northern part of Lower Styria, might help to relieve the pressure brought to bear by the Germans and collaborationists who had more or less promptly filled the vacuum created by Italy's collapse and had gone over to the offensive.

The scheme was purportedly encouraged by the Cairo SOE's man in Slovenia, the brave but gullible, tactless, and intolerably prolix Major William Jones who had preceded Maclean and Wilkinson. Having arrived on the night of 18-19 May, Jones was in fact the first British officer to reach northwestern Jugoslavia. Obviously accustomed to throwing his weight around unchecked, he came under Maclean's command by late 1943 but was not destined to keep his post beyond the next summer. He was in fact removed – fetched, bearing a haversack full of ridiculous *pièces justificatives*, by one of his successors, Lieutenant Colonel Peter N.M. Moore (D.S.O., M.C., Royal Engineers) who found the experience "terrifying" – as the result of the personal intervention of the Clowder Mission's chief. "Colonel Wilkinson enveighed against the dispatch to Slovenia by G.H.Q. [of] officers such as Colonel Jones who made all sorts of promises which had never been fulfilled and who was completely ignorant of the Slav mentality and background" was the recorded comment of a Foreign Office man who interviewed the recently returned Wilkinson in London on 8 June 1944. A number of surviving radio mesages in the PRO to and from Jones, whose station with the Seventh Corps and SNLA headquarters in Crmošnjice was called "Flotsam", confirm the judgment of Wilkinson who had radioed Maclean that the SNLA considered Jones "mad but holy".36

Be this as it may, the grandiose strategical design (if such it was) proved quite impossible to realize. The mere seventy men sent over the Karawanken, hardly an *odred* in the pan-Yugoslav sense of the word, by January of 1944 concentrated upon propaganda work and desultory patrolling, killing no more than three Nazis. Wilkinson characterizes the contingent as "skeletal" and "notional", its largely adolescent members as having been "scared out of their wits". The commandant was the Rosental-born Franc Primožič-Marko (d. 1963). Villiers described him later in the year as a former Royal Yugoslav regular (a second lieutenant) from a mountain regiment who was a very efficient staff officer, well acquainted with "all the partisan ruses, overworked, and scurvy-ridden." The influential politcommissar of the would-be *odred* was Dušan Pirjevec-Ahac (d. 1977). Like Prušnik-Gašper, he wrote about his experiences just after the war without by any means telling all that he knew. Although its other activities had little more than nuisance value, the unit did book one major success: Verdnik-Tomaž and the Istrian captain, Jože Ulčar-Mirko, were spirited across the Drau into the Sattnitz/Gure hills where they set about organizing clandestine OF committees. Regional political unity was achieved and, if only with great difficulty, contact made with the eastern sector where events of greater consequence had been transpiring for well over a year.[37]

The story of the birth of what would ultimately become the *Vzhodnokoroški Odred* is intimately associated with the names of two former partisans of the adjacent Upper Carniolan "Kokra Detachment" and members of the Slovene Communist Party: the woodcutter, Ivan Županc-Johan (vulgo Žnidar Hanzi) from Ebriach/Obirsko (a village in a latitudinal hollow or *Graben* seven kilometers west of Eisenkappel); and the Carniolan intellectual, Stane Mrhar. Other protagonists, within a short time, were Jurij Pasterk and Prušnik-Gašper, both of them natives of Lobnik, a hamlet situated in another ravine just to the east of the aforementioned market town and cantonal seat. Scampering back and forth across the old border near the Seeberg pass from early June of 1942 onward, Županc found the Eisenkappel area virtually devoid of draft-age males. Moreover, the local "Green Cadre", whether for lack of leftist political motivation or because of the risk factor, was reluctant to fight. Although assisted by Mrhar, a well-trained operative, from September onward, Županc discovered that he also had to contend with the daunting prospect of a harsh winter.

Only a few Carinthian Slovenes – Wehrmacht soldiers on leave and youths about to be inducted – could be induced to swear the binding partisan oath. The only thing to do was to pass on the recruits to the *Kokrški Odred*. A group of fifty Polish and Ukrainian POW's, one of whom was in touch with the partisans, would not join up either. The fellow Slavs were told that, at the very least, they must stop felling logs for the *Švabi* (Germans). Županc and Mrhar had better luck, due probably to the recent partisan success at nearby Robesch, in a strictly organizational sense. A hodgepodge of 250 local Slovenes, including Prušnik-Gašper who was draft-exempt as a political undesirable, was formed into a network of OF cells.

The Lobnik firebrand's personal ideological evolution was a particularly important factor in this turn of events. By 1942 Prušnik-Gašper had clearly lost interest in the KPÖ, although he did not sever relations with individual Carinthian German Communists as evidenced by later clandestine meetings with partisan spokesmen. It is quite possible, even likely, that the Nazi-Soviet Pact of 1939 was the cause of his disillusionment. The emergence of a Yugoslav alternative must have seemed a godsend to the relatively small faction of left-wing, nationalist Carinthian Slovenes. In all events, the first fruit of the association with Slovene Communists was apparently the assassination of a much hated Thurn gamewarden.[38]

The beginning of guerrilla warfare per se – a few patrols of the Kokra Detachment had penetrated the area from time to time during the preceding months – may be linked to the appearance of another crafty Communist organizer, Pavle Žaučer-Matjaž, in late November. Having been appointed OF secretary of his native Meža valley and accompanied by a puny squad of warriors from the Savinja Valley *Odred*, the party emissary – whose nom de guerre derived from the local, Slovene version of the King Matthew Corvinus legend – made his way to the environs of Eisenkappel and met Prušnik-Gašper whose parents had been expelled in April. The two men got on famously, Žaučer-Matjaž serving, like Mrhar, as a kind of guru to his less enlightened fellow countryman. About to be arrested by the Gestapo which had started to break up the OF around Eisenkappel and in the more westerly township of Zell-Sele, Prušnik-Gašper entered the lists outright. The first achievment of the so-called "Carinthian Company" was to destroy the German outpost in Solčava in the Savinja valley just across the prewar frontier. This provided excellent publicity as far north as the Jauntal.[39]

The new unit consisted of some 13 men, smallholders, lumberjacks, and miners, mainly from the Meža valley, who were about to be drafted or forced to serve in the RAD. It was armed initially with hunting weapons – the Slovene gunsmiths of Ferlach did their surreptitious bit then and in ensuing months – and a few rusty Mannlicher assault rifles Prušnik-Gašper had stashed away in a rock crevice after the clerical-fascist repression of the Austrian Socialist Party and its militia in February of 1934. By early February of 1943 the neophyte partisans had settled down in cozy, artfully concealed log and earthen bunkers on the virtually inaccessible heights of the Petzen/Peca. However, the inclemency of the season notwithstanding, orders then arrived to press on to Eisenkappel and north toward the Drau, to agitate, kill Germans, and eliminate informers.[40]

These instructions may well have been, in part, a reaction to the Gestapo dragnet which had meanwhile proved very detrimental to the Slovene cause. Profiting from the confession of a captured Carniolan courier, from papers seized after a lethal skirmish with the Second

Battalion of the Kokra Detachment near the Loibl pass, from a chance opportunity to plant several moles as well as from the arrest of a second courier (the Carinthian Slovene Peter Blažič-Melchior) who was somehow made to sing, the Nazis rounded up 180 men and women, including some of the Poles and Ukrainians. Thirteen persons, almost exclusively proletarians, were tried, convicted, and guillotined in Vienna. Those executed included two members of the Županc family, Pasterk, and the OF's Polish collaborator, Alexander Lipinski. After the war they became known, a trifle inaccurately, as the "Victims of Zell". (The latter community had already demonstrated where its sympathies lay by warmly receiving the Kranjc Battalion just before the shootout at Robesch.)[41]

The Carinthian Company's actions were more or less limited to collecting still desperately needed firearms – Prušnik-Gašper later shot a German guard point-blank in the middle of Eisenkappel during a foray of this kind – and making political hay against a background of song and dance. However, time was also found to dispose of a petty Nazi and his visiting son-in-law, a Luftwaffe captain, near Miklauzhof. By mid-March, having garnered a few more recruits, the guerrillas thought it prudent to pull back to the high alpine meadows of the Olševa just inside Slovene Styria in the face of a drive by – allegedly – some 1300 police and (unspecified) SS troops. Indeed, this manner of operation – sending out fighting patrols and then hotfooting it back to the southern Karawanken slopes – would characterize warfare in the eastern sector altogether.[42]

Reinforced by a small contingent from the Kamnik *Odred*, the eastern Carinthian partisans were thereupon reorganized on Styria's Pohorje (Bachern-Gebirge) as a battalion by the commandant of the SNLA's Fourth Operational Zone, Franc Rozman-Stane. An old-time Communist, battle-tested officer-veteran of the Spanish Civil War (like so many representatives of the hard cadre of the partisan movement), he was yet another of Prušnik-Gašper's political mentors. The battalion's own new leader was Franc Pasterk-Lenart, a decorated survivor of the Wehrmacht's Norwegian campaign and a charismatic, still fondly remembered figure. Recruited in Ebriach by his recently martyred brother, Jurij, he and his men proceeded, on April 3, to storm the town of Mežica (Mieß).

Having been tipped off beforehand, the guerrillas were able to execute four hated, local Nazi bigwigs after a drumhead courtmartial in a movie hall and to snatch a rich stock of weapons. However, the enemy quickly recovered his wits and struck back. Pasterk-Lenart was mortally wounded. The inadvisability of operations in relatively open terrain could not have been clearer. In all events, stiffened by fresh recruits from the Meža valley, the battalion continued to dart about the pre-1941 frontier area, engaging in many lesser firefights and assassinating yet other picayune Nazis and, occasionally, innocuous persons as well. Sympathetic local Slovene teenagers acted as lookouts and messengers. Jelka and a number of other women supplied information and provender to supplement the meager and unbalanced fare of sylvan life.[43] The incursions continued into the summer of 1943. Particular attention was paid to cutting off the timber supply, the "green gold", of the Leitgebs' particle board factory in Kühnsdorf, one of the largest enterprises of its kind in Germany and an important element in the wartime economy. The woodcutters were once more sent packing, and the valley station of the cable car log transport system was dynamited. (At the war's end the three Leitgeb brothers, Valetin, Walter, and Siegfried, were abducted and, since they never returned, presumably butchered.) Patrols sent out by the congeries of Nazi security organs failed to entrap the normally evanescent partisans.[44]

The Carinthian Battalion kept up its political prosyletization efforts simultaneously. Prusnik-Gasper and Županc–whom the Nazis captured, mortally wounded, in October–were buttressed by experienced Communist tub-thumpers from Carniola and railed against German factory owners and latifundaries. Local OF committees were formed. In spite of the discouragement felt over the Viennese executions, a big gathering of activists, the "Pine Forest Conference", took place on May 12-13 beneath the Bela pec overlooking the Bistra valley in quondam Yugoslav Carinthia. The expropriations that would occur in the coming postwar millenium were among the topics discussed. This was a project that appealed even to otherwise conservative Catholic hill farmers who had seen their property alienated, either by unwilling sale before the war or by seizure after the *Aussiedlung*, as part of the process of capitalist concentration within the region's agrarian economy. "Ethnic traitors" (*izdajalci slovenskega naroda*), people not necessarily Nazis but considered to be *nemčurji*, were marked down for special consideration. Indeed, as already noted, "liquidations" or "justifications", had become part and parcel of the partisan struggle. The theoretical basis for such acts was an ad hoc decree of the Slovene National Liberation Committee (SNOO), but it is not clear whether the assassinations in Carinthia were carried out by the special Communist Party security organs (the VOS, OZNA, and VDV) that were employed in Slovenia proper.[45]

It appears that certain of the victims were chosen because they had played prominent roles in the *Abwehrkampf*, that is, the military and political battle against Yugoslav annexation of southern Carinthia at the end of the First World War, or had worked to undermine the interests of the Slovene ethnic minority in the interwar period as members of the German nationalist *Heimatdienst*.[46] A total of perhaps sixty men and women was dispatched on the basis of a presumptive "hit list", often in extremely brutal fashion. Yet other persons—the Leitgebs were only the most egregious example—would be kidnapped, whisked across the frontier, and done in just after the armistice. The memory of these killings, recently publicized for propagandistic purposes by contemporary anti-Slovene circles, still rankles subliminally after half a century.[47] The bitterness is not limited to the purely Germanophone and non-Slovene oriented bilingual population. Kinship ties and personal affinities, such the close bonds formed by hunting companions, may prove stronger than speech preferences and political loyalties.

Reading between the lines of both written and oral accounts—to the extent that people, affected by what is called in Carinthia "primeval anxiety" (*Urangst*), a subliminal fear of some future political calamity— are prepared to talk at all, one begins to suspect that some killings were the consequence of personal grudges and unwarranted denuniciations. Family feuds may also have been a factor: the surnames Piskernik and Einspieler crop up more than once. Evidence was probably not weighed very carefully. There were also drumhead, death-penalty courts-martial within partisan units, the memory of which continues to gall the kin of the deceased. Perhaps the best insight with regard to these matters has been provided in literary form, Valentin Polanšek's two-volume novel entitled *Bratovska jesen* ("Brotherly Autumn"). The author, who weaves in much factual material and judges the partisans harshly for their excesses, manifests a strong revulsion for civil strife and a sense of humanity totally absent in heavily slanted, self-righteous German nationalist treatments of the subject.[48]

It is impossible to tell which of two apparent elements—the cool, deliberate adoption of terrorist methods (as in the Slovene heartland) or the unleashing of primal urges such as the squaring of accounts with gamekeepers or other personal enemies—was a more important factor in the partisans' assassination campaign. However, its effect as a political tool is at best dubious.[48] With regard to the ethical issue to the extent that it may even be raised, all that one can say is that, late twentieth century ideological-psychopathic terrorism apart, the most repellant form of organized violence is probably guerrilla warfare. To be sure, in the case at hand as in so many others, it was the consequence of social injustice, prejudice, intolerance, persecution, and military aggression.

In July and August of 1943 several dozen Wehrmacht deserters from the Zell and Eisenkappel areas were incorporated into the Carinthian Battalion. Such recruits, whether or not they wished to avoid being sent to the Russian front, were welcome additions because of their military skills. Men like them had already demonstrated their worth at the time of the

Mežica raid. Other Slovenes took to the woods for fear of being arrested, justifiably or not, on suspicion of collaboration with the partisans. Adverse socio-economic conditions in the rapidly expanding industrial towns of the Meža valley, a small but quite useful arsenal of the Third Reich, also served as a fillip. Draft-age teenagers, slave-workers, and POW's continued to be recruited, indeed appear to have become an increasingly important source of manpower as the war drew to a close.[49]

By this time the unit counted 320 men, some of them still lacking guns. Then, as a consequence of Italy's capitulation, the majority of these troops were withdrawn to to Dolenjsko (Lower Carniola), the SNLA's main base. This move was to be repeated on several occasions and seems to suggest that the Slovene high command, which momentarilly had more arms than warriors, regarded Carinthia as a kind of sideshow, at least for the time-being. It proved necessary to build up, painfully, the strength of the minuscule party remaining on the wooded heights between Eisenkappel and the Meža valley. Gradually, however, a new battalion emerged under the aegis of the Fourth Operational Zone, and guerrilla fighting resumed. Despite ever tougher Nazi countermeasures–involving *Sippenhaftung* (collective family liability) and the establishment, in the interests of better coordination, of two *Einsatz* or joint operations zones –, late 1943 witnessed many more minor and a few major shootouts, the object of the 100 odd partisans being to seize the maximum number of weapons at minimal cost. Nazi uniforms were also highly appreciated, the partisans being a disparately garbed crew altogether, identifiable chiefly by the red star affixed to their forage caps. Their adversaries hit back in November. A combined force of Nazi party liegemen, police, and Replacement Army troops swept the Meža valley and the environs of Eisenkappel but to little avail.[50]

At the end of 1943 the Carinthian Battalion was forced once again to yield some of its men, especially to the Eleventh Shock Brigade, under the pretext that there was too much chumminess. However, the ninety remaining partisans, concentrated more often than not in the Meža valley, did sustain a modicum of activity. Among their feats was an assault upon the Gestapo post near the Thurns' castle with its 300 man strong garrison. Then, on 20 January 1944, the Slovene high command directed the Fourth Operational Zone to pay as much attention as possible to its Carinthian component. The men should press ahead on prewar Austrian soil, reach Klagenfurt if they could (clandestinely, one must assume), and maintain contact with the Wild West, to which a company should be sent as reinforcment. Patrols with concrete assignments should traverse the Drau, use the Saualpe/Svinja north of Völkermarkt/Velikovec as their *point d'appui*, and lay mines along southeast Carinthia's railways. The harshly-criticized Fourth Zone command replied that it had no spare company to send but would order an advance on Austro-Carinthian territory.51

3

1944: The SOE as Protagonist

The exchange of messages between Dolenjsko and Lower Styria raises the intriguing issue of the origins of the Slovene decision to carry guerrilla warfare into the heart of the Klagenfurt basin and the Clowder Mission's putative role in it. The question is all the more interesting because of timing: Wilkinson and Hesketh-Prichard had spent the first week of January in discussions with Politcommisar Boris Kraigher, President Josip Vidmar, and staff officers at SNLA headquarters in Črmošnjice. Wilkinson believes that his interlocutors had no independent scheme for fomenting disorder north of the Drau although it bears recalling that the unfortunate Jones had apparently drawn the Slovenes' attention to Carinthia as a strategically vital communications axis on his own. (The SOE representatives met Jones on the spot, which gave them the opportunity to form the unfavorable impressions that that turned out to be the final straw for his already vexed superiors.) In any case, just after Wilkinson and Hesketh-Prichard had pushed on to the Ninth Corps in Cerkno where they conferred at length with local intelligence officers and made more specific proposals for undercover penetration of Austria (February 4), the central partisan leadership proceeded to lay the groundwork for politico-military action in a peripheral region which up to then does not seem to have interested it unduly.[52]

Almost certainly, the SNLA's chief motivation was the prospect of an increase in the as yet rather modest amount of supplies the Western Allies were delivering in return for supporting Wilkinson's project or, as actually happened, providing only minimal assistance to the Clowder Mission. A subsidiary benefit was, presumably, to relieve pressure upon Carniola, where Rösener, the SS Police, and Rupnik's new quisling régime (which functioned in the technical sense only in the former "Provincia di

Lubiana") were becoming a force to be reckoned with.[53] (The Nazi counterinsurgency campaign was crucial to the transportation lifeline of Army Group Southeast and Army Group E [Greece] as well as for maintaining links with German units in Italy.) Moreover, it might be possible for the Carinthian Slovene partisans to ensconce themselves so firmly that they could serve as the fulcrum for a later SNLA territorial coup de main.

The goals of the SOE were quite different. The idea that emerged in the course of Wilkinson's "fishing expedition" was that the pack of ragtag guerrillas (as he viewed them) fighting on the other side of the Karawanken might serve as a vehicle for entering the Ostmark and establishing contact with indigenous "Austrian" resistance groups. It might thus be possible to stir up trouble for the Nazis father to the north, perhaps as far away as Czechoslovakia and Poland, countries in which Wilkinson and Hesketh-Prichard were likewise interested because of their previous background and expertise. (Wilkinson also wished to arrange for the provision of more general intelligence data to Allied Forces Headquarters [AFHQ].) It should be stressed, however, that the Clowder Mission was not chancing all its dice on one throw. It sought to use avenues other than the SNLA – such as the Italian partisan-controlled route via the Carnic Alps – for entering the southeastern *Gauen* of the Greater German Reich.

It is imperative to point out that Wilkinson had not even heard of the principal Austro-German underground organization, the still somewhat mysterious, Communist-manipulated *Österreichische Freiheitsfront*, which was active in the industrial region of German Styria (Judenburg, Knittelfeld, Leoben-Donawitz, Eisenerz, Bruck an der Mur, Kapfenberg) and had a sporadic, tenuous link with the Ninth Corps via Carinthian German Communists and the Western *Odred*, until he reached Črmošnjice. He not only doubted the ÖFF's potential for subversion but more or less presaged that it would turn out to be a "non-event". Still, it cost nothing to pay "lip-service" to the possibility. At the moment all that the Clowder Mission's boss wanted was a secure channel for British-trained, "Austrian" agents, a network of "safe-houses". He had no premeditated intention of facilitating "irredentism" although an "element" of support for Slovene territorial aims would be the unavoidable, indirect result of collaboration with the partisans. In any case, it was obvious that the probe into Austria could not be continued without the aforementioned quid pro quo: the SNLA was the "only means" at hand. The SOE would have to requisition stores from the Anglo-American military larder.

Wilkinson's agency, it should be observed, was considerably more adept than rival services at the fine art of effecting sorties. It was capable of "high-grade drops" into remote mountain valleys or, potentially, onto the high peaks inside Carinthia since, unlike Macmis, it disposed of specially trained pilots. Luckily, Churchill's protégé did not think that the people from Baker Street (SOE headquarters in Marylebone), for whom he normally had but little use, were infringing upon his turf. To be sure, Maclean had taken some four months to decide that the Clowder Mission should be allowed into Yugoslavia at all.[54] It is a fair guess that the personally gracious and tactful Wilkinson had just as good relations – again better than the SOE overall – with MI6 (SIS). This too was a happy circumstance, for the latter organization was likewise, gauchely, poking its nose into Slovene affairs.

All in all, the Clowder Mission's head was doubtlessly correct in concluding that he had no choice but to strike at least a tacit "deal" with the SNLA. Without its cooperation there would have been no chance at all of reaching "impossible" Austrian locales, at least via Yugoslavia. It is also worth remarking that local Soviet spokesmen, unhappy about the prospect of a Western power establishing a foothold in Austria ahead of Moscow, sought to dissuade their fellow Slavs from grasping Wilkinson's extended hand and implemented a strikingly similar plan – the nominally ÖFF associated *Kampfgruppe "Avantgarde" Steiermark* – six months later. The only problem – and the evident underlying reason for the Slovenes' fundamental duplicity in their relations with the SOE – was that the long-term objectives of the two partners were antithetical. Above all, the British government's insistence upon respect for the prewar frontiers with Slovenia's neighbors, at least until the conclusion of a peace conference, was destined to envenom relations between the partisans and the world power upon which they were to become ever more dependent materially during the final stage of the war.

Be this as it may, Carinthia's enhanced significance was reflected in the formal elevation of the eastern sector battalion into an *odred* on 5 February 1944. Though much stronger than its counterpart in the Wild West, it still counted only 173 men by late March and was, in Wilkinson'words, something of a "hybrid". It sought, as best it could, to apply the classical tactics of *Kleinkrieg*: lightning raids against outlying enemy posts, attacks upon carelessly exposed columns, severance of rail links, patrolling, and recruitment. The Meža valley, from which the unit drew most of its new warriors, remained the focus of its attention. The principal pastime, of necessity, was foraging raids – although this too had military value since it compelled the Germans to adopt costly, if still only partly effective countermeasures. In all events, slowly and painfully, the *Vzhodnokoroški Odred* pressed toward the Drau and beyond. The job of extending the OF's network of cells fell to Prušnik-Gašper. Promoted on

15 March from the rank of secretary for the Jauntal to that of political chief for all Carinthia, he concentrated upon the Völkermarkt-Saualpe region where his efforts gradually began to bear modest fruit.[55]

Meanwhile, the partisans of the Wild West, the *Zahodno-* or *Zapadnokoroški Odred*, continued to fight under the very loose direction of the geographically contiguous Ninth Corps. They labored under the disadvantage of their zone's inadequate depth, exaccerbated by the especially high crest of the Karawanken. Since the Wehrmacht had already spoken for most younger men, the guerrillas could garner only a few recruits although those who did join them proved useful because of their knowledge of the local terrain. Nonetheless, there were a number of sharp, minor encounters, and some plant managers and foremen were gunned down. On January 20 the *odred* suffered a grievous loss: Verdnik-Tomaž fell, mortally wounded.

Worse was yet to come. In March the Nazis mounted a coordinated drive by their potpourri of security services. The detachment somehow survived this first blow, but, Fleckner's desperados having arrived from Russia, was largely driven back to the south and east in late April and May. It sought refuge among the summits between the Loibl and Seeberg passes and then beyond the Eisenkappel highway. Only 40 men strong by early June, helped but little by the thoroughly cowed peasantry, the remnants of the once cohesive unit were, for a while, not even in touch with their nearby, eastern sector companions. However, before all this took place, the *odred* had scored one important success. On 18 March a combat party of fifteen men under Anton Mivšek had slithered across the Drau and begun operations in the thickly wooded, already OF-indoctrinated, and hence, to some degree, hospitable Sattnitz hills.[56]

The Nazi leadership was beside itself over this turn of events and, notwithstanding Himmler's dispatch of the SS policemen, began to plan for a better coordinated and stronger response. The SNLA, with British help in the offing, was perhaps even more interested in a concerted exploitation of its Carinthian resources. Thus, on 24 April, it created the so-called "Staff of the Carinthian Group of Detachments" (*Štab koroške grupe odredov*). Its first chief, the unusually brave and talented Vinko Simončič-Gašper, who fell in battle six months later at the head of the Fourteenth Shock Division, was succeeded by Primožič-Marko within several months. Mitja Ribičič-Ciril, described by Villiers as an "intelligent, able, restless, energetic" if petty-minded village mayor type, served as politcommissar. (Another of the Englishman's piquant characterizations was of the Eastern Odred's politcommissar, Sever Franta, "a dynamic but predatory character...., the only Partisan I knew who exploited the opportunities for promiscuity offered by the common practice of sharing one's blanket with a Partizanka".) Marko and Ciril, whatever their personal credentials, can hardly be said to have had an easy time of things. To attempt to supervise the movements of two inevitably perambulatory *odredi* was a Sisyphean enterprise. As will be seen, the antediluvian, courier-based communications system, through which most messages were transmitted, precluded truly effective command. The general staff's decision not to place the Carinthian Slovene partisans on an equal footing with Styria as an "operational zone" – they remained technically, though not practically subordinate to their comrades in Štajersko – surely made sense in view of these and other adverse circumstances. With regard to action north of the Drau – crucial to the realization of the Clowder Mission's objectives –, the ŠKGO was made directly responsible to SNLA headquarters in Dolenjsko. However, the vast distance between the two locales meant that Marko and Ciril could operate more or less as they themselves saw fit.57

Despite the inauspicious prelude of the Western *Odred's* repulse, the summer of 1944 clearly constituted the high water mark of guerrilla warfare in Carinthia. There were two reasons for this. The first was the advent of Fleckner's battle-seasoned SS police troops, experts in the techniques of counterinsurgency. The second was the on-the-spot involvement of Wilkinson's lieutenants. Thereafter, the level of fighting declined noticeably, the result in large measure of a decision to sharply reduce the strength of the forces operating in Carinthia and to employ the men thus released in the fighting south of the Karawanken.

At this point note should be taken of the tactics utilized, at least initially, by the SS or "Greens" as they were called by their Slovene adversaries because of the grass color of their uniforms. Their specialty was the hunt-and-kill mission (*Jagdkommando*) or, as the Slovenes put it, *hajka*, a routine that smacked of guerrilla warfare itself. Disposing of generally high quality intelligence, the Germans plunged right into the woods and converged from three or four directions upon a partisan unit, hoping for surprise. Normally, they lingered in the area for three or four days, occupying all tactically critical positions, beating the bushes and scouring detached buildings and isolated farmsteads. The partisans' known local supporters – such as the still remembered Vivoda and Hojnik families – were shot out of hand or deported and their properties put to the torch or otherwise wrecked. Their fields denuded, other peasants had no recourse but to flee, many of them bitterly resentful toward the partisans for the travail they were undergoing. The guerrillas themselves would simply melt away and counterattacked only when Hesketh-Prichard was in charge. This was at least the later recorded impression of Villiers who had parachuted onto Ninth Corps territory on 15 May and had made his way along with Wilkinson's friend to the Logar and the Meža valleys, and the itinerant ŠKGO.[58]

The arrival of the SOE group in the Lower Styrian salient was ill-starred, to say the least. Indeed, in mid-June disaster was only barely averted. The seven-man Clowder group encountered a second British party from a competing, originally Cairo-based subversion agency, the Inter Services Liaison Department (a brainstorm of MI6), which Wilkinson had earlier agreed to assist. The ISLD people, headed by a Captain "Smith" and known to the Slovenes by the undercover name of SPAM, were not behaving with the necessary degree of tact or adequately observing partisan security rules (*konspiracija*), and there were altogther "too many bodies around" (Wilkinson). A radio operator of Austro-German origin rechristened "Sergeant Dick Black", fell into the hands of SS Police combing the area as Smith and his supernumeraries were being sent back to Fourth Operational Zone headquarters. ISLD codes and reports on conditions in Carinthia were also lost to the enemy. "Black" was probably not a Nazi double-agent, but betrayed the position of the Clowder Mission. As Villiers also later reported, "Austrians" recruited from POW camps had a "proclivity to 'go bad' under stress", that is, to squeal when subjected to the third degree. The Britons managed to escape in the nick of time from their well-concealed bunker near the hamlet of Plešnik but had to abandon their heavier communications equipment.

The Nazis thereupon expelled another Slovene peasant family, taking care to shoot its father first. "Smith", sacked for all practical purposes, returned to the joint SOE-SIS (MI6) base at Bari. (In July the Clowder Mission would come under the command of AFHQ at Caserta outside Naples through SOM or Special Operations Mediterranean, also situated in Bari.) "Although they weren't our chaps" (Wilkinson), Villiers more or less assumed responsiblity and explained that "Black" was not a British but an Austrian national. Seeking to repair his relationship with the SNLA, "Major Buxton" hastened to assure his indigenous associates that only really good people would be used in the future. However, the Slovenes now distrusted "Austrians" so much that the remaining three ISLD ones had to be placed under a form of house arrest. Villiers and Hesketh-Prichard—like Wilkinson and many other SOE personnel, articulate, sophisticated but tough-minded scions of the public school, Oxbridge establishment, the cream of the traditional, nineteenth century ruling class—were then permitted to move about in the old border area with the ŠKGO.[59]

Villiers' secret account of his Carinthian gambado (which left him sick and exhausted) is surely the single most revealing and objective primary source, published or unpublished, for the history of the local partisan movement. He readily admitted to his superiors that the impact of Clowder Mission upon the ŠKGO was "unfavourable". His party was too big. The partisans doubted that W/T (radio) communications and mobility were compatible. "Smith's" maladroit team was already there. He himself lacked the all-important YNLA *propustnica* (laissez-passer). Marko and Ciril doubted their ability to keep the Englishmen in line in accordance with Tito's orders. Indeed, "our task, as first outlined to them, was not one they were able to promote". Although the practical obstacles were overcome in time, above all because the SOE literally delivered the goods, the conflict over fundamental goals remained to the end.

The most penetrating of Villier's many individual observations deserves to be reproduced in extenso:

> I must .... refrain from a detailed analysis of the enthusiastic and naive aspirations which moved these Partisans, despite very hard living conditions, almost impossible conditions for work, and a chronic shortage of arms, food, and clothing. So you must take for granted the religious enthusiasm for NOV in POS (National Army of Liberation and Partisan Detachments), for the person of Tito and for the prospect of a Golden Age to follow the dismissal of the "Okupator", which suffused ninety percent of Partisans whom I met in Koroško.... But I would not have you think that I found the Partisans anything other than supremely selfish in their attitude to cooperation with the British and Americans.[60]

Thus, as far as the Slovenes were concerned, the principal task of the two SOE agents was to coordinate drops of containers packed with up to a hundred kilos each of supplies and armaments. The Czech-speaking, 29 year-old Hesketh-Prichard, a licensed, two-engine aircraft qualified pilot as well as a communications expert, was admirably suited for the role assigned him. Twenty sorties, three to the Western and seventeen to the Eastern *Odredi*, were realized during July and August just to the south of the prewar frontier. (The RAF was reluctant to fly over the Karawanken crest.) With the arrival of food, medicine, battledress, explosives, handgrenades, cartridges, the fiendishly ingenious Sten gun (a perfect ambush tool designed to use the German *Schmeisser's* 9 mm ammunition), and other infernal contraptions, a rapid build-up of partisan strength took place. Although there were sufficient weapons for only two-thirds of them, 250 men and women were mobilized in the Wild West and over 700 in the eastern sector.

Although, as already indicated, the two Englishmen were dissatisfied with what they regarded as the relative passivity of their Slovene comrades (whom they, like the Fourth Operational Zone headquarters, considered to be overly bureaucratic), there was in fact one genuinely sensational action: a frontal engagement at Črna (Schwarzenbach) in the Meža valley between August 18 and 24. The numerically inferior First and Third Battalions of the Eastern *Odred*, some 200 men, sought to bar the advance of a column of SS Police. The multifaceted Hesketh-Prichard – who had overcome physical handicaps by sheer willpower and was not only a yachtsman, steeplechase rider, skier, crack marksman but also a charismatic leader according Wilkinson's fond recollection of him – played a prominent role in an encounter that evidently involved as many as 700 "Greens", artillery, armor, and, on the partisan side, British-supplied PIATs (bazooka-type devices), and mortars.[61]

Perhaps a hundred Nazis were killed, many, it seems by Hesketh-Prichard himself, who replicated the feats of his renowned World War One sniper father. Črna may therefore be considered one of only two full-fledged, albeit small-scale battles fought by the Carinthian Slovene partisans. (The other occurred after the armistice and will be treated in the final chapter.) Of course the guerrillas could not tarry long in such exposed terrain and so, promptly and judiciously, withdrew to their habitual, sylvan haunts. Favorably impressed, Hesketh-Prichard radioed Bari, and the Eastern Carinthian Detachment was formally congratulated by Field Marshal Harold Alexander, the commander-in-chief of the Allied forces in the Mediterranean theater. Prušnik-Gašper later recalled this distinction with great pride although he might have been a bit less pleased with Villiers' incisive description of himself. The politcommissar was characterized as a "fearless, simple, shrewd, uneducated farmer with a genius for partisan warfare" who sported an SS uniform and looked like a "perambulatory armory". He was, however, a "pirate" who, although beloved, looted from friend and foe alike.[62]

Despite the triumph as Črna the conflict in goals between the two, ill-suited confederates was becoming increasingly evident. For some three months Hesketh-Prichard and Villiers had been importuning their Slovene associates – Ciril's "Slavic habit of dealing in half-truths" was absolutely maddening – to let Wilkinson's alter ego traverse the Drau in a do-or-die attempt to implement the Clowder Mission's "Austrian" subversion scheme. The two Englishmen knew that partisan units were already operating in the heart of the Klagenfurt basin. Indeed, Mivšek's little band had raised a huge ruckus in the Sattnitz hills, recruited a few indigenes, and evaded the SS. Moreover, three other parties (one under Franc Mahnič-Boj on June 24 and two further groups led, respectively, by Jože Belin and Ladislav Grat-Kijev [*Kampfgruppe "Avantgarde" Steiermark*] in early September). The partisans, keeping in mind their long-term political goals while seeking to wheedle as much matériel from the SOE as they could, procrastinated. Their lame excuse was that they could not guarantee "Major Cahusac's" safety. The consequent "time-lag in crossing the Drau" (Wilkinson) would have several unforeseen, interrelated effects.

What Hesketh-Prichard and Villiers did not know was that the chances of encountering the never truly widespread or substantial German Carinthian opposition to Hitler's régime and hence, potentially, the Austro-Styrian anti-Nazis had now vanished completely. Already in May the Gestapo had shattered the more or less active KPÖ organization in Klagenfurt and Villach, which by then was loosely associated with the ÖFF (in part due to the Slovene partisans' intervention). The ÖFF's sole remaining activist was the Slovene-speaking Revolutionary Socialist, Dr. Ferdinand Wedenig, and he too was was hors de combat. (As Austrian Socialist Party [SPÖ] *Landeshauptmann* from 1947 to 1965, Wedenig was destined to be politically harassed and personally vilified by Carinthian neo-Nazis both for his conciliatory attitude toward the minority and for the secret logistical help he gave the guerrillas during the war.) His principal party comrade, Erwin Scharf-Wallner, who would lead the postbellum KPÖ, had skipped to the backwoods of Slovenia on 24 August 1944, one step ahead of the Gestapo. Indeed, Wedenig himself would soon be arrested and shipped off to Dachau as part of a massive crackdown on the whole spectrum of non-Soviet-oriented Marxists. Altogether 200 prewar Social Democrats were incarcerated.[63]

In September Villiers' tour of duty (which, in the SOE, normally ran four or five months) was up, and he flew out of Slovenia by that time a relatively easy thing to do. There was no question of his returning, for, by the time he reported to Wilkinson, his superior had decided that the Slovene-centered operation was altogether "a busted flush". Nor did the Clowder Mission's chief go back himself for precisely the same reason. Villiers put to paper the joint conclusion that the plan to use the SNLA for infiltrating British-trained saboteurs was irremediably flawed. On the other hand, though the chances of actually contacting it were remote, the ÖFF was still the best bet. Thus the BBC should promote the organization on its shortwave transmissions. London should pin its hopes on Hesketh-Prichard simply getting across the river. ("Cahusac" had several inflatable rubber dinghies dropped by an Allied aircraft and, as he had been doing from the start, was applying his technical expertise to train his fellow guerrillas.) A nucleus for Austro-German resistance might be formed – and a leader found – in connection with the SNLA's Saualpe campaign. A fringe benefit was that a crucial enemy rail link, the Klagenfurt-Bruck an der Mur connection, could be threatened.

Villiers also recommended – and this, it seems, was what Hesketh-Prichard actually tried to do once he reached the Saualpe – that the Clowder Mission quickly detach itself from the Slovene partisans because they were using the British for their own (or Russian) purposes. In effect, the idea was to ride piggy-back on the partisan expedition if only for a short distance. Villiers stressed, as he did in a second, special memo on the subject of postwar boundaries, that Tito's claim to Carinthia, if based on local inhabitants' enthusiasm for the partisan movement, was "unjustified." The last statement is of course the nub of the whole business. The British desire to stimulate independent opposition to Naziism was anathema to the SNLA for strictly political reasons. The only German Carinthian guerrillas they were prepared to tolerate where those who would function as their creatures. It follows that Hesketh-Prichard's impending escapade must be regarded to have been as an audacious gamble, a veritable long shot. This judgment, it must be emphasized, is not a question of what Americans call Monday morning quarterbacking, i.e., overly facile second-guessing. Connoisseurs of the history of Allied subversion efforts in World War Two will immediately recognize that this was what the SOE was all about. Running outrageous risks was the heart of the matter.

Another aspect of the "time lag" were developments during the late summer of 1944 back in the Allied-occupied part of Italy. Alexander and AFHQ, misled by faulty intelligence according to Wilkinson (but also short of troops because of the landing in southern France), had become overly optimistic about the prospects for smashing through the enemy's northern Apennine defenses – the Gothic Line – into the Po valley. After a parallel amphibious landing in Istria, there would be an advance across the Ljubljana Gap. The Allied forces would thrust into Austria, reaching Leoben by early December and Vienna by Christmas. The latter scheme, it may be noted. much worried Tito and might well have provoked outright hostilities with the YNLA had it been implemented. On-the-spot "tactical support", put together by Hesketh-Prichard, would facilitate the drive. Wilkinson, having independently written off the SNLA by late summer, planned to use his remaining "Austrians" in two new ways: 1) through Manfred Czernin's north Italian "organization"; and 2) via air drops ahead of the Eighth Army for the purpose of fomenting coups de main. Unfortunately, the personnel at the Clowder Mission's disposal, often enlisted from POW camps, was not only of poor quality, but there both long delays and an insufficiency of numbers.

Ironically, one of but two decent agents among the twenty-nine or thirty actually dispatched was deposited on top of the Nazi security post in Tolmezzo and never heard from again. A shortage of aircraft and the need, at least on occasion, to fall back upon R and R status, "cowboy" style U.S.A.A.F bomber crews, unsuited for the delicate enterprise in question, made matters worse. The directly responsible agency (the Balkan Air Force or BAF), Wilkinson believes. was only interested in Yugoslavia, indeed had been "fairly briskly warned off about trying to gain control of special operations" anywhere else. Gone were the days when, as matter of course, he could call for sorties by the unfortunately all-too-few, specially trained RAF flyers. (Polish aviators, he stresses, were the best of the lot.) In fact, Wilkinson ascribes Clowder's ultimate failure more to this "rough deal" than to anything else though he freely admits that his project was a lesser one and that the available fleet of planes was too small for the many demands being made upon it.[64]

A further contretemps, more a nuisance than a genuine obstacle, was the fact that, by the time Villiers was on his way back to Allied territory, domestic British storm clouds were gathering over the Clowder Mission. The Foreign Office's Bari representative, Philip Broad, with whom Wilkinson was on excellent terms and who had been fully briefed by him regarding the quagmire of Slovene nationalism, informed Whitehall of Tito's open proclamation of annexationist goals in a speech to the YNLA's First Dalmatian Brigade on 12 September 1944. (However, reference was made to frontier questions as early as the 29 November 1943 Jajce declaration, of which the Foreign Office was presumably aware.) Certain bureaucrats of the Southern and Central Departments – the territorial imperative was doubtlessly a factor in this instance as it was in other, similar cases – were not pleased with Baker Street's plan for provoking mischief in Carinthia.

Seizing upon a key passage in Broad's telegram, Geoffrey W. Harrison argued on 11 October that "while from the military point of view there are obvious advantages in the proposed operation and I know that S.O.E. are keen on it, the real question is whether, if we encourage the Slovenian units (without our assistance they can do nothing) to push on into pre-1938 Austria, we shall find out later that they will use their control of this territory to present us with a fait-accompli after the cessation of hostilities." Wilkinson, who had visited Harrison "a day or two ago", could not persuade him to drop his objections. The civil servant's argument was that "we certainly do not wish to see the Austrian will to indpendence diminished be removing from her territory which was Austrian before the Anschluss".[65]

General "Luka" (Franc Leskošek), the partisan 'war minister" described by the ingenuous Jones as "tall and rugged, with a seasoned but kind face", had clearly sensed from afar the nascent opposition to Slovene irredentism. He hastened to assure Broad that the SNLA forces in Carinthia would not agitate in favor of frontier revision or otherwise prejudice an "Austrian" revolt by raising controversial topics (something which reflected a purely tactical current of opinion among the Slovene Communist leadership). Tito's statement, he explained soothingly, was only by way of guidance and added, even less plausibly, that all issues, including borders, would be reserved for the peace conference. On 21 October Broad – who was also kept au courant by Maclean's mission and forwarded his messages through the Central Mediterranean Resident-Minister in Caserta, Harold Macmillan, MP – sent another signal containing fresh evidence of the partisans' true Carinthian objectives.[66] The news can only have been grist for the Foreign Office mill. There was a certain irony of the tug of war between the staunchly anti-Communist and hence anti-partisan diplomats and the thoroughly pragmatic, victory-oriented SOE over Wilkinson's insistence upon the need, if not to ferret out the delitiscent ÖFF, at least to build up "an armed nucleus around which to gather local recruits". It was that, unlike Jones, Clowder personnel were themselves political sophisticates. Indeed, Wilkinson's original, widely circulated memorandum on Slovenia could hardly have provided a more realistic assessment of conditions in northwestern Yugoslavia and its periphery. Reference has already been made to Villier's conclusion about the postwar frontier after three months' of first-hand experience. He was even more explicit when requested to evaluate Slovene territorial claims as put forward in Tito's proclamation. In contrast to Istria, so Villiers wrote, indigenous sentiment in favor of giving the Klagenfurt basin to Yugoslvia was minimal. "At the peak of the J.A.N.L effort in Carinthia, there were never more than 1000 Partisans" concentrated along the old border, the only area where the peasantry was willing to help; "thus there would seem no reason to suppose that the plebiscite taken in 1920.... would be reversed today."[67]

At this point it seems useful to review the account published in 1980 by the Canadian historian, David Stafford, over Wilkinson's tiff with the Foreign Office. Unrealistically but perhaps understandably in light of events as they were then unfolding, says Stafford, the striped-pants set feared an alliance between the Slovenes and left-wing resistance forces in northern Italy. He goes on to depict a Clowder Mission thoroughly hamstrung by its homefront adversaries as early as 22 November 1944. Inter alia, AFHQ are reported to have specifically banned aid to the Carinthian Slovene partisans.[68]

Wilkinson finds this version of events a bit misleading. Though subject to AFHQ, and unwilling to flaunt the Foreign Office outright as a matter of principle, he and his associates retained operational autonomy. If no sorties took place after mid-November – so far there had been none at all north of the Karawanken –, the reasons were the "atrocious and unseasonable" weather and the shortage of planes, admittedly exacerbated in Wilkinson's case by the meddling of higher military quarters. (The aircraft problem was a perennial one for the SOE altogether which the top RAF command, convinced it could bomb Germany into submission, regarded as a thorn in its side). The documents reproduced in the Appendixes bear Wilkinson out.[69] Nor should the factor of his personal concern over Hesketh-Prichard's fate and, perhaps also, his close ties with the SOE director, the formidable Sir Colin McVean Gubbins, be overlooked. The Clowder Mission began to steer a more pronounced anti-Communist tack only in January of 1945 and not because of Foreign Office "bleating" (Wilkinson) but in the face of changing international circumstances and a harsh, agonizing reality: its man on the Saualpe had fallen silent.[70]

Procedural differences between British figures were of course irrelevant to the course of events in Carinthia, whether in the region south of the Drau or in the newly opened combat zone that lay beyond its northern bank. The two southern sectors may be considered first. Although the *Zahodnokoroški Odred* had been "unmasked" (Villiers) in the spring of 1944, it had not been utterly destroyed. As noted previously, certain of its members had crept across the river and were causing pandemonium in the Sattnitz hills. Other vestiges, reinforced by a company from the Ninth Corps, were on the prowl near the Faakersee/Baško jezero and in the lower Gail valley. There were also a few lesser melees in the high country between Eisenkappel and Zell. In the former instance the object was to disrupt railroad traffic. Although this proved impossible, a series of shootouts left several dead each time, thus at least demonstrating that the Nazi authorities were no longer in full control.

To the east most clashes apparently occurred near the two Obir peaks although the echo of gunfire could also be heard in the Rosental. The Germans responded in a variety of ways: with propaganda blasts, threats of retaliation, construction of new redoubts, and by stiffening the gendarmerie with levies from the Old Reich. SS *Jagdkommandos* continued to fan out, and Replacement Army *Gebirgsjäger* were positioned around Zell.[71] On occasion there were genuinely feral confrontations. Prušnik-Gašper tells of an encounter on 20 July 1944 near a chain of Nazi bunkers surrounding the wrecked summer cabin of Gauleiter Rainer on the Počula Saddle to the east of the High Obir in which a larger, if indeterminate number of the foe were taken by surprise and literally mowed down. The Germans fought to the last man with a pertinacity that elicited the begruding admiration of the tough-minded guerrillas. The area itself, near the meeting point of the Western and Eastern *Odredi*, was of special strategic significance.[72]

Fourth Operational Zone headquarters, for its part, stressed the need to cut enemy communication lines and demanded more intelligence data. Both directives seem to suggest a greater concern for what was happening on the southern side of the Karawanken. The virtual absence of radios meant, as always, that the scattered partisan units had to rely on courier-transmitted orders. Although the *Meldegänger* displayed remarkable ingenuity and courage, their casualty rate was inordinately high.[73] In early August, under its new commander, Anton Okrogar-Nestl (who had led the partisans in the Počula ambuscade), the Western Carinthian Detachment's activity diminished due to the problems of its expansion and reorganization. The ŠKGO admonished it not only to fight more but to redouble its propaganda and political organizational activity. The latter task was accomplished farther to the west, but the military effort could not be accelerated because a mere three airdops were insufficient to arm all its recruits.[74] Thus matters remained until 20 September when it was learned that the Slovene high command had decided to temporarily deemphasize Carinthia altogether.

Meanwhile, the Nazis, not satified with the recent slight alleviation of security conditions, introduced certain administrative improvements and altered their tactics somewhat. On 8 August Fleckner assumed responsibility for all counterinsurgency operations on Carinthian soil (under the overall authority of Rösener and Rainer). The network of static defenses was further strengthened. Plans were made to use the fortified posts as bases for bushwhacking partisans who tried to slip in between, especially along the Seeberg pass highway, the fundamentally successful idea being to isolate the two *odredi* from each other. Although German forces would still penetrate into more remote locales – artillery was deployed near Ebriach – there was now a greater alliance upon larger units and the strongholds.[75]

While the Nazi administration was seeking to enhance its ability to fend off attacks, in the sector east of the Eisenkappel road the late summer witnessed a vast expansion of partisan numbers, from the 229 combatants of June to the aforementioned 700 plus. Most of the fighting – the action at Črna is indicative – took place in the Meža valley rather than in Austro-Carinthia, and there was an evident reluctance to mount costly frontal assaults. The higher staffs repeatedly demanded greater aggressiveness, the result of which appears to have been more frequent strikes against enemy communications. However, the overall results were not impressive, and for a variety of reasons the new recruits did not live up to expectations. The period was also marked by a renewed emphasis upon political activity. Prušnik-Gašper was called away in late August to participate in an all-Slovene conference at Črnomelj in the Bela Krajina, the partisans' Lower Carniolan fastness. As he travelled, he had the opportunity to observe the even greater brutality of the SS Police and their native auxilliaries in Slovenia proper.[76]

4

The Last Winter: Blood on the Snow

After the Provincial OF Secretary's return from the plenary gathering south of the Sava, there was a decisive twist of fate – the previously mentioned shift in the policy of the SNLA's leadership. Tantamount to a definitive downgrading of Carinthia as a center of military operations, it signalled the beginning of what proved to be the worst year of the war for the minority of partisans who were ordered to stay behind. For some time the higher staff had been perturbed over what were called "brigade tendencies", that is, the eastern sector guerrillas' evident desire for promotion to the rank of a more prestigious "shock" formation. Dissatisfied with their dispersed, more or less static role and unhappy about the coemphasis upon political work (*však partizan naj bo tudi politični aktivist!*), they had been dreaming, their allegedly slack performance notwithstanding, of setting up their own "liberated zone". Another, probably determinative factor was that Carinthia had been sucked dry of recruits. The available human resources could be much better employed in the see-saw struggle for survival in Štajersko, in particular to reinforce its main fighting contingent, the Fourteenth Shock Division. Thus, on 20 September, the Carinthian Group of *Odredi* was abolished and broken into three parts. The bulk of the troops were sent south of the Karawanken, about 250 kept between the crest of the mountains and the Drau as the core of a new, three battalion *odred*, while another battalion of seventy choice, well-equipped warriors – Hesketh-Prichard's and Prušnik-Gašper's unit – was ordered to traverse the river and link up with the scattered, 100 odd men already on the other side.[77]

The story of the hideous struggle on the Saualpe will be better understood if prefaced by an account of developments south of the Drau during the same period of time. The long and short of it was that the reduction in strength led to a sharp decline in martial activity overall. As previously, most clashes occurred in the Meža valley. The major German offensive of 27 November-6 January in the "liberated zone" around Solčava should also be singled out, for it undoubtedly affected events in Austro-Carinthia. Joint operations by the Thirteenth and Nineteenth SS Police Regiments along with unusually adverse weather conditions including the heaviest snowfall in a number of years occasioned a grave partisan setback, the appalling details of which are graphically related in Jelka's memoirs. Among other things, Fleckner's bravos dispatched fourteen of their captives on the gunsmiths' rifle range in Ferlach, one of various war crimes for which the Nazi commander was hanged after the war.[78]

In the eastern Carinthian sector the months in question were marked by concentration upon political activity. (The notably literate partisans published an abundance of underground fliers and pamphlets although there was never enough material to suit the activists.)[79] Volunteers were few, supplies short for reasons that will be explained presently. Morale suffered. Only occasionally could patrols be sent out and ambushes staged. The fortified Nazi posts were too strong to attack. It proved impossible to obstruct road traffic, now increasingly important due to Allied aerial bombardment of the railways. It was extremely difficult to waylay motorized enemy columns. The Seeberg pass route, a major barrier for the partisans throughout the whole war, was especially well-guarded, a circumstance that helps to explain the successful German drive in the adjacent Lower Styrian salient.[80]

The logistical difficulties resulted from the previously explained, technically conditioned cessation of the SOE-sponsored, low-level airdrops into the Lower Styrian salient. It should be stressed that the personal relations between the Clowder Mission and the senior aviators of the BAF were smooth and cordial, a bright spot in what was often a tense relationship. (Wilkinson's felicitous manner must have been a major reason for this.) The total number of missions cannot be stated with certainty. Wilkinson reported after the war that there had been seventy of them but is no longer positive whether this figure or even those cited by Villiers are absolutely accurate.

The four engine aircraft used were the B-24 Liberator – a roomy, 18 container-sized, albeit explosion prone, extremely hard-to-pilot machine – and the smaller Halifax. The two-engine Dakota (DC-3), known affectionately as the old "bucket of bolts" and one of the most serviceable planes ever designed, was landed on tiny grass airstrips both in Slovenia and everywhere else in World War Two. It should also be pointed out that Prušnik-Gašper's and Helena Kuchar's criticism of the snafus inevitably associated with sorties is unfair. (Prušnik-Gašper does express gratitude.) Mountain dwellers petrified by the mere thought of deeply flowing rivers such as the Drau and the Sava and with no experience at all of air space could scarcely have imagined the problems inherent to such flights or the special skills required to execute successfully even a modest percentage of them.[81]

The situation in the Wild West was comparable to that in the eastern sector. Except for the inevitable political agitation – relations with the leaderless and quiescent left-wing Austro-Germans were equivocal, even strained –, nothing of any real consequence happened. The chief event appears to have been the mauling of the new Carinthian *Odred's* First Battalion. To be sure, some guerrillas held out in well-furnished, arboreal quarters along the old border in the so-called "Republic of Zell", tenderly nursing their wounded. Zell, it should be observed, was an ideal spot for a field-dressing station. Its sobriquet, if something of an exaggeration (especially during the last year of the war), did denote a distinctive quality. The township that gave its name to the OF martyrs of 1943 was a genuine hotbed of opposition to Naziism. The physical isolation resulting from extreme elevation and its concomitant of strong ethnic identity surely explain the relatively sophisticated partisan logistical infrastructure in a locality which even today has the highest proportion of Slovene-speakers in the whole of Carinthia. Zell's only missing ingredient was a flamboyant, literarily inclined native son like Prušnik-Gašper.

Another cluster of first-aid huts lay hidden in the vicinity of the High Obir. In the Slovene heartland as elsewhere in Yugoslavia there were equally recondite medical centers, albeit much better equipped, indeed sufficiently so that they may be considered full-fledged hospitals. Care of the wounded, based upon a traditional value system, was a striking feature of the partisan ethic and has been vividly described by Djilas and another witness-participant, Sir William Deakin. A related question is how partisan wounded fared when they fell into German hands or Germans into partisan ones. A clear-cut answer cannot be given, and the topic probably deserves further study. In Carinthia conditions may have been a trifle more favorable for the guerrillas than they were in Yugoslavia where immediate slaughter seems to have been more or less the common practice of all parties concerned.[82]

The western sector couriers – much less likely to receive treatment for their injuries or ailments in a congenial environment if indeed they survived at all – suffered heavily, while the Gestapo remained highly effective in smoking out the OF's more sedentary civilian supporters. The latter months of the war also seem to have been characterized by especially repellant Nazi atrocities. According to Prušnik-Gašper, SS policemen violated the corpses of female partisans after storming a mountainside bunker on 6 February 1945 and strung up the bodies along the road between St. Jakob and St. Peter im Rosental a warning to SNLA sympathisers. Partisans captured near the entrance to the Rosenbach-Podrožica tunnel are said to have been tortured before being murdered. Of course, as Wilkinson saw for himself, the guerrillas were just as prone to deny quarter unless their prisoners (as was often the case in Carinthia) were dragooned and decrepit militiamen.[83]

The horrors experienced south of the Drau were bad enough, but they were doubtlessly surpassed by the events of Hesketh-Prichard's and Prušnik-Gašper's ill-starred anabasis from the partisans' Lower Styrian hideaway into the highlands above Völkermarkt. Indeed, what may be called the fiasco of the Saualpe remains a highly sensitive subject even today. Most survivors of the campaign have been unwilling or reluctant to talk about it. Prušnik-Gašper's account, effusive as always, is nevertheless strangely fragmentary. Was this simply because he was there only part of the time and not a witness to everything that occurred? It seems more likely that the lacunae are deliberate, have to do with his personal involvement in what was an unusually messy business, and reflect the exigencies of postwar Carinthian and Slovenian politics.

Surely, the whole affair was highly charged politically even at its inception. Hesketh-Prichard, embarking upon an enterprise which he, like the rest of the Clowder Mission, realized was a forlorn hope in the pristine military sense of the term, could not leave until he had received personal permission from Luka (October 5). The last Westerner to see "Cahusac" was Major, later Lieutenant Colonel Franklin A. Lindsay (Ordnance Department, U.S.A), Maclean's representative in the Fourth Operational Zone. Hesketh-Prichard told Lindsay that since snow was falling in the mountains, he would be bound to leave tracks; probably he would not survive, but he had to try anyway.[84]

In all events, the SOE agent and Prušnik-Gašper were ranking members of a mini-battalion led by Ulčar-Mirko, whom the politcommissar later portrayed as a less than satisfactory commander.[85] The Drau crossing, made on the night of 14-15 October near Schwabegg/Švabek on the lower, undammed, and hence narrower stretch of the river, went smoothly enough. The dinghies were concealed, though not well enough to prevent the Nazis from discovering them a week later. Hesketh-Prichard – whom the Slovenes considered "taciturn", undoubtedly misconstruing the stiff upper lip of an Englishman who had been a page of honor to King George V – is even reported to have joked at this juncture.

Among "Cahusac's" other paraphernalia was a special, light-weight, exile Polish-designed and built, "skip-jump" radio, in the development of which he himself had played a crucial role. Operated with low-frequency signals bounced off the ionosphere, this state-of-the-art wireless allowed him to communicate directly with his superiors in southern Italy or England although the need for a detection-safe locale and the vagaries of atmospheric conditions were severe handicaps. (The Americans also employed radios of this type.) The messages were transmitted according to the "one-time pad" system. While it required a large and cumbersome supply of combustible paper, it was foolproof by the cryptographic standards of the day. Not even domestic competitors could gain access to the SOE's communications network. Hesketh-Prichard was unable to drag along either of two other novel contraptions for coordinating airdrops, the Eureka radar kit or the handy S-Phone (in the invention of which he had also been involved). Any sortie would thus have to depend solely upon the much cruder technique of lighting bonfires as beacons.[86]

Ulčar's motley party (the remnants of which would form the core of the Fourth or Northern Carinthian Battalion the next spring) was the sixth to make it across the river. It had just been preceded by a 20-man patrol composed mainly of escaped Soviet POW's and slaveworkers, equipped with shiny new Sten guns that probably derived from SOE stocks. After freeing and incorporating a bevy of fellow countrymen, this troop wreaked genuine havoc in the Lavanttal until Fleckner's cutthroats drove it back over the river in late November. Following the Russians' track, the newcomers skedaddled into the hills that lay to their northwest. On November 10 they managed to link up with three of the other dispersed units north of the Drau. These included an offshoot of Mivšek's slippery Sattnitz partisans under Gajko Gornik-Iztok but not Grat-Kijev's Soviet-sponsored, Austro-German *Kampfgruppe* which crossed into adjacent Styria and survived in the Koralpe thanks to physical junction with the Lacko Odred that was operating in the prewar Austro-Yugoslav frontier region. (Grat-Kijev was not its commander but rather a SNLA liaison officer and locally savvy guide.)

Although in the last analysis the ground was poorly chosen due its much lower proportion of Slovene-speakers, there was, especially at the outset, a modicum of indigenous support, even from an occasional, destitute Germanophone boor. Ulčar and his retinue tried hard to repress their natural proclivities and not be nationalistically assertive, highlighting rather the problems of social injustice in their logistically crucial dealings with civilians. They also fed upon the rich local herd of game, both roe and red deer. Perhaps the most important military accomplishment of the septentrional partisans, already in-mid October, was the heavy damage they inflicted upon the Philips-Valvo mica mine – the mineral was essential for submarine radar – at St. Leonhart west of Pölling and St. Andrä im

Lavanttal. The operation was carried out on 16 October by the now swollen Soviet band.

A closely associated incident that occurred the next day on a farm outside the hamlet of Lamm (near St. Leonhart) was the so-called "Spitzbauer Massacre". Whether Mahnič-Boj's party rather than the Soviets was involved is not clear. However, the affair certainly did encompass a mélange of nationalities, not only partisans but Austro-German civilians as well as errant, evidently unarmed Russian and/or Polish slaveworkers who had fled from the wrecked mine. With as many as 40 deaths, the exchange of fire with Nazi security forces was also shockingly sanguinary. The guerrillas appear to have been welcomed by at least several members of the Spitzbauer clan, but the details remain shrouded in politically colored controversy.[87]

However, the great majority of the inhabitants were indifferent or hostile, and there was no chance at all of provoking an "Austrian" uprising. The line of communications was stretched to the breaking point. Intrepid though they were, couriers could hardly penetrate the curtain of barriers along the Drau, which was also patrolled by motorboats and light aircraft. The station near the south bank atop the Kömmelgupf/Vrh was overrun by the foe on 21 October with grave loss of life: twelve partisans were slaughtered. Although so-called "legal" couriers sometimes got through and Prušnik-Gašper succeeeded, albeit only barely, in returning on 23 December, the SNLA forces in the center and on the northern rim of the Klagenfurt basin were isolated for all practical purposes.[88]

In such geographical circumstances the partisans' relative neglect of radio communications, which they regarded "as unsuitable to their type of war" (Villiers), was highly inopportune. Wilkinson's right-hand man, who had foreseen such a dénouement before leaving the region, could only report (mid-November) that "there is little information available about Partisan activity north of the DRAVA, because the crossing has up to now been a one way trip from south to north, even couriers failing to get back: this is due to German watchfulness and the Partisans' inability to combine the use of wireless with the tactics required in the early stages of the development of a territory".[89]

At this stage the picture becomes blurred. However, it is clear that Mirko's men could not remain concentrated and survive in the face of what, by November, had become a massive German military response. Whether Hesketh-Prichard and his Slovene comrades quarreled outright will probably never be known for certain, but, given the dire straits in which they found themselves, it is conceivable, even likely, that there was disagreement. The partisans continued their policy of "justifying" local Nazi party hacks, indeed with extreme cruelty if one may accept the witness of their surviving kinsmen and friends. (One Hitlerite's life may have been spared because he had protected Slovene nationalist neighbors at the time of the *Aussiedlung*.) The homes of the defunct NSDAP worthies were pillaged, and forced requisitioning was commonplace. Supply shortages were endemic although a bit of help – explosives, gear, and medicaments – ultimately came from those of Wedenig's colleagues still in a position to elude the Gestapo. Dogged by the enemy, always on the move with his wireless, and cursed by bitterly cold, nigh impossible flying weather, Hesketh-Prichard was able to arrange only one airdrop to the station dubbed "Trigger" by the SOE. Yet he would not live to hear the drone of the circling aircraft's engines.[90]

Late November was altogether a period of deteriorating relations between the British and the SNLA. An order was actually issued, though not implemented, for the wholesale expulsion of liaison officers save at corps level.[91] The partisans were displeased with Hesketh-Prichard's efforts to recruit, non-Slovene "Austrian" resisters, something that seemed to them a far cry from Tito's hypothetical objective of letting the SOE into Carinthia in order to favorably dispose the British toward a future frontier rectification. Wilkinson believes that his logistically bereft friend had become an "embarassment", in fact "was endangering the lives of everyone he came into contact with". On 3 December "Major Cahusac" sent his last signal, and this is the presumptive, approximate date of his demise. His personal message for the Clowder Mission's chief was: "Give my love to all at White's [club]; this is no place for a gentleman", a kind of old-boy cliché alluding to the complete lack of civilized amenities.

When interrogated by the British shortly after the war, Prušnik-Gašper and several other guerrillas swore that their English mate had fallen in battle. The story did not ring true. The investigators concluded that almost certainly their missing fellow countryman had been assassinated by his companions.[92] It is fair to assume that the instructions to liquidate him, which somehow reached the Saualpe (perhaps via a "legal" courier), emanated from a higher political quarter. The judgment of those who knew "Cahusac" best was that Britain had lost one of her best and brightest. Howarth has written that: "In the work of SOE, as in other forms of warfare, action had to be preceded by reconnaissance; even [when it] proved negative casualties occurred; and the lives of the ablest were not spared; Alfgar Hesketh-Prichard was a victim of this requisite of war".[93]

It must be emphasized that the Carinthian German nationalist version of what was an inter-Allied tragedy is replete with error, indeed is pure "cock" according to an indignant Wilkinson. The most serious misstatement, as the data previously cited make crystal clear, is the assertion that the Gestapo had succeeded in cracking the SOE code and learned of a breakdown in Hesketh-Prichard's morale. However, the report that the six foot one inch skeleton later found in the Bärenschlucht near Eberstein-Diex/Djekse and bearing bullet holes through the throat and back of the head was "Cahusac's" is probably correct despite the unavailability of corresponding British documentary records.

That the Clowder Mission agent did succeed in recruiting or at least in animating a few non-Slovenes before he was killed is suggested by a surviving Austrian gendarmerie report of 1946: 29 Germanophone partisans supposedly fell fighting the Nazis near Eberstein in late 1944 and early 1945. This group's existence could have been the primordial cause of the Englishman's murder. Conversely, Wilkinson is persuaded that the crucial factor was the Clowder Mission's total inability to supply him. Had there been sorties during the fall, many more local Austro-German recruits, he thinks, "would have emerged almost instantaneously", like bees attracted to honey: such was the SOE's experience under identical circumstances elsewhere.[94]

As for the Slovene guerrillas, only a hard core withstood the rigors of the unduly inclement winter and the even more vigorous Nazi countermeasures that began on 6 December. The SS Police, Replacment Army soldiers, *Volkssturm* contingents, and odd vestiges of battle-hardened front line units not only garrisoned strategically pivotal localities but went after the partisans on their own ground. As many as 2000 troops, some on skis, may have been involved. All of Ulčar's companies suffered frightening losses. The wounded were sometimes stomped to death by the Germans. Women warriors were among the fallen. Prušnik-Gašper reported that his harried ex-comrades sought to maintain their flagging morale by communal singing, an archetypical Slovene pastime.

The sortie arranged by Hesketh-Prichard prior to his putative death took place on 27 December during a brief break in the weather. The stores collected by the partisans may have been all that kept them alive at a point in time when Wilkinson and Villiers, suspecting a radio malfunction, had not yet given all hope for their compatriot. Only in mid-April, having barely survived a SS sweep near St. Oswald above Eberstein, did the tattered remanants of the Northern Battalion emerge from their remote lairs and make their military presence felt again, albeit weakly. The British made three additional drops shortly thereafter, but the containers fell into Nazi hands.[95]

In order to fully understand the outcome of Carinthia's guerrilla ordeal in the spring of 1945 as well as the end of World War Two in southeastern Europe altogether, it is necessary to glimpse at events in the Slovene heartland from mid-1944 onward. Fortunately, for the historian, the human caliber and the intellectual capacities of the different Allied officers assisting and spying upon the SNLA were very high. It is also a stroke of luck that many of their perceptive secret reports, the most relevant of which are part of this book, have survived. Lindsay, and Deakin, then a lieutenant colonel as well, were only the most outstanding of a group of men whose dispatches tended to be mutually corroborative and carried great weight in London and, presumably, Washington. (Lindsay served at the end of the war as chief of the U.S. military mission in Belgrade.)

The OSS, while it ultimately managed to infiltrate a few intelligence-gathering-agents into pre-1941 Carinthia and other parts of Austria, was stymied in its initial effort to mount an operation from the Lower Styrian salient. The partisans evidently trusted the party that wished to traverse the Karawanken in Hesketh-Prichard's footsteps even less than they had the Clowder Mission.[96] Only the Austrian Communist *Kampfgruppe* in the Koralpe, though it proved to be of neither military nor political value, enjoyed their support. (However, Peter Kuchar and his confreres in the Eisenkappel area did rescue several downed U.S. fliers.)[97] Despite the all-pervasive suspicion and restrictions, the astute Lindsay, head of Maclean's team at Fourth Operational Zone headquarters, was remarkably well informed about indigenous circumstances as the material reproduced in the Appendixes demonstrates. Indeed, he radioed messages about Slovene territorial ambitions early as the summer of 1944. The PRO likewise contains two anonynous OSS appraisals of overall conditions in Slovenia. Although politically rather unsophisticated, they are literate, generally informative, and quite useful for their portrayal of the idealistic features of the partisan movement.[98]

Moore, a professional soldier, could be called the doyen of the Allies' SNLA liaison officers. He was first sent to the region in late 1944 as a kind of itinerant demolitions expert and to "have a look at Jones" (Wilkinson), briefly taking the Canadian's place and then following his own, wounded successor, the American Captain James Goodwin (November 1944). A participant in numerous partisan actions, the new man was later described by the head of Macmis as being well-acquainted with local personalities and issues. Maclean's postwar account of Moore's accomplishments and of the partisan fighting effort in 1944, when there were devastating ground and air attacks upon Axis rail links in Slovenia (especially at Litija), was no less laudatory.[99] Moore himself, in a report dated 29 June 1944, described the partisan blow against the Štampetov viaduct on the Ljubljana-Trieste line as "a great example of Ptz efficiency in planning and execution" and "a model of its kind".[100]

What is important in the present context is the fact that by late 1944

Lindsay and Moore had become thoroughly disillusioned with the SNLA as a military force and were more certain than ever about Communist political objectives. Moore's detailed aviso of 10 February 1945, also printed in the Appendix, was received by the Foreign Office's influential Deputy Permanent Undersecretary, Sir Orme Sargent, on 27 March and may be summarized more or less in the bureaucracy's own words. The Slovene partisans, after fighting well the preceding summer were relatively inactive and had been unsuccessful in the little they did undertake to do thereafter. Their obvious intention was to husband their strength and wait for the collapse of the German army group in Yugoslavia in order to seize Ljubljana, Primorje, and Carinthia. Therefore Allied support for them, was no longer militarily justifiable. (Moore actually recommended a scaling-down rather than a complete cutoff.) It was recognized that these views were especially unpalatable to Field Marshal Alexander (then on the best of terms with Tito), but Maclean himself had "no hesitation in accepting Lt. Col. Moore's evaluation of the situation".[101]

This analysis – though it seems unfair, or at least inadquate, to Yugoslav military historians who underscore the potency of the various Nazi counterinsurgency campaigns in Slovenia during 1944 and early 1945 – was also proffered just after the war by one of Moore's colleagues, Captain J.C. Lammie (Royal Engineers), who was serving with the Ninth Corps and fell into German hands on 1 April. The junior officer stated that partisan sabotage units had attempted to sever German communications lines, destroying locomotives and rolling stock. The Slovenes had mounted small, local ambushes and had assaulted out-of-the-way garrisons. However, at no time had they used their main striking force as they could have. They had never employed their full resources to block the foe's advance into the liberated zones. Their policy had been to play for time, conserve their energies, and await the moment of the Nazis' capitulation.[102]

The reaction to Moore's report of another top Foreign Office man, J.M. Addis, was not only to favor terminating assistance but to observe, in good Machiavellian style, that: "If, on the collapse of Germany, Tito can be kept busy for two or three months with a civil war against the White Guards, it would be an admirable situation".[103] The PRO does not seem to contain any evidence that the Allies encouraged such a outcome. Indeed, it is hard to imagine that they could have channeled the rapidly and autonomously flowing stream of history to their liking anyway. Nevertheless, Addis' cynical *Wunschtraum* was soon to be realized, after a fashion, within a strictly Lower Styrian and Carinthian context.

Deakin's memo of 28 April 1945 – also to be found in the Appendixes – reached Macmillan and Anthony Eden too late to have especially affected what by then had become a torrent of interrelated events. Nevertheless, it is as historiographically valuable as Lindsay's and Moore's missives because of its characterization of Carinthian circumstances and the hard stance toward Yugoslavia which the Western governments had now unequivocally adopted. Deakin, the prime minister's prewar assistant in researching the well-known Marlborough biography, was an Oxford-trained scholar and, in later years, has been a prominent academician. As Churchill's onetime confidant he was in a position to play a key role, while a member of the SOE's flamboyant Cairo staff, in the decision to downplay Draža Mihailović's Chetniks and, tentatively, help the partisans. During the summer of 1943 he saw duty on the ground in Montenegro and Bosnia, demonstrating along with his fellow Britons a physical courage which much impressed his equally imperilled comrade-in-arms, Tito, and the memory of which may have influenced the Yugoslav leader at the time (1948) of his break with Stalin.

After heading the SOE's Yugoslav Section back in Cairo, Deakin was seconded to the Foreign Office's Bari dependency and attached as an adviser to the then brand-new BAF. (The Balkan Air Force did more than its name implies: it was an RAF commanded, inter-Allied organization responsible for all land, sea, and air operations in southeastern Europe). His next job was that of British embassy secretary in Belgrade, liberated on 20 October 1944, a period that he recalls today as having been marked by extreme confusion. All that needs to be noted here is the stress his memo placed upon the Yugoslav (rather than Soviet) satellite function of the ÖFF apparatus that had been transplanted to Slovenia.

There was considerable irony in this, for it was the RAF that had flown the exiled Austrian Communist leadership – Franz Honner was so fat that he became stuck in the aircraft's door – from its refuge in Russia to Črnomelj in the first place (November 1944). Another incongruity was that the Austrian battalions formed from the summer of 1944 onward and attached to the SNLA turned out to be mere paper tigers because their Slovene dompteurs questioned whether they could make them perform the required tricks. Deakin's express warning (a confirmation, to be sure, of what had long been suspected) about the plan to seize and annex the Klagenfurt basin should also be underlined. However strong his Yugoslav sympathies, the English diplomat was every whit a *Realpolitiker*, in which respect of course he hardly differed from his friend, Tito.[104]

Another Foreign Office record of approximately the same time (9 May) is equally helpful in depicting what was happening and therefore may be quoted at length:

> This report that Yugoslav troops are preparing to enter Austria has been followed by the report in Mr. Macmillan's telegram 825 that they are actually arriving in the Villach-Klagenfurt area. The Prime Minister has already urged Field Marshal Alexander to press on into Austria, and Caserta telegram 827 reports that British troops may have reached Villach last night.
>
> It looks therefore as if a situation very similar to that in Venezia Giulia is going to arise in Carinthia, and we must hope that our troops arrive before the Yugoslavs have formally established themselves or set up their own administration. There are of course important differences between the two cases. In Venezia Giulia the Yugoslav territorial claims are in part at least justified, and they can count on the sympathy and support of the majority of the local population. In Carinthia the Yugoslav claims are flimsy, and all our evidence goes to show that the local population have no wish to be incorporated into Yugoslavia. Besides it is our stated policy to restore a free and independent Austria, and it has been agreed in principle between the Four Powers that Austria within her 1937 [sic] frontiers will be occupied and controlled by the Four Powers. We therefore cannot condone, as we have done in Venezia Giulia, the establishment of Yugoslav administration, and we must insist on withdrawal of Yugoslav troops, whether regulars or partisans, as soon as operations against the Germans are over. As stated above, British troops are pushing ahead as fast as they can, and I do not see therefore that any further instructions to AFHQ are required. Some diplomatic action in Belgrade does, however, seem very desirable, but if it is to carry weight the Soviet Government must be brought in.[105]

5

The Vernal Finale: Opera Buffa

While high British and U.S. officials were bracing themselves for a confrontation with Tito – Churchill agreed to a gradual cutoff of all deliveries to the Yugoslav Army "on the best pretext there can be found" already on 18 April[106] – the hibernally quiescent Slovene partisans were once more beginning to stir. The thread of military operations, an unravelling one for the SNLA historiographically speaking, must thus be picked up anew.

Perhaps the most striking feature of the war's end on the Balkan front was the skilfully conducted, echeloned withdrawal of the 400,000 man strong German Army Group Southeast (by then amalgamated with Army Group E) commanded by the Luftwaffe general and later (1946) Yugoslav-executed war criminal, the Austrian-born and trained Alexander Löhr. Staffed mainly by officers of Austro-German, indeed Imperial Austro-Hungarian background, this host, belligerent as ever, had pulled back to Croatia with the Yugoslav Army and its turncoat Bulgarian confederates in hot pursuit. Moreover, Soviet divisions were closeby in Hungary and approaching or already in the adjacent, eastern part of Austria, the self-scuttled ship of state which the Allies had agreed to raise from the political vasty deep. Löhr had mingled his men rather adventitiously with some 200,000 Ustashi, a term that now meant all Croatian quislings not merely *Poglavnik* Ante Pavelić's genocide squads. The only recourse for the vast traffic jam of Axis soldiers was to put itself beyond the prewar frontiers and thus escape the massive retribution they suspected would accompany Communist Yugoslav captivity. The fear generated by guilty consciences was, of course, an especially powerful motive for many of them.[107]

It is impossible to broach here the many, still open questions regarding the final campaign.[108] However, the Slovene role must be described if only in outline form. It should be emphasized again that, notwithstanding its high-faluting, nomenclatural edifice of corps, divsions, and brigades dating from 1943, the SNLA remained an essentially guerrilla organization. Although the Western Allies had endowed it with a limited amount of heavy equipment, it was ill-suited for crossing swords with the still more or less well-caparisoned, partly-motorized formations of the Nazis and, up to a point, their native helpers. In all events, Tito's strategy seems to have been to use the Slovene partisans, bolstered by whatever regular Yugoslav Army contingents could be pushed ahead of the main body of his troops, as the wings of a huge pincers that would close upon Carinthia. The special task of the Fourteenth Shock Division was to plug the gap between the prongs of the extended scissors.[109]

However, this scheme harbored two fatal flaws. The seizure of Primorje and the strategically crucial port facilities of Trieste was an equally important Yugoslav objective which necessitated a major diversion of military resources. Control of the city and hence a secure line of communications northward was of course simultaneously an indispensable precondition for the Western Allies' position in postwar Austria and a problem that began to concern Alexander as early as 6 April, three days prior to his planned breakthrough into the Po valley ("Operation Grapeshot" which terminated on 22 April). In all events, the relative numerical weakness – a maximum of perhaps 40,000 men – and the manifold hardware deficiencies of the SNLA were a guarantee that it could not execute its dual mission of halting the retreating enemy and seizing control of Carinthia prior to the arrival of the forward elements of General Richard McCreery's Eighth Army, namely, the 55,000 plus troops of Lieutenant General Sir Charles Keightley's Fifth Corps (Sixth Armoured, Seventy Eighth, and Forty Sixth Infantry Divisions).

The military historian will also recall that Major General Sir Bernard Freyberg's New Zealanders, part of Lieutenant General Sir, later Field Marshal Lord John Harding's three division-strong Thirteenth Corps (also Eighth Army), were pushing with all due speed toward the Isonzo/Soča river and Trieste. Their task was to forestall a coup de main by the 50,000 man-strong Yugoslav Fourth Army which, with Anglo-American logistical and air support, had pushed German and Croatian collaborationist forces northwestward along the Dalmatian coast from Zadar – faster than AFHQ had expected – and had swept into Istria and Primorje in order to bolster the SNLA's relatively impuissant Ninth Corps. The first New Zealanders reached Trieste on 2 May, the day that the separate surrender ("Operation Crossword") of German Army Group Southwest (Italy) went into effect, but found it already partly occupied by Yugoslavs who had come the preceding day. Control of its port facilities had now become an issue of overriding importance.[110] The Carinthian Slovene partisans were meanwhile trying to contribute their moiety. At the beginning of April they received fresh orders to disrupt German communications, the purpose of the SNLA high command not being to expel the foe, whether Nazi or quisling, but to crush him on Yugoslav Slovene soil. This was a third strategic objective – indeed a fourth one if the seizure of state power at home is taken into account –, and it naturally resulted in further depletion of what was very slim military capital to begin with, even with the help of the Yugoslav Army. (The intricate question of the SNLA's relationship to Tito as supreme commander lies beyond the scope of this study.) In any case the immediate problem was that the Nazi rear was still well-manned, even after the transfer of the bulk of the Thirteenth SS Police Regiment to eastern Austro-Styria in order to assist in the OKW's vain attempt to blunt the Soviet thrust.

A mishmash of other policemen, militia, border guards, and second-rate Wehrmacht units – Territorials as well as Replacement Army troops – was still at hand. So were the 5000 boorish and refractory troops of the training regiment and other Carinthian detachments of the Volunteer Waffen SS Grenadier Division "Galicia", recently rechristened in extremis "First Ukrainian".[111] Having been employed, inter alia, to build the makeshift barriers of the Führer's illusory, last-ditch "Alpine Fortress",[112] they fought on, despite a certain propensity to go over the hill, until noon of the day after the general armistice. Little Eisenkappel was chock-a-block with a garrison of some 500 men. Another impediment for the guerrillas was a severe shortage of food stocks, the consequence of the gradual influx of Axis forces from Yugoslavia and Hungary. However, the Carinthian *Odred* did receive reinforcements of a kind: local Austro-German Johnnies-come-lately, leftists whom the Slovenes called, symptomatically, the "German Battalion". This contingent was evidently unrelated to the Austrian battalions which the ÖFF and their Yugoslav Communist patrons cobbled together, causing Deakin what turned out to be unnecessary concern.[113]

The Carinthian Slovene partisans, upon emerging from the bush, experienced great personal exhilaration but played only a minor military role as the war ended. The shattered Northern Battalion, by then containing a mere dozen and a half Slovenes and revived by a troop of Soviet irregulars who had come from Austro-Styria, could move about more freely after the departure of the SS and sparred with the Ruthenians. However, at least before the armistice, it dared not push southward and challenge the throng of retreating Magyars, Germans, and assorted

Yugoslav quislings. Below the Drau, around Zell, there were lively OF doings.[114] The area was considered a kind of liberated zone, and a politcal conference was held in nearby Hintergupf/Zavrh (above St. Margareten im Rosental/Šmarjeta v Rožu) in early April. Shortly thereafter the handful of Nazis remaining in Zell, SS according to Prušnik-Gašper but more likely gendarmes, were shooed out. However, the action was of tactical significance only.

A Replacement Army artillery unit was ordered (2 May) to substitue for the "Greens" and positioned itself along the Loibl pass highway. This strategically expedient move was most likely mandated by Löhr who was now in charge of what had become the front-line. In all events, the purpose was clearly to safeguard a land route that was more important than ever. German and quisling forces were congregating around Ljubljana and would have to travel over it in order to escape from Slovenia. (Franc Krener replaced Rupnik as commander of the White Guard on 5 May in the course of a farcical, eleventh hour coup d'état.) The road would also serve as the emergency exit for a multitude of terrified civilians, supporters of the so-called "Slovene National Committee" recently installed by Rösener.[115]

Another apparent obstacle to SNLA operations were the evidently unconcerted actions of a senior gendarmerie officer and the local Wehrmacht command. (By this time Carinthia was largely cut off from the Reich Government and even from the other *Gauen* of the Ostmark, Vienna having fallen to the Soviets already on 13 April.) Lieutenant Colonel Josef Stossier, who would soon redon his old-Habsburg style uniform as the head of a new "democratic" police force, was well aware of the perils facing Carinthia from his prior involvement in Nazi counterinsurgency operations. Lieutenant General Ferdinand Noedelchen not only led the Replacement Army's 438th "Special Use" (*zur besonderen Verwendung*) Division which had been fighting the partisans but was also in charge de facto, if ultimately under Löhr, of all other armed forces in the Gau of Carinthia. He was assisted by the Reich German Colonel Meng, military governor of Klagenfurt and chief of the 139th Light Mountain Infantry Replacement Regiment. Field and company grade officers of the latter unit, especially the "Austrians", knew that the end was near and began to take steps to prepare for it, first on their own and later with the tacit support of their superiors.

Stossier met with partisan representatives on four separate occasions in April. On 2 May Captain Hans Mayer did the same, threatening, as had Stossier, that the Wehrmacht would continue to fight vigorously with the numerous forces at its disposal. The purported effect was to bluff the guerrillas into momentarilly hesitating. The latter charade, at any rate, was linked to frantic, last-minute maneuvers by Carinthian German civilians, egged on the Nazi "surrender faction", to depose the distracted and vacillating Rainer, hardly the right man for welcoming Keightley to Klagenfurt. The chief objective of all concerned was to avoid the resistance à l'outrance advocated by NSDAP fanatics and to enable the British to the enter the province before the Yugoslavs. The military were doubtlessy also anxious to help Löhr's soldiers safely reach the pre-1938 frontier.[116]

The fact of the matter was that the Nazi police state was still in place. Indeed, it did not relax its stranglehold until virtually the last day of the war. The Gestapo and SD, efficient as ever, had worked throughout the winter and early spring arresting and prosecuting régime opponents of every stripe (especially left-wingers), both German and Slovene. In the Eisenkappel area patrols were still beating the brush in the hope of spooking coveys of guerrillas, especially when there was precise knowledge of where the quarry had gone to ground. Special mention should be made of the bestial massacre of the Sadovnik family (25 April) by a vestigial SS party, evidently because of its its ties to local partisans. They were lolling about the farmyard as the Germans approached but were able to flit into adjacent woods. (The writer has met an emotionally disturbed survivor, Ančka, who was bayoneted and left for dead in the heap of corpses next to her burning home as a child). The site of this atrocity, at Koprein Petzen/Pod Peco, is now a partisan museum and a shrine to the minority of Slovenophone Carinthians who had the strength of will and the opportunity to resist Hitler's "New Order".[117]

While the war's end cannot be a focus of this book, the Carinthian Slovene partisans and their Yugoslav compatriots were nevertheless at the center of the major international crisis – inextricably related to the explosive situation in Venezia Giulia and Trieste – that developed over Austria's southernmost province in May of 1945. It thus deserves to be passed in review, all the more so because the account can be based, at least in part, upon previously unavailable or inadequately, even meretriciously employed primary sources.

Advance parties from the Sixth Armoured, debouching from the Canale valley at Tarvisio at the first light of dawn on 8 May won the forty-five mile race to reach Klagenfurt shortly after 10:00 a.m, thirteen hours before the armistice – signed in Reims and 2:41 a.m. on 7 May – took effect locally. (It began thirteen hours later on the eastern as opposed to the western front.) The American-built Staghound armored cars of the Second Reconnaissance Battalion, followed by others of the Seventh RB, rolled smoothly on their distinctive, giant rubber tires into the city's centrally situated New Square. Wilkinson, alone save for his driver, had shot ahead of them in a

Ford station wagon as head of Number Six Special Force (Staff Section), the name used for the Clowder Mission since March. The SOE's representative, who was either the first or the second Allied officer to arrive in the city, was already in the courtyard of the *Landhaus*, conversing with a group of deferential civilians. They claimed to be the "Austrian" Provisional Provincial Government and were clearly seeking to curry Allied favor as other German Carinthians had done with the guileless American Miles Mission in the spring of 1919.

The Britons beat local guerrillas by only three hours and the Upper Carniolan Kokra *Odred*, which had trudged over the mountains into the Rosental and commandeered a train, by only five to six. (The Sixth Armoured hastened to effect a "blow" on the railway the next day.) A motorized detachment of the Yugoslav Fourth Army, made up of 75 British and American-supplied vehicles, was not far behind. It had followed a round-about route via Kranjska Gora (Krainburg), Tarvisio, and the Wurzen/Koren pass after having been stopped by the British from entering the Canale valley over the Predil pass. The Clowder Mission chief, however, was momentarily less concerned with the "Tits" than with other matters. He was hoping against hope to find Hesketh-Prichard alive. A secondary concern was to collect "loose chaps" dropped into central Styria, useless though his uniformed Austro-German "Joes" had proved to be.[118]

The individuals – "strange characters" – with whom Wilkinson briefly parleyed prior to the appearance of a gaggle of other British army and intelligence functionaries were none other than the aforementioned civilian plotters: they had just assumed what they fancied was executive power thanks to the initiative of the Nazi "surrender faction". Rainer, mesmerized by the belief that he might still play some kind of politico-military role, had abdicated only the night before upon returning from a conference in Graz with Field Marshal Kesselring who had apprised him of the absolute futility of any resistance after Germany's overall capitulation. It had been the less benighted *Gauhauptmann* Meinrad Natmeßnig who took steps to form the provisional provincial government on 5 May, allying himself with a heterogeneous cluster of more presentable, pre-Anschluß politicians and, indirectly, with the Stossier and Noedelchen factions.

Having whispered among themselves for a month or so in certain knowledge of the Third Reich's imminent demise, the civilians sloughed off their wartime cocoons and flapped their wings for Wilkinson and his comrades in the morning sunlight. Sir Peter especially recalls Stefan Tauschitz, a third-rate Talleyrand, whose unsavory past the British were quick to uncover. The office-hungry conspirators are sometimes referred to collectively but much too generously as the Carinthian "resistance movement" or as "Austrian patriots" in contradistinction to the by then superfluous, "moderate" Nazis. The only one among them to have actually put his life on the line was Wedenig, freshly returned from Dachau. The person picked to be the new *Landeshauptmann*, Hans Piesch, turned out two years later to have served as a functionary in the local Nazi agency for denationalizing the Slovene minority and had to resign his sinecure in order to spare the Austrian Foreign Ministry further embarassment in the face of Yugoslav claims upon southern Carinthia.119

Contrary to what official Carinthian historiography would have posterity believe, these odd bedfellows were in no wise responsible, though they strove to contact the Western Allies in various ways, for the prompt arrival of the British Army. Their only tangible achievments were the prevention of several projected Nazi demolitions and the stopping of a few executions. The closely related claim of Walzl that the Britons dithered and dawdled simply to please Tito, whose willing tools they supposedly were, is a singularly unfortunate misinterpretation deriving from both an evidently casual examination of the records stored in Kew and a seriously defective knowledge of World War Two literature. Having known about the SNLA's objectives at least since mid-1944, the Western Allies could not have been more strongly motivated than they were to reach Carinthia as soon as possible. The immediate reason for the Fifth Corps' being in a position to ward off the SNLA was also simple enough. As Walzl himself notes, Globocnik and other Nazi officers, especially the rough-and-ready Waffen SS General Heinz Harmel famed for defending the "Bridge Too Far", commanded almost 33,000 still battle-worthy troops in the heavily mined and fortified Canale valley but offered only token resistance to Keightley's advance, a decision ratified by Löhr ex post facto on 7 May.120

Seconded by Villiers who had made his way separately to Villach via the Isonzo-Soča valley, Wilkinson was quick to perceive the cant being dished up to the British although he stayed for only five days before leaving "Buxton" in command of his platoon-sized "private army" and departing for his new job as comptroller of the Political Branch of the British High Commission for Austria.121 (Major Edward Renton, Captain Patrick Martin-Smith and Lieutenant Finlay Lockhead were some of the other Sixth Force members employed in Carinthia.) Seeking to assert its authority with the help of Stossier's new "Austrian" policemen - *tempora mutantur et nos mutamur in illis* -, the democratic régime *malgré soi* sought to compete with: 1) the immediately established British Military Government; 2) a Yugoslav Army administration; and 3) an OF polity headed by a much respected Völkermarkt physician, Dr. Franc Petek, who was supported by a few Austro-German Communists.

Carinthia's provisional provincial government, like its Yugoslav-sponsored rival, was destined to be short-lived. After the withdrawal of Tito's forces two weeks later, it was relegated to the category of a consultative body. (However, it managed to exercise considerable influence all the same and was later permitted to assume real authority.) The Slovene partisans, for their part, busied themselves, rapine apart, in different ways. They placarded Klagenfurt with proclamations of their rules and intentions, which the British proceeded to tear down. The guerrillas also disarmed and bludgeoned the rebaptized Germanophone cops while encouraging local Yugoslav adherents to stage pro-annexation demonstrations.122

The muddle was neatly summarized by the urbane Macmillan in a telegram from Caserta to his London superiors dated 9 May:

> 1. In addition to trouble over Venezia Giulia Tito is engaged in a scamper into Austria. As you will have seen from my telegram under reference Yugoslav Brigade [Eleventh "Miloš Zidanšek" Brigade of the Fourteenth Division] follow our troops and are generally engaged in an attempt to make good their claims by de facto possession. As you know, these include the Klagenfurt area.
>
> 2. Situation is becoming very embarassing to local British commanders. It seems undesirable to use force at the moment, but incidents may occur or be provoked.
>
> 3. Field Marshal has so far merely reported the situation to the Combined Chiefs of Staff. But some clear instructions must soon be issued as to whether he is to order 8th Army to close Austrian frontier and eject them from the positions into which they have infiltrated. Presumably the frontier as at 1937 is the right one.
>
> 4. Since zones of Russian, Italian [sic], French, and British occupation of Austria have been virtually agreed at European Advisory Commission, intentions should presumably be communicated by United States and United Kingdom Governments to the Soviet and French Governments.
>
> 5. Field Marshal and I feel this is in a different category from Venezia Giulia. Austrian occupation has been agreed between the four powers, and principle that the powers and these only should be charged with the task has been accepted. There has been no such agreement about Italian territory.123

By 10 May it was apparent at AFHQ that the situation was even graver than described in Macmillan's signal of the preceding day. Keightley asked Eighth Army Headquarters for permission to **shoot** at the Yugoslavs

The Vernal Finale: Opera Buffa 63

although, as matters developed, he and McCreery, were forced to hold their fire and extemporize. There was as yet no choice in the matter. Two days earlier Alexander had sent his chief of staff, General William Morgan, to Tito in order to persuade him to pull back from from the western part of Venezia Giulia. The reason was that Harding had secured no more than a toehold there, and AFHQ had to control not only the deep-water Trieste harbor but also the region's railways and roads in order to secure its line of communications to Vienna. (Carinthia was of course equally significant in this regard.) Taking no chances, the Mediterranean theater commander simultaneously began to plan an eleven division-strong strike against Yugoslavia and to solicit the support of the highest Allied political and military authorities.[124]

Alexander was seeking to make Tito adhere, in modified form, to a personal commitment (February) to permit Anglo-American governance of Venezia Giulia, inluding the old Austro-Hungarian naval base at Pula, until peace negotiations determined its permanent fate. The Field Marshal's emissary, flown to Belgrade in a B17, proposed that Yugoslavia accept a compromise, de facto partition of a territory which for Slovenes and Croats was the Littoral and Istria, not Venezia Giulia. The so-called "Morgan Line" would not only suit AFHQ's military requirements but also, supposedly, accomodate both Yugoslav and Italian ethno-political interests.

The effort met almost immediately (9 May) with failure although AFHQ did not give up hope entirely and the Yugoslav Army pulled back from the western shore of the Isonzo-Soča on 11 May. The prospect of a new war thus loomed ominously. There was much to worry about. If the Russians intervened, Keightley would be exposed on two flanks, northeast along the rail and highway route into Styria and east along the course of the Drau. Other potential problems – those of supply and of troop morale resulting from a seemingly incomprehensible order to turn about and fight a propagandistically canonized ally – were also formidable and in the latter instance the source of great concern not merely in Caserta but in London and, above all, Washington.[125]

What happened over the succeeding, tumultuous eleven days – the Yugoslavs began to leave Carinthia on 21 May – is vividly recorded in a series of wirelesses sent by the major personalities involved, especially "Supermac" and Alexander. On 11 May the Minister Resident reported that Tito was demanding that the major powers allow him to participate in the occupation of Austria; however, Yugoslavia's strong man had received a favorable reply only from Moscow. Macmillan added wryly that the Communist leader was hardly an "unprejudiced participant". The Foreign Office replied that while the matter was still under consideration, it certainly could not concur. The next day Alexander specifically requested Tito to withdraw Yugoslav troops from Carinthia because of the establishment of an Allied Military Government. The field marshal promised to "administer the area impartially and without prejudice to any claim you may wish to make....". The real military reason was of course the protection of his "L.C.".[126]

On 13 May London was told that the Yugoslav Army was pulling back, but it soon became evident that this had only to do with a reshuffle of forces, probably related to the battle of Ferlach (10-11 May) and continuing action against the Ustashi in Slovene Styria. The first of many reports of partisan looting in Klagenfurt and elsewhere – mainly food, it appears – were also passed on.[127] (The capital city, battered by Allied bombing raids, had many unsecured buildings.) Meanwhile Churchill had asked Truman – the American were at first unwilling to support the British who had had to go it alone in Greece the preceeding December – to backstop the British, but the President had already decided to reverse U.S. policy of his own accord. Word of the change reached London on the evening of 12 May but was not immediately forwarded to Caserta. The assent of other governments – those of Brazil, Poland, and the Commonwealth, troops of which formed part of Alexander's command – would also be necessary.[128]

On 14 May the British embassy in Belgrade reported that Tito was arguing that things had changed since the Moscow Declaration. Yugoslavia had suffered immeasurably, and "it would therefore be unjust to deny the Yugoslav army the right to pursue the enemy over the pre-war frontier and to occupy the territory liberated from the enemy". The Yugoslavs were pursuing a foe who had not capitulated (Ustashi and *domobranci*). In an attempt to make the arrangement sound more attractive, the meaningless promise was made that they would be put under Alexander's command.[129] Whatever domestic political considerations weighed on Tito's mind – and the urgent need to satisfy peculiarly Slovene aspirations must have been the paramount one – he had to keep to himself.

Also on the fourteenth Macmillan confirmed that Keightley's soldiers were firmly installed in Carinthia but were unable to contain the Yugoslavs' "minor reign of terror". The Britons could hold out until they were strong enough to clear up the whole area, but meanwhile, concerned about their exposed line of communications back to Italy, they could not prevent "high-handed actions". "Mac the Knife" – as he was called after he became prime minister – certainly knew what he was talking about, for he had just returned from a quick tour of Eighth Army command posts, including a three hour, flying visit to Klagenfurt and conference with Keightley (13 May), an episode that lies at the root of what has become a major historiographical, political, and indeed legal fracas.

The purpose of the trip, it is now finally clear, had been to pursue Alexander's suggestion that local British generals be "put.... in the political picture", opaque because of the Americans' transitory unwillingness to sanction the use of force against Tito. It was absolutely essential to tell the field commanders to continue following the policy of restraint until inter-Allied differences were resolved. (Macmillan was unaware of Truman's about-face on the day in question.)[130] The dilemma of the Fifth Corps was especially troublesome and of inordinate proportions, Carinthia having been inundated with as many as half a million surrendered enemy troops and refugees, "displaced persons" in the bureaucratic jargon of the era.[131] By this time the crisis was at its peak: Churchill wrote to Sargent that "the change in the situation is enormous....; [there is] acute tension between us and Tito.[132]

On 15 May Macmillan, back at AFHQ since mid-afternoon of 13 May, radioed that the Yugoslavs were now firmly implanted in Völkermarkt, the headquarters of the Fourteenth Division. The latter unit comprised some 6000 effectives, major reinforcements for the 1500 man strong Motorized Detachment and the perhaps half as many partisans of the Carinthian and Kokra *Odredi*. The Sattnitz guerrillas, for their part, were proudly standing watch over the Ducal Chair, a hoary symbol of Slovene nationhood, located on the Zollfeld-Gosposvetsko polje, about ten kilometers northeast of Klagenfurt near Maria-Saal. The closest Yugoslav regular formation was the Third Army, but it was temporarily tied down mopping up the roughly one third of Löhr's army and the bulk of the Ustashi trapped inside Yugoslavia. Another cause for worry, though nothing came of it in the end, was a second flurry of hesitation on Washington's part.[133]

The next two days brought even more inauspicious news. The post-armistice battles in Slovene Styria and the Meža valley now over, an additional 2000 Yugoslav Third Army regulars had slipped into the border town of Lavamünd/Labot, and two divisions of the Fourth Army were being readied to support them. Bulgarian forces were also just inside the frontier and the Soviets close by. However, there was no obvious change in the local situation. The partisans seemed to be confused and out of touch with their superiors. Alexander, a superb professional soldier, remained concerned about their rough demeanor, the fragile line of communications back to Italy, and the shaky disposition of the Fifth Corps. Spread out over a wide region, Keightley's men were also responsible for shepherding the masses of surrendered enemy personnel into huge holding pens ("cages") and provisioning them. However, they could not be sustained locally for long, and to send them southward, where food stocks were equally insufficient, would "paralise" what was already an only barely functional logistical apparatus crucial to the projected offensive operations.[134]

By 18 May the Americans were preparing to leave for Carinthia in force at Eisenhower's explicit command. Contingency planning had apparently begun some time earlier, i.e., before the war had actually ended. Five divisions from the U.S. Third Army would be concentrated in the Enns valley, buttressed by the Ninth Air Force, and sent to assist Keightley. A red alert was issued on 20 May and not cancelled until 21 June, the original target date for the strike against Tito. (A few American reconnassance units involved in what was called "Operation Coldstream" actually did penetrate into the upper Drau valley as far as Spittal although they were forced to by snow-covered passes to detour via Innsbruck and the East Tyrol.)[135] The tension had now reached the breaking point. Alexander reported, also on 18 May, that:

> the behaviour of the Yugoslavs is making a very unfavourable impression upon the troops, both British and American. The men feel that by being unable to prevent actions which offend their traditional sense of justice they are condoning such behaviour. As a result feeling against the Yugoslavs is getting stronger daily.

It was clear, he added, that the responsibilities of occupation could not be shared under conditions of this kind.[136]

6

The Aftermath: A Legacy of Bitterness

Wilkinson, back in Italy for a while and indignant over what he had witnessed during his short stay in Carinthia or had learned since he left, wrote a personal letter to Gubbins. The partisans' deportations of native Carinthians were horrific. Sixty people had been abducted from Völkermarkt and Feistritz im Rosental. (The actual total was 263 persons.) The victims were decent folk, not Nazis. POW's were being treated relatively humanely, however. While brigandage was the order of the day, there had been no blood baths. Even the SS and Nazi party members were not being molested. Reality was more complex, however. Several minor massacres did occur, apparently unbeknown to the British, and a large, if indeterminable proportion of the persons spirited away were in fact full-fledged Nazis. There were in all events a wide range of reasons for picking the individuals in question. It is clear that the pent-up rage of the partisans toward exploitative capitalists or "ethnic traitors" and the wartime, nationalist-tinged message of social revolution was only part of the story.[137]

While the special SNLA security detachments were checking off the names of Carinthian German civilians on their sometimes inaccurate hit lists, a strange British-Yugoslav covenant regarding another category of former enemy was taking shape – gradually, by happenstance, and, in the last analysis, as much on the intergovernmental-diplomatic plane as on the various levels of military command. Though a succession of Fifth Corps documents make it seem at first glance that there was an outright trade-off or quid pro quo – Tito's forces would leave the Klagenfurt basin while Keightley would send back the remaining, sundry Yugoslav quislings who had escaped to Austria –, appearances are deceiving. The actual circumstances were singularly entangled and complex. To begin with, the lower or Carinthian level discussions were conducted by possibly battle-fatigued officers whose communications with their superiors back in Italy were marked by great confusion and contradiction. The local talks began on 15 May, just two days after Macmillan's fleeting visit, under the pressure of the rapidly escalating international crisis.

On the same day AFHQ, at McCreery's initiative of 14 May ("suggest Croats become Tito's show"), was instructing Macmis in the Belgrade embassy to inform the Yugoslav government of its willingness to "turn over" 200,000 Yugoslav nationals. They were said, incorrectly, to have "surrendered" to Keightley and were, it appears, the Croatian forces that were piling up on the Yugoslav side of the pre-1941 (1938) frontier near Bleiburg/Pliberk rather than other much smaller, non-Croatian collaborationist units already on Carinthian soil. The entirely pragmatic reason for the offer, in the aftermath of which the Croats were converted, willy-nilly into all kinds of Yugoslav quislings, was the Eighth Army's physical inability to handle them under the prevailing conditions of logistical stringency and preparations for engaging in fresh warfare. Air Vice Marshal Sir Arthur Lee, who had "untidily" (Deakin) succeeded Maclean in March, was working from the so-called "Office of the Supreme Allied Commander's Representative with the Yugoslav General Staff" in the British Embassy building and was by all accounts ill-suited for his post, proceeded to execute Caserta's orders. He broached the issue to his Yugoslav counterparts on 16 May.

Written confirmation of acceptance came from Major General Ljudrag Djurić the next day: "Kindly inform us where our delegates are to meet the delegates appointed by Field Marshal Alexander for the handing over.....". Deakin, Ambassador Ralph S. Stevenson, and Lindsay–by then head of the U.S. Military Mission in Belgrade, with whom Lee was in touch on other occasions–were not informed and did not even discuss the issue among themselves. (Most documents in the relevant WO file bear the notation "copy to Col. Deakin" but not in the case at hand.) Thus it was that the phlebotomy that Wilkinson could not discern in Carinthia would occur on Yugoslav soil instead. The troops affected were destined to be only about an eighth of the aggolermation of Ustashi opposite Bleiburg and but would also include Serbs and Slovenes. Had anyone bothered to consult Maclean back in London, so he has told the writer, his answer would have been that the Fifth Corps' grab-bag of captives faced "certain death".

By 19 May the Carinthian-Istrian powder keg was about to explode. Macmillan informed London that with the final capitulation of the mass of Croatian collaborationists on Yugoslav soil–a prelude to which was the largely but not fully effective blocking action (15 May) of the Thirty Eighth Irish Brigade outside Bleiburg–five of Tito's divisions were already in Austria or about to enter. Orders went out to SACMED (Supreme Allied Commander Mediterranean) to dislodge the Yugoslavs by "force from the area we require". However, with only verbal support from a peeved Stalin to whom he was already unwilling to toady and unable by himself to prevail militarily against the hand that only so recently had been feeding him, Tito informed indefatigable Ambassador Stevenson, also on 19 May, that his forces, a probable total of 16,000 men on Carinthian soil, would go back to their own country. (The Yugoslav leader, says Deakin, was later rumored to have sat up all night waiting for a telephone call from the Kremlin that never came.) The makeshift, haphazardly coordinated combination of diplomatic pressure-exercised simultaneously by the West's Moscow representatives-and a firm military posture had worked like a charm. To what extent Tito was apprised of the impending use of force against him must remain an open question.

Keightley's adjutant, Brigadier A.R.W. "Toby" Low (Lord Aldington) next met with Belgrade's two local spokesmen: the freshly arrived Lieutenant Colonel Doko Ivanović (Third Army) and the already present Lieutenant Colonel France Hočevar (Fourth Army). A two part agreement was made "in an atmosphere of great cordiality", subsequently enhanced by a Yugoslav-donated case of champagne. Ivanović, at 7:00 p.m., 19 May, and Hočevar, at 11:00 a.m., 20 May, both promised an an immediate Yugoslav withdrawal from Carinthia. Low, for his part, would return left-over Ustashi – their evacuation had begun already May 17 – along with captive Serbs and Slovenes, having been told that they would be fairly treated. A request to repatriate Serbian quislings who had fought under Globocnik's command in Istria and the Littoral and had surrendered to the British on the west bank of the Isonzo/Soča was tactfully rebuffed. The Fifth Corps saw no reason to extend the accord to less threatened northeastern Italy, its responsibilty in any case.

The second half of the compact, summarized in writing but not subscribed, may be characterized as a **fortuitous** consolation prize or windfall: there are no grounds for concluding that Tito left Austria simply because of a payment in human flesh. However, the opportunity to maintain for a short while the standoff over the more important Littoral and Trieste, concerning which the Allies were still planing a resort to arms and which was provisionally settled only on 9 June, could also have affected his decision.138

The disillusionment of rank-and-file Slovene partisans could hardly have been greater after three years of travail and sacrifice. Among other things, the members of the Carinthian *Odred* were told that, if they did not break camp along with the other Yugoslavs, they would be quartered in the POW "cages". Taking their swag with them–the British did relent and permit collection of what was strictly *praeda militaris*, especially the (deliberately disabled) vehicles and artillery so necessary for transforming them into anything like a regular army –, the SNLA guerrillas recrossed the frontier *z grenkobo v srcu* ("with bitterness in their hearts").139 The Irish soldiers could barely trust their eyes, especially with respect to the guerrillas. The Thirty Eighth's war diary states: "What was not so certain was whether the odd bandit groups operating independently would also comply".[140]

The irony of using a Nazi expression (*das Bandenwesen*) will not be lost upon anyone conversant with the source materials or indeed with the story of Hitler's rule in Europe altogether. The adoption of the term was also a harbinger of the attitude of the freshly installed British occupation authorities toward the OF leaders. It should be noted in passing that Prušnik-Gašper and others hastily shed their piebald uniforms and stayed behind as Austrian citizens in the technical sense of the word. They set about forthwith revamping their still illegal organization which proved almost as repugnant to the province's new masters as it had been to the old. By 1947 the inveterate Lobnik conspirator would be serving another stretch in the Graz calaboose where the clerical fascists had deposited him ten years earlier.[141]

Before attempting to assess the historical significance of Carinthia's *petite guerre*, an epilogue must be added, for it will help the reader to understand even better the resentment, wrath, and sorrow experienced by the departing SNLA troops and those of their comrades who chose to remain. The post-armistice donnybrook at Ferlach, though a mere scuffle when compared to other encounters of World War Two, was the only major action on Austro-Carinthian territory and the second of but two pitched battles involving insurgent Carinthian Slovenes (the first having been fought at Črna).

From the guerrillas' vantage, the engagement was a disaster or, in their own words, a tragedy representing the "last crimes of the traitors". From a military historical perspective, it was simply another illustration of the validity of the basic precept that irregulars should not make a stand in the open, above all when faced by superior numbers. Another negative factor was the partisans' apparent lack of organizational cohesion. The indigenous troops included most of the Carinthian *Odred*, fleshed out by many last-minute volunteers, and the understrength "German Battalion". Made up of Gestapo-harassed Social Democrats (who were also called the *Kärntner Partisanen*), the latter unit was evidently connected to the recently founded, still little studied "Austrian Freedom League" or ÖFB which had just seized control of Ferlach's municipal administration.[142]

Of course, it must be granted that, as is so often the case in combat, the initial circumstances were quite accidental. The native Carinthians and the "Mirko Bračič" or Thirteenth Brigade of the later patriotically canonized "Štirnjasta" (Fourteenth Division), which rushed to the scene in order to assist them, were not actually looking for a fight. Seeking merely to accept the surrender of hostile formations – some 10,000 Nazis and 20,000 quislings ostensibly commanded by a German colonel and rechristened, in his own name, the "*Korpsgruppe* Werner von Seeler" – that were pouring over the Loibl pass from from Carniola, they fell victim to a skilfully coordinated, surprise assault, backed by artillery. The foe, including many inveterate killers and war criminals (of whom Rösener was only the most prominent), were desperate to escape the SNLA and the Yugoslav Army that was coming to its aid.

The first enemy unit to appear, evidently on 9 May, was the Thirteenth or "Artur Phleps" Regiment of the mainly ethnic German Seventh Waffen SS Volunteer Mountain Division "Prince Eugene", which passed over the adjacent Drau river bridge at Hollenburg/Humberk after the murder of a Carinthian *Odred* parliamentary in Ferlach's Hotel Just.[143] Other contingents, of strictly Carniolan provenance but technically part of Army Group Southeast since 25 April, followed, and the guerrillas began, willy-nilly, to expropriate much needed heavy equipment and vehicles. The troops who had begun to lay down their weapons encompassed elements of the evanescent Rösener's three Carniolan SS Police Regiments (the Seventeenth, Nineteenth, and Twenty-Fifth), Waffen SS odds and ends, part of a flak division, *Feldgendarmerie*, border guards, non-SS paramilitary police with tanks, and a regiment of the infamous Brandenburg "Special Use" Division (a counterinsurgency, "dirty tricks" outfit).

Behind and/or intermingled with the Nazis was a gallimaufry of collaborationists: a horde – perhaps as many as 13,000 men – of Krener's *domobranci*, the "Wariag" Regiment of the Russian Liberation Army or ROA (*Vlassovci*), two regiments of the so-called Serbian Volunteer Corps (*Nedici, Ljotici*), 4500 White Russians of Anatoli Rogozhin's *Schutzkorps Serbien* or *Ruskii Korpus* as its members preferred to think of themselves, 400 Mihailović Chetniks, and – according to Prušnik-Gašper – some Ustashi as well.[144] An estimated 6000 anti-Communist Slovene civilian refugees tagged behind under the most trying conditions.

The surrendering Germans, apparently infuriated over finding the nascent SPÖ in charge of Ferlach and in cahoots with Slovene guerrillas, grabbed their guns again as part of an attack that began at 5:00 p.m. on 10 May. There was savage combat in the streets of the cannon-battered, burning town. Once again the SS gangsters (Twenty Fifth Regiment) trampled their wounded foes to death, throwing the corpses into the Drau. The Germanophone leftists, who included not only a leavening of a few, ideologically sympathetic local gendarmes but some *Volkssturm* men, were decimated. (The great majority of the gendarmerie had prudently departed southern Carinthia along with other Nazi troops.) The Slovene irregulars, though reinforced by the Fourth Army's Motorized Detachment, which lost several of its totally inadequate Honey or Stuart tanks (a light vehicle equipped only with a 37 mm peashooter) to *Panzerfäuste*, had to recoil in the next morning's fighting and let their adversaries follow the path of the "Artur Phleps" Regiment across the river. The brutalized Germans and their Slavic puppets thus managed, during the rest of the day and on 12 May, to achieve their undoubted objective of surrendering to British troops waiting at Hollenburg, merely idle bystanders as far as the partisans were concerned.

Supervised by a squadron of the First Derbyshire Yeomanry (Sixty-First Infantry Brigade, Sixth Armoured), the victorious fascists trotted off to internment at Viktring/Vetrinje outside Klagenfurt. Von Seeler, a tidy-minded staff officer, remained in command although his Slovene cohorts, always rather petulant, soon became fractious. Up to that point, he had in fact served as a kind of straw man: Rösener, along with Krener, almost certainly supervised the whole Ferlach business à perte de vue although he had formally given up his Slovene post already on 8 May. The Higher SS and Police Leader thereupon (11 or 12 May) took a powder dressed as a common soldier. Why the SNLA did not blow up the bridge, which had been secured five days earlier by other SS soldiers (probably from the Sixteenth Panzer Grenadier Division) but was in its hands at the time of the fighting, is something of a mystery.[145]

The partisan dead probably totalled well over 200 dead. The Carinthian guerrillas including the author's friend, Peter Kuchar, who was there, and the Yugoslavs were understandably incensed over casualties of such magnitude, at least by their standards. Relations between them and the British, who had been specifically enjoined by Keightley (following instructions that stemmed in the last instance from Churchill) well in advance to combine firmness with fair play and the utmost degree of tact, took a decided turn for the worse. Burdened by Anglophobic memories altogether, the Carinthian Slovenes still speak of a Perfidious Albion. The fact that the Derbyshires' Major I.H.P. Dolan twice drove to Ferlach (9-10 May) and engaged in discussions with the Germans lies at the root of this impression of deliberate betrayal which, paradoxically, they share with *schadenfroh* neo-Nazi Carinthians.

However, considering the host of difficulties with which Keightley had to contend, armed intervention, as opposed to (abortive) mediation, was unquestionably impossible. Even if his forces had not been overextended, the grand tactical problems – a crossing of the artificially broad and deep Drau at more distant points and lateral disposition in elevated, forested terrain – would have been virtually insuperable. Wilkinson's comment on the affair (and he was in Carinthia when the battle took place) is that, since the armistice was mutually binding upon the British and the Germans, any direct involvement of the Fifth Corps would have been illegal. It was "their bird", in other words, a matter for the Communist Yugoslavs and their opponents to thrash out for themselves. It must of course be granted that an SLNA setback was scarcely an inconvenience for the sorely tried Fifth Corps.[146]

To be sure, the final exertions proved to be vain for the great majority of the quislings who had retreated from Slovenia. (The civilian refugees were entirely spared but only at the last minute.) AFHQ had issued orders already on 14 May to repatriate all Yugoslavs who had fought for the Germans. This was a preamble to Caserta's aforementioned (15 May) offer to Tito, which, it must be stressed again, the labyrinthine documentary record shows to have been made not in order to bribe the Yugoslav leader but for reasons of logistical and operational expediency. The intention was to exclude "Chetniks" – understood, naively it seems, as any kind of anti-Tito Serb – in keeping with stated Allied policy, but the message actually sent to McCreery and Keightley failed to mention this. (Morgan visited Klagenfurt on 16 May in conjunction with preparations for the strike against Tito and became more cognizant than ever of the burden the surrendered Yugoslav collaborationist personnel represented.)[147]

The last Croatians were packed off on 23 May. The Serbs came next. Roughly 11,000 Slovenes were hindmost. Lulled into acquiescence by the lie that they were being shifted to Italy, they were coerced only upon learning of British cozenage through the escape of a few earlier "repatriates". Jammed into sealed railway cars at Maria Elend/Pod gorje, they travelled through the Rosenbach tunnel into Yugoslavia and, like the non-Slovenes, were largely immolated. Why Tito did not honor Ivanović's and Hočevar's guarantee of a humane reception is still hard to explain. Was the killing done merely for vengeance and domestic policy reasons or, as seems more plausible, mainly because of the continuing Trieste crisis? In all events, Djilas noted later, cryptically, that "massacres are the fruit of bitterness and of the calculations of leaders". [148]

A similar fate befell the maleficent Cosssacks of Hellmuth von Pannwitz' Fifteenth SS Cavalry Corps, who had smashed their way into the Völkermarkt area after the armistice, as well as a wide variety of other Nazi-employed Soviet citizens and even a few "White Russians" (a term imprecisely used by contemporaries). The existence of the Yalta Agreement or rather the repatriation accord arising from it meant that virtually all of them were forcibly sent back to the USSR as Soviet nationals – a category that proved difficult to define in practice despite the official yardstick of the 1939 frontiers. In order to accomplish this, Keightley had to authorize the use of force. The "repatriates" – in Yugoslavia's case as well – were mostly but by no means entirely soldiers: the designation "camp follower" could also lead to the deadly consequences which the British Cabinet itself foresaw and decided to overlook already in latter 1944. As far the quisling warriors were concerned, the procedure was collective classification – whole formations – rather than individual selection, impossible under the current conditions of military duress. Thus it was that Rogozhin's men escaped the fatal lot of their Serbian comrades-in-arms.

The largest single contingent of Soviet returnees consisted of approximately 25,000 other, evidently not quite so noxious "Cossacks" – an equally vague appellation – and just under 5000, ill-reputed "Caucasian" legionnaires (Georgians, Circassians, and Avaric tribesmen). They were led by the ex-Red Army general, Timofei Domanov, and had been encamped in the upper Drau valley near Lienz in East Tyrol since their flight from adjacent northeastern Italy across the Plöcken and Gailberg passes. An associated formation, were the odd 1400 Kuban Cossacks of the Russian Civil War general, Andrei Shkuro. Like the Foreign Office, the Nazis had feared that the Italian and Slovene partisans might join hands and had settled the anti-Communist "Russians", along with many women and children, in Venezia Giulia, Friulia, and Carnia the previous summer. Supposed to function as a kind of cordon sanitaire, they had constituted a veritable colony known as Kazachi Stan or "Cossack Land".[149]

It is not possible to probe this abstruse, polemical, and emotion-laden topic in any depth here. All that can be said is that the thesis of a "conspiracy", a nefarious plot instigated by Soviet intelligence and brought to fruition by Macmillan acting through a pliable Keightley and Low, has been refuted most recently beyond any reasonable doubt. The new sifting of evidence fully confirms the thesis that pragmatic, if heartless, indeed ruthless military considerations were determinative: it was necessary above all else to "clear the decks", as Alexander, seeking to shift the onorous responsibility to Churchill, stated in a signal of 16 May 1945 and to "apply simple rules of thumb" as Britain's scrupulously researched, official campaign history puts it.

It may be worth adding that there was a perhaps subliminally influential paradigm for Keightley's and Low's strictly technical reasoning. In an earlier, very thorough policy discussion involving Deakin in Belgrade, the BAF and Caserta, Allied intelligence officers had weighed both the political and logistical implications of granting asylum to collaborationists captured by the few Anglo-American troops on Yugoslav soil (Land Forces Adriatic) and had recommended against it.[150] Of course ratiocination is one thing and reality another. One cannot overlook the fact that the cunningly and brutally conducted fulfillment of the different agreements with Tito and the Soviets sickened many of the Fifth Corps soldiers involved, burdens the conscience of those of them who are still alive, and somehow weighs upon the British Army's corporative sense of honor. It is only scant comfort that every national host has at least one, if not more such skeletons in its closet.

A further reflection seems apropos. Since Keightley's and Low's actions were affected by the advice of the civilian Macmillan during his lightning visit to Klagenfurt (that occurred before the Yugoslav quislings had become a major problem and apparently related only to the worsening military crisis and the already encamped "Cossacks"), they should likewise be viewed politically and this notwithstanding the dissenting view of

Macmillan's official biographer, Alistair Horne. Indeed, the higher ranking Generals Alexander and Morgan as well as Western diplomats outside Italy were implicated to an even greater degree in the Carinthian-Istrian emergency, which thus appears altogether to be a prime example of the inevitable concatenation of war and politics according to the classical definitions of Clausewitz.

The contemporary notations of a lower-level observer seem to support this bipolar interpretation. Captain Nigel Nicolson, the First Guards Brigade intelligence officer whose chatty "sitreps" and logbook are useful sources for the history of the Fifth Corps, wrote on 13 May that return of the collaborationists was sure to result in their deaths. However, only eight days later, having been sharply reprimanded by Major General Horatius Murray (Sixth Armoured) for opposing the policy, having accepted Ivanović's and Hočevar's assurances that no harm would come to them and apparently reflecting a commonly held staff viewpoint, he persuaded himself that "in Carinthia at least, the Tito problem has been ended by an arrangement which is highly satisfactory for ourselves". (Nicholson's wording suggests that he thought at the time a deal had been struck.) In all events, the consequence was that many personally innocent quislings were doomed to die alongside genuine war criminals. Krener, it is worth noting, caught wind – rather late – of what was afoot, protested, and then faded from view, dying thirty two years later in an ideologically more congenial Argentina.[151]

Yet another way of viewing the Carinthian-Istrian imbroglio is that of soldiers practicing *Realpolitik* although the case at hand represents an especially risky variety. Was it not better to take a chance with the captives' lives and, having rid one's self of an impossible manpower and logistical impediment, be able to reduce the casualties that outright expulsion of the Yugoslav Army would entail? Multilateral hostilities, perhaps a humiliating defeat, and a third world war were also quite conceivable at the moment in question. After all, the responsible commanders could not have known in advance that Stalin would refuse to pull Tito's Slovene chestnuts out of the fire. It bears recalling once more that the Fifth Corps, in conjunction with the whole Fifteenth Army Group in Italy and the U.S. "Coldstream" forces, was already furtively preparing what was dubbed "Operation Beehive" while it was shipping back the first lot of Croatian quislings to Yugoslavia and sparring verbally with Tito's representatives (i.e., before 19 May).

The furious debate over alleged British "war crimes" may now subside since the doctrinaire, right-wing advocates of the conspiracy theory have been shown to be such inadequate researchers, to a degree that raises doubt about their very capacity to think dispassionately and analytically. Nevertheless, it is a matter of elemental justice to observe that the rancor felt by the thwarted Slovene partisans was anything but unique. The bilious legacy was shared with their Germanophone and bilingual adversaries, wartime targets of assassins' bullets as well as post-armistice victims of abductions and yet further "justifications". The same thing holds true for the families and friends of the 6000-7000 *domobranci* butchered upon their return to Slovenia, especially at the "Pits of Kočevje".[152] Their "repatriation" – approved by Alexander in patent violation of the declared policy of the British and American governments – and mass occision are a painful subject that not only Britons must confront. Present-day Slovenia, indeed all of Yugoslavia if the likewise systematically slaughtered Serbian and Croatian quislings are included, must ultimately come to terms with its blood-stained origins.

Nor should one overlook the grief of SOE men, however obliquely expressed, over the loss of a fondly remembered comrade, one of several hundred fallen standard-bearers of Britain's underground struggle against the evils of Hitlerism. The stricken consciences of certain aging Fifth Corps soldiers, especially those who had to manhandle and even shoot the disarmed "Cossacks", bear recalling too. Deakin, looking back from the special vantage of someone who has been soldier, diplomat, and historian, has seen fit to reiterate Bismarck's gloomy, admittedly condescending dictum that the Balkans were not worth the bones of a Pomeranian grenadier.[153] Clearly then the harvest of war savors ill to all who partake of it.

Conclusions

What may be inferred from the chain of events described hitherto? First, it seems that Carinthia's guerrilla war reflects what is known about the reciprocal relationship between incipient capitalist economic development, social class formation, and its concomitant of a dynamic social psychology. Under the extreme conditions of totalitarian rule, persecution of the underclass easily leads to physical resistance by persons who might otherwise have resigned themselves to a fate of gradual assimilation. Admittedly, it is unlikely that armed opposition would have gone beyond the level of the "Green Cadres" had there been no political, ideological, and military organization from the contiguous Slovene heartland and, more importantly, logistical support from the SOE. The contrast with Burgenland's passive, even phlegmatic Croats comes readily to mind. Clearly, the thickly wooded, Alpine terrain was also an indispensable factor. Finding cover out on the plains was a quite different matter as SOE agent Basil Davidson was quick to discover in the Hungarian-ruled Voivodina.

The strictly military facets of the story should also be borne in mind. The fighting undoubtedly fits the classical pattern of guerrilla warfare with its ghastly spiral of stealthy assaults, counterblows, reprisals, and atrocities. Goya's etchings in the Prado, awesome to behold, are more telling than anything that has ever been written. ("Guerrilla" is after all a Castilian word.) Nazi counterinsurgency, which presupposed the active collaboration of at least a portion of Carinthia's Slovenophone population, proved highly effective even if the partisans could not be eradicated. Although there was wide support from nationally conscious Slovenes including persons who hearkened to the voice of the clergy, the dissidents, unlike their Napoleonic-era Spanish precursors, represented only one, probably lesser element within the province's overall linguistic minority. The lethal contempt felt for *nemčurji* is indicative of this.

Another question is whether the guerrilla struggle in Carinthia facilitated the Allied victory in a meaningful way, especially since subsequent

Yugoslav territorial claims were partly based on such an assertion.[154] As indicated, the equivalent of an enemy division was prevented from fighting elsewhere. Downed British and American aviators were rescued.[155] Substantial material damage was inflicted although it appears that on balance the partisans did not impede a significant wartime expansion of the Carinthian economy. Clearly, they had no effect at all upon the progress of the huge Drau river power project. In all events, the greatest harm was done was in the Meža valley as well as in "Carinthian" Gorenjsko.

A further issue, which almost certainly will never be satisfactorily resolved, is the "body count". It is highly improbable that 3855 enemy were slain as Slovene spokesmen have long asserted.[156] Even if the figure were halved, it would need to encompass actions outside Austro-Carinthia and assassinated civilians. Conversely, a total of 1080 partisan dead sounds right, especially if one includes couriers (many of whom were killed by avalanches), OF agents, Carniolan, Styrian, and Meza valley Slovenes as well as the locally-recruited slave laborers and POW's. However, one should emphasize that the current Carinthian German nationalist disparagement of these sacrifices on the grounds that the majority of the casualties were not Austro-Carinthian Slovenes is a crude distortion of the given historical circumstances. Carinthia's 14,000, euphemistically labeled *Fremdarbeiter* were not enjoying a holiday in the fancy hostelries along the shores of the Wörthersee. The treatment meted out to the French, Polish, Soviet, and (1941) Yugoslav POW's was even worse, so appalling in fact that the British could barely restrain them from taking vengeance upon their tormentors after the armistice.[157]

In summary, it may be said that the Carinthian Slovene partisans suffered horrendously and exhibited impressive fortitude in the face of Nazi repression. This remains true notwithstanding the fact that their involvement in "dirty", Balkan-style comabt caused a few of them to commit acts that were not only questionable but also, historically speaking, counterproductive. The fighting in Carinthia was not just a manifestation of *Kleinkrieg* but reflected several other kinds of organized, socially legitimized violence as well. As in central Slovenia (where conditions bore a certain resemblance to those in Spain under Napoleonic-French occupation), the struggle was a kind of civil war that embraced other Carinthians, German-speaking and bilingual. It was no less a revolutionary upheaval insofar as the Marxist leaders, obdurately opposed to the existing social order, were bent upon seizing power, a goal that probably loomed larger in the minds of many of them than that of uniting all Slovenes into one state. Finally, the conflict was part and parcel of a world-wide conflagration because of a conservative, status quo-oriented Britain's intimate association with it and clashing power-political interests in southeastern Europe.[158] Among other things, it was a mirror of the essential, partly subliminal, partly deliberate (in Wilkinson's view) quality of British strategy in World War Two – the desire after, the insane carnage of World War One, to reduce losses by using indigenous surrogates and nibbling away at the edges of the Third Reich.[159]

A final reflection is in order. Shortly before he died the inimitable Prušnik-Gašper told Žaučer-Matjaž that he hoped, among other things, that "Austria's fateful Nazi past would not be allowed to lapse into oblivion".[160] How ironical it is that when he uttered these words there seemed little chance of his wish being fulfilled. Now, only nine years later, due to the irrepressible opportunism of an intimate, ex-associate of Löhr, the former UN Secretary General, and officially certified accessory to war crimes, Kurt Waldheim[161], the great historical myth, created in the first place (1943) by the Allies themselves, of Austria as Hitler's victim has been laid bare for the whole world to see. The fact that his fellow citizens, in an outburst of xenophobic pique and their traditional, virulent anti-Semitism, have elected Waldheim Austria's federal president only underscores the point. *Unbewältigte Vergangenheit* – confronting the distasteful issues of national history – is not just a British, Yugoslav, or, for that matter, an American problem.

PART TWO

Documentary Appendixes

APPENDIX A

Memorandum on the Revolt in Slovenia

Lieut. Colonel P.A. Wilkinson, O.B.E. Royal Fusiliers

27 April 1944 [PRO FO 371/44255, R98160]

TOP SECRET
R. 1934

INTRODUCTION

1. There are few things more individual than a partizan movement, and few subjects on which it is less safe to generalize. This paper is based on personal experiences during a 1,500 mile march through Western Jugoslavia, North Eastern Italy and the newly formed Gau Kärnten which I made with Major A.C.G. Hesketh Prichard, Royal Fusiliers, between December 1943 and March 1944. It is confined to the revolt in Slovenia and is not intended as a review of the Partizan movement as a whole, which my limited personal experiences do not qualify me to attempt.

SLOVENIAN WAR AIMS

2. The key to any revolt is the motive which inspires it. Slovenian war aims are twofold:

First, and above all, to establish a free and democratic Slovenia stretching from Trieste to the Karavanken Alps and embracing all Slovene speaking peoples. The geographical limits of this area are more precisely described in Appendix I.d [a map of Slovenia not reproduced here].

Secondly to help create a free federated Jugoslavia in which this liberated (and enlarged) Slovenia can play its part without fear of domination by a Serbian military oligharchy.

3. With these aims in view the Slovenian Partizans have transformed a revolt, which began as a struggle for existence, into what is now virtually a national Crusade.

4. The ideal of an independent Slovenian nation dates from before the last war, when Slovenia was still a province of the Austrian Empire. Although under an alien rule, the Slovenian speaking peoples were at that time at least geographically united. When the Austrian Empire collapsed, a quarter of Slovenia was, by the Treaty of Rapallo (1920) handed over to Italy. In the same year the Korosko Plebiscite resulted in the Slovenians north of the Karavanken Alps being incorporated into the rump of Austria.

It is the restoration of these two territories (including the port of Trieste) after a quarter of a century of foreign rule which the Slovenians so earnestly desire.

5. As for the concept of a federated Jugoslavia; this is no idle aspiration and Marshal Tito and Dr. Ribar have already evolved the necessary centralistic machinery in which the Slovene representatives play an active part. Moreover, the formal influence of this central government is growing daily.

For those who are interested I have set out the details of this somewhat complicated political organization as it affects Slovenia at Appendix I.b. of this report.

INTER-ALLIED RELATIONS

6. As far as the Slovenians' attitude to the Allies is concerned, they have a blind (and almost pathological) admiration for the U.S.S.R. (especially for the Soviet Army), a somewhat chilly respect for Great Britain (in particular for her democratic parliamentary institutions), and an indifference almost amounting to contempt, for the Americans. Nevertheless it is noteworthy that they always listened to the B.B.C. in preference to Moscow, and even avowed anglophobes had the highest possible opinion of the objectivity of British news, and the general fairness of the British standpoint.

7. My reference to the chilly respect for Britain refers of course to the official attitude (which nevertheless is becoming more cordial every day). Personally, like most other British officers, I received a warmth of welcome wherever I went which I found profoundly moving. Indeed, this universal friendliness and hospitality, especially among the poorer people I

met with on the roads, was quite the outstanding and most precious memory of my trip.

RELATIONS WITH THE COMMUNIST PARTY

8. One cannot leave the subject of inter-allied relations without touching on Slovenia's affinity with the Communist Party.

9. Ninety per cent of the Slovenian Partizans describe themselves as Communists. In fact, the majority are nothing of the kind. However, all are well aware of the debt they owe to the pre-war Communist organization in Jugoslavia.

10. In the absence of any other allied secret organization the Communists provided the original framework and mechanism of the whole Partizan movement; the organizers, the coordination, the requisite funds and sufficient political encouragement to fan the first sparks of resistance into flame. This sense of gratitude is one of the first lessons in the 'political education' of the Slovenian Partizan recruit.

11. Apart from all this, there is throughout the Partizan movement an important backbone of what can best be described as professional anti-fascists – mostly trained in the Russian Staff School followed by practical military experience with the International Brigade in Spain. This cadre of experts fills many of the key appointments in the Partizan Army and includes Tito himself, six of his ten Corps Commanders and a large number of senior medical officers, sappers and other technical personnel. Apart from a handful of ex-regular Jugoslav officers, these experts represent the only trained or professional military element I came across: for the average Slovenian Partizan soldier is essentially an amateur.

12. On the other hand, it is not only an account of this sense of indebtedness that 90% of the Slovenian Partizans describe themselves as Communists. While the majority are emphatically not ideological Communists, (which is, anyway, not a creed suited to a nation of smallholders, like the Slovenians), there is nevertheless a very general desire to associate themselves with Russia. They rightly feel that the advance of the Soviet armies is the most (and almost the only) unmistakeable token of an early Allied victory and the liberation of their country. In the U.S.S.R. they see (somewhat ingenuously) the champion of the small state in its struggle for national independence, and the epitome of successful national resistance to the Fascist bully. Also they see a vindicator of the Slovenian man-in-the-street in his long conflict with his own bourgeoisie and with the pre-war clique of Serbian business men (to whom they attribute a malevolence they were hardly numerous or important enough to deserve). Finally, as in all Slav countries, with the notable exception of Poland, there is a traditional tendency to look to Russia for salvation.

13. Hence, to sum up, while it is untrue to say they are Communists, at least 90% of the Slovenian Partizans are the most ardent admirers of the U.S.S.R., whose political and military leadership they unquestioningly accept.

14. This Russian influence may prove significant if, after the war, there is a revival of Russian imperialism. For we should remember that Greater Slovenia stretches from Trieste in the West to Villach and Klagenfurt in the North; and after Czechoslovakia, Slovenia offers Russia her most important gateway to the West.

15. At the present moment the Communist influence is increasing, but if you will refer to Appendix I.b. you will see that the Christian Socialists are well represented in the Izvrsni Odbor, and if there is a post-war reaction, the ultimate emergence in Slovenia of something resembling a Christian Socialist government (while unlikely) is not impossible.

16. At the same time, it is worth noting that over 50% of the practicing Catholics are fighting with the White Guard against the Partizans.[162]

ATTITUDE TO KING PETER

17. There remains one major political question outstanding: this is the Slovenian attitude to King Peter. Provided they are not asked to have him back, which they would resist to the last man, they are not very interested in him. They are certainly not in the least vindictive against him. To show what I mean, supposing one fine day King Peter arrived by parachute on Slovenian free territory, my guess is that (after the inevitable consultation with Tito Headquarters) he would be kept in polite house-arrest until he could be handed over to the British as one of their unwanted agents, with the request that he be shipped back to Italy without delay. I admit that the Partizans would gladly shoot some of his entourage, but the Slovenians look on the King with pity rather than with hate. They see in him an unfortunate young man born in a century when kings are no longer fashionable.

II. MILITARY ORGANIZATION

18. The Partizan military effort depends on maintaining a nice balance between political and military control. It is a peoples' army, one of whose avowed aims is the overthrow of the pre-war Serbian military despotism. They have no wish to replace it by another, (which the Partizan movement could easily become,) and are determined to keep the army under control. For this purpose they have evolved a diarchical system of command, whereby in every unit from a Corps to a Company the Kommandant and

the Politkommissar are interdependent, and no order is valid unless signed by them both. Tito alone combines in one person political and military sovereignty.

The practical disadvantages of such a condeminion are manifest, especially since both Kommandant and Kommissar are technically equal in status, (though in practice the Kommandant always has the last word).

THE KOMMANDANT

19. By and large the Kommandants are splendid chaps: non-political, as far as one can be when popularity plays so large a part in one's appointment, brave to a fault – three divisional commanders were killed in action last winter while leading their troops in person into battle. The Kommandants of Corps and Divisions are invariably good officers, many of them trained at the Russian staff school and with International Brigade experience. Brigade and Battalion Kommandants are generally sound practical soldiers with over twenty months continuous experience of guerilla fighting. Owing to the rapid expansion of the Slovenian Army most of the Company Kommandants are rather inexperienced and lightweight. But taken as a whole the Slovenians have every right to be proud of their Kommandants. Those that fail to make the grade do not last very long, and there is a high standard of professional competence and personal leadership.

THE POLITKOMMISSAR

20. Despite fundamental disagreement on almost everything except our dislike of the Boche, I got on very well with most Kommissars. Nevertheless, on the whole they are a noxious class. The senior ones are exceedingly intelligent, some of them, such as [Boris] Kraigher and [Ales] Baebler [Bebler] (who were both charming men), Communists of international reputation; most of them sharply critical of Britain's contribution to the war (and indeed of almost everything, which, as a regular soldier, I hold sacred). Some are personally ambitious, and therefore most conspicuous among the Slovenian Partizans, whose movement must be one of the most selfless crusades in history. The junior Kommissars are of the type of discontented elementary school teacher, socially frustrated, ambitious and venomous.

21. Nevertheless, the Kommissars are all brave men and vie with their Kommandants in leading their troops into battle. All are trained soldiers as well as being trained politically, and frequently act as seconds in command of their unit. In fairness it must be said that many units are

devoted to their Kommissars and the characteristics which repelled me are not necessarily repulsive to the Partizans.

22. The Kommissars are responsible for the morale as well as for the cultural and political instruction of their troops (who, in theory, have at least one hour's political training daily!). They are responsible for security, propaganda and very largely for recruiting. In the larger formations they have intelligence duties as well, and it is the Kommissar who handles the conspirative side of the movement including the development of courier lines and subversive organizations in the towns and, above all, liaison with the Communist party.

23. In conclusion, the Politkommissars as a class are the Partizan element most unsympathetic to British ideals and most hostile to our work in the Balkans. The Partizan official English version of them as 'welfare officers'is somewhat misleading.

HEADQUARTERS ORGANIZATION

24. Partizan Headquarters are small both because they have to be mobile and because of the decentralization inherent in guerilla warfare: also of course there are no Corps Troops. Take for instance HQ. IX Corps: there was a Kommandant (graded as a full Colonel), a Kommissar (2nd. Class), a Chief of Staff (graded as a major and known locally as the Nacelnik), an intelligence officer (captain) and a signals subaltern. On the administrative side there was an Intendant (Captain) charged with victualling and quartering the Corps HQ. and with the general provision of such warlike stores (particularly from enemy and secret sources) as units were unable to obtain locally. There was a doctor and a group of ten propagandists (Agitprop) and finally an itinerant judicial department consisting of two officers (known as Referents) whose judicature ranged from trying cases of high treason to arbitrating the claims of peasants for goods forcibly requisitioned by the Partizans.

25. In Slovenia even the HQs. of higher formations are nomadic, their itineracy being conditioned less by enemy action than by the capacity of the countryside to feed and maintain them. For the most part they are located in villages and the higher HQs. are often in the neighbourhood of some German occupied area on which they depend for many of their black market supplies.

SLOVENIAN ORDER OF BATTLE

26. The Slovenian Command consists of two Corps, the VII and the IX Corps. The inter-Corps boundary is the railway from LJUBLJANA to TRIESTE.

27. VII Corps comprises the 14th, 15th, and 18th Divs. and 8(?) Odreds, and is responsible for ISTRIA (north of the River DRAGONIA and south of the inter-Corps boundary), NOTRANSKO, DOLENJSKO

and UNTERSTEIERMARK (anglice Lower STYRIA and in Slovenian STAJERSKO).
28. IX Corps comprises the 31st and 32nd Divs. and 6 Odreds. These troops are located in the Slovenian area of North East Italy (known as PRIMORSKO), OBERKRAJN (Slovenian GORENJSKO) and Carinthia (Slovenian KOROSKO).

STRENGTHS

29. Some confusion may have arisen in the past over the nomenclature of Partisan units.
30. A Corps is normally commanded by a full Colonel and contains some 10-15,000 men.
31. A Division is commanded by a Lt. Colonel and numbers between 3 and 4000 men (e.g., the 32nd Div. is 3800 and 31st Div. 4000 strong).
32. A Brigade is officially 1,000-1,500 strong and is commanded by a major.
33. A Battalion is between two and five hundred strong.
34. Odreds are normally commanded by a Major and have a strength slightly less than that of a Brigade. They normally comprise two or three Battalions.[163]

BRIGADES, ODREDS AND ODBORS

35. In Slovenia the Partizan troops are organized into three categories: Brigades, Odreds and Odbors, each of which has a special role.

(a) Brigades

A Brigade consisting of three Battalions is the normal Slovenian tactical unit for offensive operations. It is rarely if ever employed in a static role and unless employed on a special task, such as a convoy or recruiting drive, its normal tactics are to roam through the neutral marchlands, which separate the German from the Partizan safe territory, so to speak, looking for trouble. This may take the form of raiding or investing an isolated German garrison, attacking a railway line or ambushing a convoy. Like all guerrillas they quite rightly avoid pitched battles at all costs and when so threatened they melt into the woods and reform elsewhere.

(b) Odreds

An odred is the normal Slovenian garrison unit. Normally consisting of three Battalions it differs from the Brigade in that its role is predominantly static and defensive. Its task is garrisoning and policing the liberated areas and preventing any enemy encroachments. It is composed of full time soldiers, though these are frequently drawn from the district the odred is defending. Now that offensive operations in Slovenia are on the decline the Odreds are on the whole attracting a better and more experienced type of Partizan than the Brigades. Although this role is defensive the Odred normally yields to superior strength, and, like the Brigade, avoids pitched battles at all costs.

(c) Odbors

These are groups [committees] of part-time local defence volunteers, closely resembling our Home Guard, and with many of the same merits and limitations. They all have rifles, and wear Partizan caps but no uniform. There is one of these civilian patrols in all the larger villages not occupied by the enemy, and on the approach of the enemy it is their responsibility to give the alarm in time to enable any Partizans to escape. Only very rarely is this civilian patrol required to oppose by force the Germans' entry into their village, and normally having given the alarm they take to the woods with the other Partizans. The Odbor is also required to provide local guides.

SLOVENIAN TACTICS

36. The Slovenian Partizans (far more than the Bosnians or Croatians whose forces approximate more nearly to a regular army) are masters of guerrilla warfare in the classic style: "invulnerable, intangible, without front or back, drifting about like a gas". Their success lies in a clear realization that (to continue quoting from the Seven Pillars of Wisdom), "a regular soldier might be helpless without a target. He would own the ground he sat on and what he could poke his rifle at"; but nothing else. In short, Slovenian tactics are essentially evasive and they only fight a pitched battle when cornered.

37. By exploiting their own mobility, the inaccessibility of the terrain and their local knowledge they avoid, if possible, even giving the enemy a target to hit with his superior fire power and equipment.

38. It is a fair criticism to say that they have an irrational and almost primitive fear of tanks and aircraft, and altogether, at the present time, they tend to err on the cautious side. However, we must remember they are largely fighting their own war. Also there is growing an understandable desire to survive the present campaign. This means that as the pressure on Germany increases from other quarters and they relinquish their grip on the Balkans, the Partizans are slower to take advantage of the situation than they were, say, nine months ago. This tendency may

decrease when the impending shortage of food and supplies and the probable lengthy duration of the war becomes more generally known to the rank and file. But for the present they are still digesting the fruits of the Italian capitulation, and they are very war weary: not only in mind but physically exhausted as well.

39. During the four months I was in Slovenia I personally witnessed the railway line between Zagreb and Karlovac blown up with H.E. from an unexploded aerial bomb; one small patrol attack in Istria, which was very successful, the Germans losing one killed and five prisoners (four Mongols and a German N.C.O.) for one Partizan killed; one small fire fight when a German company unexpectedly attacked a village (VINICA) in which I was passing the night, and were repulsed with no apparent loss to either side; and one rather larger engagement when a German battalion occupied CIRCHNO for two hours, killing 40 Partizans whom they found there, and finally withdrew when threatened by reinforcements amounting to two Partizan divisions. The latter made no serious effort whatever to harrass the German withdrawal, despite their numerical superiority.

40. At the same time there is considerable 'Kleinkrieg' activity on the LJUBLJANA-KOCEVJE road and railway, and on the 2nd. March the KOCEVJE garrison was alleged to have been invested and to have been without food for seven days. Nevertheless, I suspect that the incentive for much of this activity is the booty it provides; particularly cigarettes, of which there is a complete lack in NOTRANSKO and DOLENJSKO. On this occasion a strong relieving column was sent out from LJUBLJANA, which was entirely immobilized en route by an unexpectedly heavy snow storm. Despite this the Partizans were unwilling to take advantage of this situation and allowed the column to withdraw virtually unmolested.

41. It would be unwise to attach too much importance to these incidents, and I may well have been unrepresentative in my very limited personal experience (though I fancy not). In any case, in fairness to the Partizans I must stress that I was never any length of time with a fighting unit, and was most anxious myself to avoid becoming engaged with the enemy, which would have jeopardized my proper mission.

42. The formation of the original Slovenian Partizans was very largely a process of integrating the various resistance groups which had sprung up spontaneously in different parts of the country. Alternatively small parties of Partizans were sent from time to time to organize some territory which had hitherto been barren. Thus in the autumn of 1942 sixty-two Partizans under BRACIC made their way from DOLENJSKO to PRIMORSKO and by Spring 1943 had already raised two Brigades in North East Italy. By the end of the same year these two Brigades had grown into two divisions which form the present IX Corps.

43. In either case the limiting factor was more often lack of arms than lack of men.

44. Then, suddenly, came the collapse of Italy, and without warning the Slovenian Partizans were presented with more arms and equipment than they could possibly dispose of in the time available. At that time they only had two divisions; and this windfall meant that they could arm a further three divisions and bring their strength up to two Corps. There was now a serious shortage of recruits.

45. The *ISVRSNI* [*izvršilni*] *ODBOR* [Executive Committee] accordingly made a decree whereby everyone male and female between 18 and 45 years old was liable to conscription into the Partizan forces, but the response was disappointing. As a result of this the Brigades were despatched on a recruiting drive and those that wouldn't volunteer were, if necessary, pressed into service. This had an important sequel in that during the German autumn offensive, which immediately followed this drive, many of these conscripts deserted, and it was on account of these desertions that the Slovenian partisans were so anxious to enlist any British escaped P.O.W.s who passed through their territory, thereby keeping up their numbers (or at least their paper strength, for many of the British prisoners were in no physical condition to fight).

46. At the present time recruits are mainly either volunteers or refugees from one of the German 'Wehrmannschaft' mobilizations. In February I myself watched a party of the latter being shepherded down from Carinthia by the Partizans. Apart from a sprinkling of young boys, they were most of them middle-aged farmers roused from their beds in the middle of the night and forced to fly for their lives–unshaven and frozen from their first night in the open, unarmed, resentful and thoroughly miserable, it seemed impossible that they would ever make useful soldiers, but I was informed that this unpromising material after a month with a Brigade and a course of 'political instruction' became as resolute and enthusiastic as the rest of the Partizans. Hm, perhaps.

47. Although the bottom age for mobilization is 18, volunteers are often much younger. (Particularly in Croatia where I have had to carry on my shoulders a twelve-year-old warrior deputed to escort me across no-mansland to prevent him getting submerged in a snow drift!) Even in Slovenia one frequently comes across individuals of 12 or 14 and section or even company commanders in their middle teens in charge of men more than twice their age. Major Generals are in their middle thirties, divisional commanders in their late twenties–often with staff officers ten years older than themselves. When I discussed this with one of the Partizans he reminded me laughingly that Marlborough was a commander in chief when under thirty and Pitt a Prime Minister at 24, and that in

guerrilla warfare, at least, infallibility was in no sense recognised as the privilege of seniority. Indeed the "under-twenties" could and did air their views at meetings as loudly and long as the Kommandant himself, and were always listened to with patience.

48. Training normally consists of a ten-day course in rifle, L.M.G. and grenade, after which the so-called trained soldier is posted to a Brigade. Nevertheless for a guerrilla force the Slovenian Partizans take their training very seriously, and the first military school was started near Ljubljana as long ago as autumn 1941. They now have an officers' school (nomadic like the rest of their institutions) with a six weeks course, and a capacity for 20 students at a time. The syllabus includes tactics (up to a Battalion level), drill, fire control and demolitions. In addition, at Slovenian HW, there are reputed to be regular signals, sapper and artillery courses (although they have no guns), but I never heard any exact details of these. For the most part the Slovenians choose their specialists on account of their peacetime vocational experience, and rightly make no attempt to train raw material for technical jobs.

49. Small formations also have schools: for intance, IX Corps ran a guerrilla school at which Simic Stanislav, a Slovenian trained by us in the Middle East, had been appointed sabotage and demolition instructor.

50. For the most part the instruction given at all these schools is severely practical and relies on rule of thumb methods (which the Partizans have reduced to a fine art) rather than on theoretical knowledge.

51. Marksmanship is not up to British regular standards, and fire control is somewhat amateur, targets being frequently engaged at fantastic ranges despite the limited ammunition available. The standard of W.T. operating, of which we had, unfortunately, extensive experience, is quite deplorable.

52. In Slovenia literacy is over 95%.

53. To sum up the standard of training is well below that of a regular army (even where patrol tactics are concerned) but infinitely better than I had imagined possible in a guerrilla army.

DISCIPLINE

54. Where anti-social offences are concerned (for instance theft or rape) discipline is extremely harsh. On the other hand, obedience is not a Slovenian virtue; and I have had some uncomfortable moments while the entire patrol debated on the desirability of carrying out some urgent order. A Slovenian commander must be sure that any order he gives represents the wish of the majority under his command or he will not last long in his appointment.

PRISONERS

55. The Slovenians take no prisoners, and informed me that they themselves are invariably shot by the Germans (though from Prisoner of War sources I rather doubt this to be the case). On two occasions the Germans have approached Slovene HQ and suggested some exchange arrangements should be made. But both times this was scornfully rejected in principle by the Partizans. Nevertheless, important personages are undoubtedly exchanged from time to time.

PERSONAL EQUIPMENT

56. Ninety per cent wear Italian uniforms – most of them in good repair. All Partizan troops (and most of the villagers) have good boots, either of Italian or of local manufacture, but new boots are fairly hard to come by. (For instance we found the greatest difficulty in providing boots for escaped prisoners of war.) When I left, leather for repairs was beginning to run short.

57. There is a good cobbler attached to every unit, and at the larger HQs. there is a tailor as well. About half the troops have Italian overcoats, and a proportion of the remainder have probably rejected an overcoat as being too heavy to carry round. All carry at leat one blanket and most have an Italian waterproof sheet as well.

58. When I arrived all Slovenian staff officers were expected to wear Italian uniform but others might wear British Battle Dress if they could obtain it. I believe that this order has since been rescinded and Battle Dress may now officially be worn by all.

SMALL ARMS

59. Everyone – even the Local Defence Volunteers – has at least a rifle, and a grenade slung from his belt (generally by the safety pin!): officers and N.C.O.s frequently have a S.M.G. Weapons are an important item of prestige and the Sten is viewed with great disfavour because it looks so obviously cheap. My own Colt Super was almost my best passport.

60. The average Company with a strength of 100 men normally disposes of 2 Heavy and 10-12 Light M.G.s and at lest 1 Light Mortar.

61. There appears to be no shortage of S.A.A., but of course there are only limited reserves beyond what a Partizan actually carries on his person. The extent of these reserves, which have been hidden by individuals and units in various parts of the country, is quite impossible ever to assess.

ARTILLERY

62. The nature of the terrain makes the use of anything but pack artillery impracticable. The few pieces which they captured from the Italians after the capitulation they lost in the subsequent German offensive. They now have no artillery whatever, and their only supporting weapons are a few Heavy Mortars – about two per Brigade.

ANTI TANK

63. There is less than one anti-tank rifle per battalion. Their normal defence against tanks is to take to the woods. Needless to say they describe every tracked vehicle as a 'Tiger'.

SAPPER WORK

64. Their bridge demolitions seemed awfully good and were very numerous. Their anti-tank obstacles, with several notable exceptions, would have been ineffective against any modern tank, and were incidentally an appalling inconvenience to the Partizans, as they effectively barred the roads to cart transport, which meant that everything had to be carried on packsaddles or by porter.

65. They take their train derailments very seriously and use the following:

(a) A mine of 8 – 16 lbs.
(b) 3 or 4 charges each of 2 lbs., 4 metres apart.
(c) 3 sleepers lashed together (see Appendix I.C.)

66. As to their methods: they like the sleeper technique best. When using H.E. they maintain that, while two sticks of plastic will undoubtedly cut a rail, experience has shown that a fast moving train will jump such a cut, especially on a curve, where it carries on on one rail owing to centrifugal force. (Which rail this will be is unpredictable since it varies with the speed and weight of the trains.) They also find this whereas 1 lb. of plastic H.E. will destroy 1/2 a metre of rail, the train will not be derailed with any certainty unless 4 metres are destroyed, since the explosion does not always take place when the wheel is directly overhead, and it is possible to jump a 1/2 metre cut.

67. The Partizans have a permanent demand for H.E. which they put to a number of unconventional (and not always economical) uses. The Slovenians are particularly short of H.E. at the moment since most of their enemy sources have dried up (particularly since the Italian capitulation).

Appendix A
COMMUNICATIONS

(a) Radio

68. Slovenian H.Q. has W/T communication with the following:
Tito's H.Q.
Croatian H.Q.
H.Q. VII Corps.
H.Q. IX Corps.

Corps has normally a wireless links with Division (mainly captured Italian material) and occasionally Division has a link with Brigade; but this is rare and generally inefficient. As stated above the standard of operating is exceedingly low.

(b) Telephones

69. Unlike Bosnia and Crotia, where there is a first class telephone network, in Slovenia telephones are extremely rare. The only area where I found them being used at all extensively was in the neighborhood of IX Corps H.Q., (and of course in the BELA KRAJN, though here only between the main towns like SEMIC, CRNOMELJ and METLIKA).

(c) Couriers

70. The outstanding feature of Slovenian Communications is their courier system. This is largely in the hands of boys between the ages of 14 and 20, who man the various stages, living often in conditions of grave danger and almost invariably of acute discomfort. They are responsible for carrying mail and providing guides for official travellers. The average march is between 6 and 12 hours a night – if all goes well, but one must be prepared for anything up to 20 hours, which we were forced to do on half a dozen occasions. (The worst non-stop march was 37 hours!)

71. Using the official courier lines it is possible to travel from Slovenian H.Q. to PRIMORSKO in 10 days, to STEIERMARK in 10 days; and from PRIMORSKAN H.Q. (IX Corps) to KLAGENFURT in 8-10 days and to ISTRIA in 5 days.

72. This courier organization is the most efficient and secret activity which I encountered during my trip, and, as far a I know, nothing on the same scale exists in Bosnia or Croatia where most of the communications run through safe areas.

73. I have a vivid recollection of a courier rendezvous some twenty miles east of TRIESTE. It was a small lean-to hut of wattles and fir branches in a wood overlooking the TRIESTE – LJUBLJANA railway.

Every now and then the sky was lit by a giant flash from an electric locomotive laboriously drawing a train up the winding, snow-covered track from TRIESTE and the night was made noisy by a continuous chatter of small arms fire from German patrols on the railway a mile or so down the valley. When we arrived the Istrian courier was already inside the hut, crouching in the snow over a tiny fire, and five minutes later the courier from Jugoslavia came sliding and stumbling through the trees, rather breathless for he had been chased over the railway line by a German patrol – for the third time that week, he told us. He was about eighteen and the other boy looked rather less – to all appearances a pair of English schoolboys on a skiing tour.

74. It took an hour to sort the mail. There were letters from Austria, from Italy – even from Albania; important-looking packages from Tito Headquarters, and simple letters from Slovenian peasant mothers to their sons fighting in Carinthia. Each one was carefully registered and signed for by the new courier. It was a most impressive example of the extent and indeed of the efficiency of the Partizan movement.

75. We were travelling from Primorskan H.Q. to ISTRIA and there had been a heavy fall of snow, which had already exhaused us, though only a third of our night's march was done. So we were glad to wait till the mail was finished – even though, by this time, the Borea had frozen the sweat on our backs, and our snow-soaked and freezing feet had become so exquisitely painful that we wondered if we should ever walk again.

76. After wishing each other a lucky journey – the normal greeting on the road – the other two parties moved off. We stopped for a moment to remove all traces of the fire, and then having laid a false trail or two in the snow we too set off for the 'Strecke', guided thither by the bomb flashes and orange Verey lights of the German patrols.

PAY

77. Partizans do not receive pay of any kind. In the Partizan free areas money has virtually been abolished, and nothing is for sale except wine (at 20 lira per litre). In the marchlands there is little enough for sale, but money still has some meaning. Lira are the accepted currency. It was usual to pay 'indirectly' for a night's lodging (though this was often refused), by means of a parting gift. Coffee, tea, sugar and cigarettes, if you have room to carry them, are far more valuable for this purpose than money – the use of which I felt tended daily to remind Partizans we were a nation of shopkeepers in these circumstances.

Appendix A
PROVISIONING

78. The Partizan army in Slovenia is entirely dependent for its maintenance on the civilian organizations. Food, civilian transport, etc. is provided by the village committee who are responsible for the maintenance of all units in their district. No praise can be too high for the way the civilian population uncomplainingly accepts the sacrifices imposed on them by the exigencies of the Partizans, whose rapacity almost equals that of the Germans. The gladness of heart with which they handed over their few remaining possessions for the good of their cause was, for me, the most convincing evidence of the popularity of the revolt, and of their devotion to its purpose.

79. It is obviously impossible for an army of this size to live exclusively on the country, and for provisions as well as for warlike stores and medical equipment which is not available locally they depend on the following:

(a) Captured enemy stores.
(b) Stores dropped by British aircraft.
(c) Most secret sources of supply from the German occupied towns.

LJUBLJANA is now completely closed to the Partizans and almost everything has to be obtained from TRIESTE. Now that the Germans have taken over from the Italians, all this traffic has got far more hazardous and difficult, and British air supplies are therefore all the more eagerly awaited.

FOOD SUPPLIES

80. When I was in Slovenia, for the troops at any rate there was ample meat and potatoes, a complete lack of fresh vegetables or fruit, (and, incidentally, of soap and tobacco), a diminishing supply of bread and no salt or sugar. The diet was adequate, though not very healthy and desperately boring; it is best described as 'honest prison fare'.

81. Now I can well believe the Partizans are beginning to face a food shortage, for, counting on an Allied invasion early in the Spring to relieve them, they have been criminally prodigal of their supplies: eating their seed corn and seed potatoes, killing their stock without regard to breeding, and so forth.

82. Travelling through NOTRANSKO last February there were already signs of acute shortage among the civilian population, and in January the Secretary of the Primorskan Narodni Svet told me they had only two months food left. This was an exaggeration for I myself remained in Primorsko for six weeks and fed excellently all the time, and so did the villages through which I travelled.

83. Nevertheless, when dealing with any Partizan provisioning problem one must appreciate that what you see on the plate is all there is, and there is very rarely any more where it came from. The Partizan lives from day to day and from hand to mouth, and however frugal he may wish to be (though economy is not a virtue the Slavs admire) his nomadic life and the uncertainty of his movements make it impossible for him to put by anything against a rainy day. Normally he merely has the choice whether he fasts full or empty.

MEDICAL

84. Although very largely without soaps, anaesthetics or antiseptics the doctors do the best they can. Provided the patient can stand being moved across country by unsprung peasant cart or slung across a pack horse, and can endure the long night marches with only a thin blanket (and not always that) to protect him from the snow and above all from the freezing wind, the primitive nature of the hospital arrangements need have no particular terrors. Hospitals are always chosen on account of their inaccessibility and generally consist of a requisitioned mountain village or a hutted camp in the forest.

85. Luckily the average patient is pretty tough (and we should remember they had to sleep two in a bed in Jugoslav hospitals in peacetime). None the less the number of casualties who survive both their wounds and the treatment is astonishing.

86. Clearly the wounded present an appalling problem in a guerrilla army, and a means of evacuating the badly wounded to Italy is one of the most urgent of the Slovenian's requirements.

87. As far as diseases are concerned there is practically no Flecktyphus in Slovenia. Consumption is pretty general and on the increase. Coughs are universal. You can hardly fail to pick up some streptococcal infection of the skin, throat, nose or eyes – as everything you touch is infected. The normal process is to scratch for lice, start a sore, infect the sore – and so on. M. & B. tablets are a veritable panacaea in Slovenia, and quite essential.

88. I personally suffered fairly frequently from rheumatism in my hip joints, and believe this too is a common Partisan complaint, especially after sleeping out in the woods. It is rather more serious than it sounds in view of the distances one has to march.

INTELLIGENCE

89. Nowhere is the essential difference of outlook between the Partizans and ourselves more apparent than over the question of

intelligence. With the possible exception of tito's H.Q., which is daily increasing in importance, the Partizans have no requirement for strategical intelligence, or indeed for any intelligence not directly connected with their local operations. The value of accurate order of battle reports is lost on them; moreover, though prepared to strip a dead or indeed a wounded enemy of every item of clothing and equipment, they superstitiously insist on burying his pay book with him! Not that their neglect of intelligence work is entirely due to ignorance of indifference. To collate modern intelligence in a useful form requires a skilled and numerous filing staff and extensive archives, both of which are out of the question where a nomadic Partizan H.Q. is concerned. Nevertheless, they could have done far more, had they seriously tried, and might have been of great help to us had they been given practical guidance by the various B.L.O.s, most of whom had had no intelligence training whatever.

(a) *Field Intelligence*

90. Tactical intelligence is good and local cross-examination of prisoners during the battle compares favourably with our army. As I have already said all intelligence other than tactical is totally ignored. Nevertheless while at Slovenian H.Q. I was asked to revise the field intelligence syllabus for the officers' school, which shows at least they are waking up to its shortcomings.

(b) *Secret Intelligence*

91. This is closely bound up with the Communist organization and is by no means easy to penetrate. The Slovenians in 1943 had several well placed sources in LJUBLJANA, but when in Spring 1944 LJUBLJANA was entirely "abgesperrt" they found the greatest possible difficulty in maintaining contact with them. This is not helped by the shortage of radio equipment and suitably trained operators. On the whole the Partizans appear to know surprisingly little about German intentions in Slovenia proper. On the other hand, contact with TRIESTE is regular and good. There is also quite an extensive organization of agents in Northern Italy, especially around VENICE. The information from these sources in Italy is filtered through H.Q. IX Corps. On the whole the results are rather impressive and the material far more professional than most received from Partizan sources.

92. Considering their possibilities, the information received from Austria by the Partizans is most disappointing – political waffle and Communist propaganda for the most part. In fairness it must be said that now they know what we want the Partizans are trying to develop their

organization to meet our requirements, and just before I left they informed me they had an embryo train watching organization on the LJUBLJANA-TRIESTE railway which was showing great promise.

93. On one thing the Partizans are resolved and that is to prevent Allied personnel contacting their subsources direct. The only terms on which they will accept our intelligence officers are that these shall sit at formation H.Q., accept the official Partizan "hand out" and make the best of it. They will not tolerate any individual snooping, but on the other hand they are more than ready to co-operate with us as best they can – on the basis of an official exchange of information.

(c) Security Intelligence

94. This was the responsibility of the Kommissars. By the time I arrived in Autumn 1943 most of the unreliable elements had already been liquidated (and in February 1944 a decree was issued formally disbanding the Secret Police – doubtless lest such an organization might grate on Anglo – American susceptibilities). As is inevitable, an immense amount of malicious and defamatory information is lodged by private persons. This is sorted out by the Kommissar, and if he considers there is a case the accused is arraigned before a Referent (see para. 24).

(d) German Penetration

95. Undoubtedly the Germans have penetrated the Partizans. Recruits from GORENJSKO (alias OBERKRAJN) nearly always include a number of German agents, though apart from general subversive activities their value to the enemy is limited by the very primitive communicational facilities. I know of one case in IX Corps where they discovered that a Brigade Kommissar was a German agent. Indeed, there is no question that the Germans have well placed agents among important Partizans, and the latter's occasional reluctance to let us cross-question individual German Abwehr agents, whom they have captured, may be attributed to their wish to keep their dirty washing to themselves, at any rate until they have had time to deal with the culprits.

Conclusions

96. Taken by and large the Slovenian Partizan intelligence organization has considerable possibilities, but is at present woefully undeveloped, and I doubt if we shall ever persuade them to make the most of thei "Agitprop" department.

97. The standard of cypher security is very moderate. Between Corps

and division they have a letter substitution system, which an intelligent cross-word reader could break in an hour. Between the various higher formations they claim to use a double transposition method, but I suspect a total ignorance of the security limitations of such a system.

98. As far as our personal movements were concerned a sort of "bush telegraph" system used to work between the villages which at times was quite frightening (especially on the few occasions we were trying to keep our presence secret).

99. On the other hand, where the really conspiratorial aspects of the movement were concerned (i.e. courier lines, locations of H.Q., penetration of occupied towns and liaison with Communist organizations) the security was quite bafflingly good. It sometimes took three days to make contact with a H.Q. which you knew couldn't be more than five miles away. Similarly, if one ever lost one's courier (through being surprised and having to scatter) it might take up to a week to regain contact with the courier line.

PROPAGANDA

(a) The Political Education of the Partizans

100. The importance of the psychological factor in guerrilla warfare cannot be overemphasized. Col. Lawrence called it the third factor in command and says of the Arabs, "We had to arrange their minds in order to battle, just as carefully and as formally as other officers arranged their bodies".

101. The strength of the Slovenian revolt is due in great part to the care taken over "Political instruction".

102. It must be remembered that many of the Partizans have joined the movement either to evade German conscription or because their houses have been burnt or requisitioned, and they see in service with the Partizans an immediate means of livelihood and a possibility of saving something from the wreck after the war. Others have often been forcibly conscripted by methods reminiscent of the 18th Century Pressgang. To be able to ring this rather unpromising material up to the high standard of morale the Partizans achieve is a notable tribute to the persuasiveness and efficiency of the machinery of their "Agitpropr" department.

103. "Agitprop" (in extenso Agitacijski propagandin odsek) is a department of the General Staff and is the responsibility of the unit's Politkommissar. Corps, Divisions and Brigades have their own Agitprop section. At IX Corps H.Q. there were ten Agitprop personnel – twice as many as the G. staff, which indicates the importance they attach to it. They

are responsible for cultural training, the organization of "Meetings" (on the Communist pattern) and the production of unit newspapers. The Communist party have their own Propaganda units.

104. As far as cultural training is concerned, every Partizan other rank is required to have one hour's "Political instruction" daily. Officers have Political instruction according to their needs.

105. The Meetings take place in the various villages in the unit's area and consist of a political harangue, followed by two or three one act plays, the first generally a classic, the second a local piece with a heavy moral underlining the need to join the Partizans, and the third a piece of slapstick comedy. The whole atmosphere is rather mediaeval. Then follows patriotic songs and dancing.

106. As for the newspapers, every unit down to Brigade and sometimes even to Battalion produces its own cyclostyled edition. Apart from these there are the following which are produced regularly by Slovene H.Q.: SLOVENSKI POROCEVALEC, which is the organ of the Freedom Front; KMECKI GLAS, for peasants; NASA ZENA, for women; MLADINA, the Youth organ; SLOVENSKI PARTIZAN, for the Army; LJUDSKA PRAVCA, the Communist official organ. These are produced weekly and are beautifully printed (far better than, say, the Daily Telegraph!) and often illustrated.

107. In addition I have personally seen 50-60 special productions issued by Agitprop including a medical journal, an engineer journal, a literary journal, etc. etc.

108. A summary of the radio news is typed and circulated daily down to Company level and also by courier to all village committees.

109. Partizan units (down to Brigade H.Q. have Broadcast receivers, but in Free Territory these are virtually no wireless receivers other than those in official use. B.B.C. reception is almost always good.

(b) Leaflets

110. The Partizan attitude to our leaflets was rather as we should have felt had the Americans insisted on dropping leaflets on Great Britain urging us to greater efforts: they considered the whole thing rather an impertinence on our part. The more so since in one case the leaflets were written in Serbian!

(c) Propaganda against the Germans

111. The Partizans do very little of this – far less than against the Italians. To begin with they are resolute in their determination to offer the Germans no future except a slit throat – which is an inadequate induce-

ment to desert. Secondly they have not yet grasped the possibilities of disseminating a propaganda addressed to the Germans ostensibly by Germans; but now it has been put to them they like the idea.

(d) The German Propaganda to the Slovenian Partizans

112. The overt variety was was pretty stereotyped and made the following points:
   (1) Dangers of Communism.
   (2) Partizans were paid by Russian (sometimes even by British and American) gold.
   (3) They were traitors to their nation.
   (4) Those forcibly mobilized by the Partizans should desert and join the Domobrans – offering a Passierschein.
   (5) Rommel would soon clear up the Partizans anyway.
   (6) The Big German Nation, not Soviet Russia, offered the real anti-plutocratic front.

113. The German black propagana was rather well done. Here are two examples:

Example I. The following was clandestinely delivered to several Partizan H.Qs. in IX Corps Area: Partizan 3rd. Alpine Zone.

Order of the Day

Italian treachery has resulted in Tito's capture while inspecting Partizan units in PRIMORSKO.

This is a critical moment in the Partizan movement, and you should hold on, but above all don't fight until you get further orders.

We shall pay back the Italians for their treachery!

Example II. This was ostensibly a White Guard leaflet and made a very considerable impact on the Partizan rank and file. The argument was as follows:
   (1) Our aim is to form a Jugoslav State.
   (2) We hope to unite Croat, Slovene and Serb.
   (3) The King and Government in London are building up this new state and to this end have created the Royal Jugoslav Army.
   (4) You should therefore follow the King against the Communists.
   (5) The Anglo–American recognize the King, and this ranges Jugoslavia on the side of the Allies.
   (6) When they invade and liberate Jugoslavia the Anglo–Americans will only recognize the followers of the King.

(7) Anyhow, it is obviously unjust that the political programmes of 16 political parties should be sacrificed to the selfishness of a small minority party like the Communists.

Both the above examples were inspired by the Germans but actually produced and disseminated by the Blue Guard Propaganda centre in GORENJSKO.

114. As far as subversive work generally is concerned the Partizans are rather a disappointment. The reasons for their inactivity (or at leat for their unwillingness to co-operate with us) are as follows:

- (a) Any action which cannot clearly be attributed to the Partizan army results in the Germans wreaking their vengeance on the civilian element. As the entire Partizan provisioning system depends on civilian co-operation the Partizans are at great pains to keep them sweet. (This for instance precludes the use of camouflaged tyre busters, etc.)
- (b) The only areas where subversive work can usefully be carried out is in the towns or in similar German occupied areas. Here the organization is generally entirely in the hands of the Communists who already have their hands full with their own projects, and have no time or inclination for those that are British inspired.
- (c) The Partizan Movement is at present in the throes of an adolescent fervour of righteous patriotism and they are for the moment temperamentally unreceptive to any forms of warfare that are not 'sans peur et sans reproche'. In a guileful, cruel and perfidious world it is refreshing (if somewhat alarming) to find a nation battling for its life in the best traditions of the Boys Own Paper.

115. Such sabotage as there is is carried out by coup de main parties (e.g. the destruction of the IDRIA quicksilver mine last February), but the opportunities for this sort of operation are very few, as there are so few industrial installations in Jugoslavia.

116. During my trip I managed to awake some interest in the possibilities of carrying on subversive propaganda among the German troops of occupation. However, when I left it was too early to see whether this was going to have any practical results.

117. The real value of Slovenia as far as S.O.E. is concerned is as a base from which to penetrate Austria (and thence Central Europe) and North Eastern Italy. Provided Tito's approval can be obtained for the necessary framework organization of British personnel safe lines can be established without great difficulty. This has been dealt with at length in another paper.[164]

Appendix A

III. THE GERMANS
STRENGTH

118. As for the Germans, we spent most of our time avoiding them. Moreover, nothing was more difficult than to obtain exact information about the enemy from Partizan sources.

119. My estimate (which is hotly disputed by the Partizans) is that there are not more than 20,000 Germans permanently employed in the Slovenian theatre (including TRIESTE, GORIZIA and the area in North East Italy which the Germans call the KARST). I freely admit that there are often a great many more temporary troops than this, but the balance is made up of training units, rest camps and above all troops in transit between Italy, the Balkans and the Eastern Front.

120. According to sources which I think reliable this 20,000 is made up as follows: 10,000 Germans (at the very maximum); 7,000 Foreign legionaries (Mongols, Poles, Czechs, French, etc.); 3,000 Italian Fascists.

Though nominally they mostly belong to the 162 Legionary division,[165] these troops for the most part have no real divisional organization and consist of detachments whose task is to garrison towns, communications, and other vulnerable points.

LOCATION

121. On February 8th the German garrison of TRIESTE was 1,500 German troops, 150 S.S., 300 Legionaries and 200 Italians. In PRIMORSKO most market towns above the size of, say, AIDUSSINA, have a garrison of about a company. The same applies to ISTRIA. The main railway lines and all main roads are normally patrolled – but with a few exceptions there is no difficulty about crossing them.

122. GORENJSKO, which has now been incorporated into the Greater Reich and labelled GAU KÄRNTEN, is more heavily garrisoned than any other Slovenian district – mostly by police troops and by the S.S. Both of these are zealous and vindictive and cause the Partizans a lot of trouble. Even quite small villages have German garrisons (as I discovered to my cost!)

123. In NOTRANSKO and DOLENJSKO apart from the main railways and a few hedgehogs such as NOVO MESTO and KOCEVJE there are no permanent German garrisons.

MORALE

124. The Germans consider Slovenia a passive theatre and the morale of the real Germans (as apposed to the legionaries) was pretty high. At

the present time a German soldier's morale is, roughly speaking, a function of his distance from the Russian Front. From the few I spoke to it was clear that, while they no longer expected to win the sort of victory they had hoped in 1940, there was still no reason why this war (which in any case was only the first phase of a larger struggle) should not have a perfectly satisfactory outcome. To be faced with unconditional surrender was unthinkable, and a further impertinence on the part of their arch enemy Winston Churchill. Those of them whom I saw after being taken prisoner by the Partizans without exception faced certain execution with great fortitude. They were 'korrekt und soldatisch' to the last.

125. As for the legionaries, it was another matter. Most of them had chosen service with the Germans as an alternative to a concentration camp. For sheer opportunism, bestial cruelty, and general untrustworthiness the Mongol legionary can have few equals. Nor was the prospect of falling prisoner into their hands particularly alluring. And yet despite several cases of betrayal (at GORIZIA Mongol deserters gave the Germans information which led to the arrest of the entire TERENSKI Odbor) the Partizans welcomed these proselytes into their ranks with a father's welcome for a prodigal son. I have seen them kiss Mongols whom they have just taken prisoner, calling them "Brother Russians" (despite the fact they were patently not of Slav origin and anyway I personally would have been prouder of my relationship with the Barbary ape). But I quote this as another example of the somewhat uncritical attitude of the Slovenian Partizan towards the U.S.S.R.

126. The Germans for their part have got the Mongols well sized up order them about at the pistol point and discipline them with the lash.[166]

GERMAN EQUIPMENT

127. I saw a lot of captured German equipment which all appeared first class.

GERMAN TACTICS

128. For the most part the German sticks to the roads and the Partizan to the mountain tracks: possibly by tacit agreement. There are exceptions to this – particularly German Police and S.S. units, both of whom go looking for Partizans even in the forests themselves. The Partizans for their part never stick their necks out!

129. But the normal form is for the Germans to move down the valley, surround a village, shoot any Partizan who has been too idle to take to the hills, burn a few houses of well known Partizan sympathisers, requisition

and pillage what they can, and then withdraw; perhaps taking a few boys and girls with them to send to forced labour in Germany.

130. During this operation they may or may not be harrassed by the local Partizan unit. Unless it is a definite encroachment into what the Partizans consider their safe areas, the chances are the village will be left to its fate.

GERMAN ATTITUDE TO INHABITANTS OF OBERKRAJN

131. Having annexed this wholly Slovenian province the Germans are now trying to persuade the inhabitants they are misguided Germans who have forgotten Germany (but who have not, needless to say, been forgotten by Germany). A typical case of the Germans' complete incomprehension of their subject peoples.

REPRISALS

132. The normal practice is to burn any house in which arms or ammunition is found.

133. The shooting of hostages is growing daily and is a source of the greatest consternation to the Partizans. Between the 8th. and 31st. of January 155 hostages were shot in LJUBLJANA.

134. When I was in the neighborhood of SKOFIA LOKA in early February 50 hostages were shot for the murder of one German Gestapo official.

GERMAN CONSCRIPTION DRIVES

135. The Germans are making every effort to recruit all possible manpower in the Occupied countries. It is to evade this that many of the peasants are forced to join the Partizans.

136. I was personally caught in one of these Wehrmannschaft drives in GAU KARNTEN and can pay tribute to its thoroughness, which almost resulted in me being packed off myself to Germany as a (very) Foreign Worker.

IV. THE SUMMING UP

137. I make no apology for the length of this narrative. The Slovenian revolt is too important a movement to dispose of summarily. Indeed, in Central Europe (for Slovenia is essentially a part of Central Europe rather than a Balkan country), it is probably the most important event of its kind

since Andreas Hofer raised the Tryol in revolt during the Napoleonic wars.

138. Politically its aims are purely nationalist, linked with those of a Federated Jugoslavia more as a matter of political convenience than because of any sentimental tie, though Slovenian Partizans are all unanimous in their acceptance of Tito as their Leader. Above all, it exemplifies the new political feeling abroad in Europe today: nationalist, strongly left-wing, anxious to break for ever with the pre-1939 social structure, and above all with the pro-war King and Government which represented it.

139. But the importance of the Slovenian experiment lies less in its aims, which are common to all, than in the fact that they have managed to reduced them to a function of practical politics. Shaky as their political structure may be, it works. Even under the shadow of enemy occupation they have got a complete civil administration (revolutionary, if judged by pre-war standards) yet smoothly functioning for all to see – and, if they wish, to copy.

140. It is this empiricism in their affairs which makes Slovenia a political bridgehold in Central Europe and explains why the political importance of the Slovenian revolt transcends its military value (which is, at best, only a means to an end).

141. This, I think, Russia has appreciated better than we, and this is why her all-pervading influence in Slovenia is significant.

142. By the same token Slovenia is of paramount consequence to us during the war as a base, from which to make contact with resistance elements in Central Europe and North Italy. This feature also in my view exceeds in importance the Slovenians' intrinsic military value (as an aggressive force, at any rate). The Slovenians are only too willing to co-operate in this penetration, since it asks nothing of them which is in any way incompatible with their own interests, and helps to widen their sphere of influence. Our failure to exploit these possibilities more rapidly is due in no case to any hesitation on the Slovenians' part, and must be attributed mainly to delays in obtaining Tito's sanction for the introduction of the necessary British staff.

143. Taken as part of the united nations pattern their military effort is important too. There is no doubt that if the Slovenian Partizans were prepared to reverse their policy and concentrate their forces they could, at a given time provided the German reserves were committed elsewhere, virtually paralyse German rail and (to a lesser extent) road communications through SLOVENIA, ISTRIA and PRIMORSKO for several days, and possibly even for weeks. But they would be unwilling to attempt this unless given the strongest inducement (such as the promise of

TRIESTE) since their forces are for the present dispersed, and employed in what is for them, for political as well as for military reasons, the more important task of keeping the enemy out of their free areas, on which they depend for physical as well as for political existence.

144. There is one further point which deserves consideration, and that is the use of Slovenian liberated areas as safe harbours for Allied parachutists. From there they could attack the main strategic railways at the critical moment, afterwards returning to the safe areas for subsequent evacuation by air.

145. But these are special cases. The present value to us of the Balkan resistance movements lies in the number of German divisions they contain. While at the moment this policy is not incompatible with Slovenian aspirations, and the Slovenian revolt is undoubtedly diverting large numbers of enemy troops, we must never forget that as far as the Slovenians are concerned, this diversion is largely incidental; indeed little more than a tiresome and, they hope, temporary necessity. They have no wish to play even the smallest sacrificial role in our grand strategy.

146. Further, in assessing the military value of the Slovenian Partizans we must never lose sight of the fat fact that, far, far more than the Croats or Bosnians, they are irregular troops, and must be judged by irregular standards.

147. There were three propositions put forward by Lawrence concerning the employment of guerrilla troops. "Firstly that irregulars would not attack places, and so remained incapable of forcing a decision. Secondly, that they were as unable to defend a line or point as they were to attack it. Thirdly, that their virtue lay in depth, not in face".

148. There is another side of the Slovenian campaign which resembles the Arab War. It, too, is geographical, and like the Turkish army, the Germans are 'an accident'. "Yet killing Turks would never be an excuse or an aim. If they would go quietly our war would end. If not we would try to drive them out ..... but as cheaply as possible for ourselves, since the Arabs were fighting for freedom, a pleasure only to be tasted by a man alive".

149. These conditions explain much that has been criticised in the Slovenian's tactics – especially their 18th Century determination to avoid pitched battles by finesse. Since, despite the smallness of their forces, this war is complete for them in itself, they can keep their mind on its ultimate aim, to which battle is only a means. In this they follow Saxe rather than Foch.

150. In Slovenia today one lives an 18th Century existence: horse and cart provide the fastest means of transport; one often depends for light on melted pigs' fat in a hollow turnip; surgery is performed without anaes-

thetics or antiseptics; communication is by courier; even the sanitation is Georgian in construction and convenience; it would therefore be unfair to judge their army by any but 18th Century standards, which means that Clausewitz' thesis and his metaphysics about battles simply do not apply.

151. If we accept his premise, it is clear that the value of Slovenian military resistance lies less in its tactical success than in the fact that it straddles the main German communications between Italy and the Eastern front. In December 1943 the German approached the Slovenian H.Q. and proposed an armistice. They promised the Slovenians freedom from molestation in return for a free passage of German troops along Slovenian roads and railways. They even offered the Primorskan Partizans the freedom of GORIZIA.

152. The offer was rejected with scorn, but it is significant of the value the Germans attach to what has never been in the past, and, in my view, never will be in the future, more than a potential threat.

Appendix 1.a

History of the Slovenian Partizan Movement

1) The Slovenian Freedom Front (known as the "Osvobodilna Fronta") was founded on April 27th, 1941, in Ljubljana. Unlike the Serbs, who rushed headlong into military action before their resistance movement was properly organised, the Slovenians built up a subversive organisation in Ljubljana and the surrounding district before attempting any overt resistance. The first guerilla action took place in June, 1941 in Gorenjsko.

2) By August 1941, there were 800 Partisans actively fighting in Gorenjsko on Jelovec, a mountain covered with thick forests situated some 25 miles north-west of Ljubljana.

3) In the autumn of 1941 the first groups were formed in Dolenjsko. The first large action carried out by the Slovenian guerillas was on October 19th, 1941, when – under Sercer, one of the heroes of the movement – they attacked Loz, killing 100 Italians.

4) That autumn the first Slovenian Partisan military school was started near Ljubljana. By the winter there were 1,000 active partisans in South Gorenjsko and a number of organised groups, each of 30-40 guerillas, which were active in Dolenjsko. All these were armed and organised from Ljubljana.

5) The winter of 1941-2 was extremely hard, and the partisans were forced to leave the mountains in Gorenjsko and move down into Dolenjsko.

6) While this military development was taking place the Freedom Front had been extremely active politically, and by the autumn of 1941 they had formulated the political framework on which the present Slovenian organisation is based.

7) As a result of the steady growth of the Partisan movement during the winter, in April 1942 the Partisans felt strong enought to start an offensive against the Italians. This was very successful throughout Dolenjsko and forced the Italians to retreat into Notransko which is the area lying west of the Ljubljana – Kocevje road.

8) During the summer of 1942 there were between 5 and 10 thousand Partisans in Dolenjsko, and in May the first "free territory" was organised round Kocevje, where the Slovene parliament and General Staff was established on May 18th. Meanwhile, Gorenjsko, which had been abandoned by the original Partisans, started to form a new organisation. Unfortunately the German offensive in Gorenjsko that summer all but wiped out this resurrected Partisan organisation. Meanwhile the Partisans who had left Gorenjsko for Dolenjsko (see para. 5 above) migrated to Steiermark and started a Partisan organisation there to evade the German mobilisation drive. This was successful.

9) In 1941 the company, with a strength of 100-150 men, was the bas unit and these companies were loosely formed into three main groups: one in Notransko, one in Steiermark, and one in Dolenjsko. At this time not everyone had a rifle, and there were approximately 2 L.M.G. per company.

10) The Italians next launched two extremely successful offensives, first in July and the second in September, and employed new tactics which consisted of attacking each village and locality in turn.

11) As a result of these offensives the Partisans felt the need for rather larger tactical unit than the company. During the early summer the first brigades had been formed in Bosnia and in July 1941 Slovenia followed suit and the first brigade (the "Tomsic") was formed in Dolenjsko. In September and October three more brigades were formed (the Gubceva, Cankarjeva, and Sercerjeva Brigades). In the autumn of 1942 the Sercerjeva brigade had 13 L.M.G.'s.

12) Autumn 1942 marked the arrival of the first Staff Officers from Tito's H.Q.

13) During the winter of 1942 the Partisans launched another offensive against the Italians, this time with less success.

14) During the autumn of 1942 the Italians organised a "White Guard", known as M.V.A.C., which was recruited from Slovenes in concentration camps in Italy.[167] From then onwards village garrisons were generally half Italian and half White Guard.

15) It is noteworthy that in the autumn of 1942 a party of 11 Partisans went north to organise resistance in Carinthia. This was very successful and by the spring of 1943 a battalion had already been armed and organised and was actively fighting the Germans.

16) About this time too, 60 Partisans under Bracic went to Primorsko and by the spring of 1943 two brigades had been formed which have since expanded into a corps of two divisions.

17) In January 1943, Josip Widmar succeeded Boris Kidric as President of Slovenia.

18) By the spring of 1943 the Partisans had established a real superiority over the Italians, and it was a normal practice to post brigades in turn to Dolenjsko to enable them to capture sufficient arms and equipment to make up their deficiencies and allow them to expand.

19) After the collapse of the Fascist Party in Italy the Slovenians appreciated that Italy was on the verge of surrender. They therefore withdrew all their brigades into Dolenjsko and formed two divisions which they held concentrated ready to take advantage of the Italian capitulation.

20) As soon as this capitulation took place, which resulted in the surrender of 6 Italian divisions in the Ljubljana area, the Partisans collected enough arms and equipment to expand their two divisions into two corps of two and three divisions respectively.

21) In September 1943, a German offensive opened in Primorsko and Istria. 5 German divisions were involved and during October they reached Dolenjsko. The German aims was to establish small German "hedgehog" garrisons throughout Dolenjsko and this plan the Partisans claim to have defeated. The campaign lasted 6 weeks.

22) At the close of this offensive the Partisans again established free areas which in December 1943 included the Kocevjske Rog and most of the Bela Krajn, which they hold to this day.

23) An important meeting of the Slovenian Parliament was held at Crnomelj during February, and this marked the final development of the Slovenian Partisans' political organisation.

Appendix 1.b

THE PARTIZAN POLITICAL ORGANIZATION

1. It is beyond the scope of this paper to deal extensively with the Partizan parliamentary organization but the following will suffice to serve as a background for the study of Slovenia.
    (a) *AVNOJ* [*Antifašističko veče narodnog Jugoslavije*]. This is the Partizan Parliament of all Jugoslavia and has 300 members.
    (b) *The Presidential Committee.* The physical difficulties of convening AVNOJ under present conditions made it essential to evolve a somewhat smaller wartime Parliament. This Committee is presided over by Dr. Ivan RIBAR and includes the following representatives: 23 Serbs, 20 Croatians, 10 Slovenians, 4 Bosnians, 9 Montenegrans, 4 Macedonians.
    (c) *The National Committee (NACIONALNI KOMITET OSVO-BITVE JUGOSLAVIJE).* This is the executive Government and is made up of the following members (Slovene members members marked thus: *):

President
   Josip Broz-TITO. (War)
Vice Presidents
   Edvard KARDELJ (Sec. of Communist Party of Jugoslavia)*
   Vladislav RIBNIKAR (Propaganda)
   Bozidar MAGOVEC
Members
   Josip SMODLAKA
   Vlada ZECEVIC
   Edvard KOCBEK (Education)*
   Ivan MILUTINOVIC (National Economy)

Dusan SERNEC (Finance)*
Sreten ZUJOVIC, CRNI [nickname of above]
Milivoj JAMBRISAK (Health)
Todor VUJASINOVIC
Anton KRZISNIK (Social Politics)*
Franc FROL (Justice)
Mile PERUNICIC
Rade PRIBICEVIC
Sulejmin FILIPOVIC

2. Now as far as Slovenia itself is concerned there is:
   (1) OSVOBODILNA FRONTA, or Parliament
   (2) IZVRSNI ODBOR, Executive Committee [izvršilni]
   (3) OKROZNI ODBOR, Regional Committees [Bezirk]
   (4) RAJONSKI ODBOR, District Committec [Kreis]
   (5) TERENSKI ODBOR, Village Committee [Ort]
3. Up till February 1944 PRIMORSKO and ISTRIA each had a NARODNI SVET (or National Committee), but these were abolished as the Italian Slovenes were suspected of separatist tendencies.
4. Slovenian CARINTHIA has a POKRAJINSKI ODBOR. [Gebiet]
5. The composition of the IZVRSNI ODBOR is as follows:
   President
     Josip VIDMAR (Independent)
   Vice Presidents
     Edvard KARDELJ
     Edvard KOCBEK (Christian Socialist)
     Josip RUS (Communist)
   Secretary
     Boris KIDRIC (Sec. Slovene Communist Party)
   Members
     Marjan BRECELJ (Christian Socialist)
     Tone FAJFAR (Christian Socialist)
     Franc LESKOSEK
     France LUBEJ (Communist)
     Zoran POLIC.
6. The Primorskan NARODNI SVET used to consist of:
   President
     [France] BEVK
   Vice President
     [Jože] WILFAN [Vilfan] (a lawyer from KRAJN)
   Secretary
     [ALEŠ] BAEBLER [BEBLER] (a well-known international Communist)

Appendix 1.c

[contains diagram of "sleeper" mine laid unter rail tracks]

APPENDIX B

Report of Operations Military Sub-Mission to Fourth Operational Zone Jugoslav Army of National Liberation

Franklin A. Lindsay

[PRO WO 202/309]
14 May to 7 December 1944, 15 January 1945

15 January 1945
Submitted by: Franklin A. Lindsay, Major, Ord. Dept.
Dist: HQ 37 Military Mission
Internal: Comd
A/Q (2)
G(Ops)
G(Int)
G(L) (3)
SORE

TABLE OF CONTENTS

INTRODUCTION	1
PARTIZAN STRENGTH	1
PARTIZAN OPERATIONS	2
PARTIZAN ORGANIZATION	4
USE OF MILITARY EQUIPMENT BY PARTIZANS	5
AIR OPERATIONS	6

SUPPLY 6
GERMAN OPERATIONS 7
INTELLIGENCE 8
AUSTRIAN PENETRATION 9
POLITICAL NOTES 10
RELATIONS BETWEEN MISSION AND PARTIZANS 11
AIRFIELD 12
ALLIED PERSONNEL 12
NARRATIVE ACCOUNT 13

INTRODUCTION

This report covers the operations of the Military Sub-Mission to Fourth Operational Zone, Jugoslav Army of National Liberation, a sub-mission of the Military Mission of Brigadier MacLean to the JANL. The period covered is from 14 May, 1944 to 7 December 1944.

It is hoped this report will assist in bringing about a more objective and unbiased attitude concerning the contribution of the Partisans to the defeat of the German Army. In general the conclusions reached are:

a/ The Partisan Forces of Fourth Zone contributed greatly to the disruption of enemy communications between Italy, the Balkans, and Germany.

b/ This contribution was not as great as it could have been considering the supplies, and man-power available to the Partisans and the weakness of the German opposition. This was especially true after September when the Partisans almost completely failed to hold the initiative.

c/ By obstructionist tactics and indifference the Partisans of Fourth Zone prevented the Allied representatives from obtaining more than a small fraction of the available intelligence on enemy movements thru this vital area.

d/ The Partisans on the whole blocked every effort of the Allies in their efforts (1) to obtain intelligence from Austria, (2) to infiltrate agents into Austria, and (3) to stir up an Austrian Partisan movement against the German occupation.

e/ The inefficiencies and carelessness of the base in matters of supply resulted in the failure of many sorties and often reduced Partisan effectiveness by failure to deliver urgently needed supplies at the right time and place.

The report is divided into topical sections covering the various phases of the Mission activities. A narrative of the experiences of the Mission personnel has been included.

Appendix B
PARTISAN STRENGTH

In 1942 and 1943 small groups of Partisans were formed in the mountains of this area. Two small brigades grew out of these groups and in Feb. 1944, the Fourteenth Division was transferred from Dolinska (Seventh Corps) to Stajersko. During the winter and spring the Germans carried out several offensives against the Partisans and at the time of my arrival the total Partisan strength of Fourth Zone was probably under three thousand. Between June and November approx. two thousand men per month were recruited. The majority of these recruits were sent to Seventh Corps as insufficient weapons were available in Fourth Zone for the entire number. By the end of November, Fourth Zone strength was estimated to be about 8,000 men.

Battle Order Fourth Zone 1 December 1944. (Strengths are estimated.)

14th Division	2700
1st Slovene Brigade (Tomsic)	900
2nd Slovene Brigade (Sercova)	900
13th Slovene Brigade (Mirko Bracic)	900
6th Slovene Brigade (Slandera)	1000
11th Slovene Brigade (Milos Zidancek)	1000
Lasco Odred (north of Drava between Maribor and Dravograd)	100
Korosko Odred (area between Solcava and Drava river)	400
Kosanske Odred (area around Koze [Kožje] northeast of Zidani Most	700
Kamniske Zasavske Odred (area between Kamnik and Zagorje on Sava river)	600
Kokrski Odred (area north of Kranj)	500
Miscellaneous Chetas and Kommando Mestos	1000
	8000

The estimated increase in strength roughly agrees with the total number of weapons delivered by air plus weapons captured.

In October the Sixth and Eleventh Brigades were ordered across the Sava and were temporarily attached to the Seventh Corps.

PARTISAN OPERATIONS

Partisan operations are of two types; operations against enemy lines of communication and operations to liberate and hold territory.

From the time of my arrival in Stajersko in June until September, the Partisans were aggressive and quite successful in their attacks against lines of communication. After this date, although they were stronger and better equipped, attacks on lines of communication were weak.

The early successes were partly due to the surprise achieved. Our first load of explosives, eight tons, was dropped in the middle of June. The rail lines were weakly guarded as the Partisans had been unable previously to make any major attacks.

On June 22, I accompanied a Partisan battalion on an attack against a large masonry bridge at Mislinje on the Celje–Dravograd line. We were able to reach the bridge without detection and found it completely unguarded although an enemy garrison of two hundred was less than two kilometers away. Charges were laid at the base of three of the seven columns against the "uphill" side, thus achieving partial tamping. The first charges did not completely cut the columns and it was necessary to lay a second set. As soon as the first charge was detonated Partisan machine gunners opened up on the German garrison from a nearby hill. The garrison, thinking they were under attack, manned their garrison bunkers and did not interfere with the laying of the second charge, although they were much stronger than the Partisans. A half hour later the second charges were fired and the columns destroyed. A gap of a hundred yards had been made with eighteen hundred pounds of explosive and without a single casualty. This bridge has never been repaired.

The following night units of the Fourteenth Division attacked and destroyed a portion of a tunnel near Polcane [Polčanje] on the main Celje-Maribor line. Only five guards were found in the area and these were quickly disarmed. Charges were placed in charge holes which had been constructed along the walls when the tunnel was built. The earth above the tunnel was quite sandy and the effect of the charges was to drop the entire height of the hill into the tunnel shaft. Todt workers, working under the threat of death penalty, required six weeks to open the tunnel for single track traffic. Minor sabotage operations were carried out on the rail net continuously during July and August.

During the first week of September a concentrated attack against rail lines was made at the direction of Marshal Tito. The following targets were selected by the staff and myself; tunnel at Polcane (previously damaged) and a nearby bridge on the Celje-Maribor line, bridge across Savina River at Tremerje, three miles south of Celje on the Zidani Most line, bridge across the Sava at Litija on Zidani Most-Ljubljana line, and five kilometers of road bed along the Sava on this sector.

Operations were delayed on the Celje-Maribor section because explosives were not delivered until the night of 2 September. During this period, Lieutenant Bush was with the Fourteenth Division which had been assigned this sector. Division HQ requested air support through him for an attack against the Polcane tunnel. When the base advised that no support was available, the Division dropped plans for action against this line and moved away from the line. During this period no attacks of any sort were made on this sector although Bush reported that in his opinion much could have been accomplished by small sabotage groups. Similarly, no attempt was made against the Tremerje bridge.

During the same period Sergeant Welles was with the two brigades assigned to the Zidani Most-Ljubljana sector. The Zone commandant advised me on 6 September that the Litija Bridge had been attacked, unsuccessfully, however, because the enemy garrison at Litija numbered about fifteen hundred men. Sergeant Welles later reported that no attack was made against the bridge, although local Partizans stated that the garrison was not more than two hundred men. In Welles's opinion a successful attack at this time could have been made. Successful attacks were made, however, on cuts and embankments between Zidani Most and Litija. Traffic was stopped on 1 September and the line has not been reopened since.

A few weeks later a second attack under the direction of Seventh Corps was made against the Litija Bridge. This operation probably has been covered in Captain Goodwin's report. However, it is believed that its lack of success was due to the repeated postponements and that the enemy learned of the plans for the attack.[168]

After September attacks continued on the Zagreb-Zidani Most-Maribor and Maribor-Klagenfurt lines, but were confined to cutting rails and blowing small bridges. Delays in traffic were from a few hours to two days.

Until December almost no traffic moved over the main Celje-Ljubljana road. On 6 December the road was blocked for three days and very heavy troop movements took place in the direction of Maribor. The road was again blockaded on the tenth of December to cover a second enemy movement. During the first period and probably the second no attempt was made by the Partizans to mine the road although I am quite sure a few mines could have been laid quite easily each night, and would have been most successful in disrupting the enemy movement.

As in the case of operations against lines of communications, in operations against German garrisons the Partizans were quite successful before September. After September they lost the initiative almost entirely and no large engagements took place except on the initiative of the enemy.

Until 1 August no liberated territory existed in the Fourth Zone. When we arrived in May we found the Partizans operating only in the mountains.

Every village had a German garrison and movement was possible only at night. The chief Partizan concentration was on the top of the Pohorje, but the enemy was able to move troops in groups of two to three hundred through this area almost at will.

On 1 August a highly successful attack was carried out by nearly all the Partizan units of Fourth Zone against the German garrisons in Solcava, Luce, and Lubno in the upper Savinska valley and against Gorni Grad and Bocna in the Dreta valley. In two days all these garrisons were eliminated. German losses were one hundred killed, forty five captured (later released to return to Celjo as "propaganda"), two hundred and seventy five Wehrmänner captured, all of whom joined the Partizans. Partizans lost ten killed and seventeen wounded. On 13 September this liberated territory was further enlarged by the capture of the garrison of Mozirje.

In October the Odred which had been operating in the Pohorje was forced to withdraw by a large German force. Since then the enemy has had almost complete control of this area, and no Partizan unit has been able to remain there more than two or three days at a time.

In September a small area around Laze, north and east of Zidani Most, was liberated; this was used as a base for operations against the rail line Zagreb-Zidani Most-Celje.

Partizans claimed, after the elimination of a few small garrisons between the Sava and the main Celje-Ljubljana road, that this area was almost liberated. Although they enjoyed relative freedom of movement here, it was not really liberated as the Germans continued to move through the area from time to time with little opposition.

In addition to units in Stajersko, Fourth Zone also controlled two Odreds operating in Carinthia. The West Odred operated relatively freely in the Karawanken Alps south of Klagenfurt until August. At this time a military zone was established and Partizans were forced out of all territory west of a line Kamnik-Eisenkappel.

On 1 December a German offensive was undertaken against the liberated territory of the Upper Savinska valley with the purpose of eliminating the Partizan threat to the rear of their retreating forces. This offensive succeeded in recapturing all liberated territory and in driving the Partizans into the mountains.

PARTIZAN ORGANIZATION

As the Fourth Zone is much smaller and the liberated territory less secure than in the other Partizan commands military and civil organization was less fully developed than elsewhere.

No schools existed for the training of officers or sergeants and all trainees were sent to schools in Seventh Corps.

The weakest link in the military organization was the junior officers and the junior commissars. Many of these men achieved their position primarily because of long service in the Partisan ranks. Many appeared to be "political" appointees with little qualification in leadership. The rank of an officer was regarded usually as a position of privilege rather than responsibility. There is far greater differentiation between officers and men in matters of clothing, food, equipment, shelter, and privileges than is found in the British or American armies.

These junior officers take advantage of their authority to get the best of the meager supplies available for themselves. Nearly all officers had "Tito" jackets tailored from British and American greatcoats, then took second greatcoats to wear over the jackets. Meanwhile, the troops shivered in ragged remnants of civilian clothes and German uniforms. At Zone headquarters all the couriers and girl secretaries had British battledress and at the same time I saw whole fighting brigades without a single piece of Allied clothing.

The same situation existed in the issuing of food. Separate messes existed for officers and men and normally there was a very great difference in both quality and quantity. Officers seldom carried their own rucksacks on the march but had their equipment carried by their personal couriers.

Apparently Partizans have a definition of responsibility quite different to our concept of military responsbility. On several occasions I made requests for certain actions to the Zone Commissar and to which he agreed. Later, if the action was not carried out, the reply would be in essence, "Well, I gave the order, and if it was not carried out it was not my fault. I can't be everywhere at once." One day during a drop I asked the lieutenant in charge of the area to replace a signal canopy which had been taken away by mistake. The order was passed down through six people before a fourteen year old boy was sent out. Meanwhile, a Mission sergeant had done the job.

Civilian organization appeared to be quite comprehensive. Collection and distribution of food was the chief task of the local administration. The Partizans, however, seldom helped in the cultivating or in the harvesting, although units would often rest at a farm house for a week or more.

Soon after liberation of each village a "free" election of local officials was held by the Partizans. However, only one candidate for each office appeared on the ballot. This apparently was not considered inconsistent with political freedom.

USE OF MILITARY EQUIPMENT BY PARTIZANS

Military equipment used by the Partizans in Fourth Zone included:
Hand grenades
German, British, and Italian rifles
Schmeisser and Sten sub-machine guns
Boyes AT rifles
German MG 38 and 42 and Bren light machine guns
Breda heavy machine guns
Two inch and three inch mortars
Piats [Projector, Infantry, Antitank, less effective British bazooka]
U.S. Anti-tank Rocket Launchers
Italian 75MM field gun
Plastic, 808, and accessories

The rifle and light machine gun were the basic weapons for the guerrilla type of fighting in this area. Large numbers of Brens were delivered and were very popular and effective. The chief difficulty was in training the Partizan soldier to use it economically.

Mortars were not used particularly effectively due to lack of training. Apparently little attempt was made to use fire control instruments and tables. Fire control consisted mainly of rule-of-thumb correction on observed fire. However, the mortar bombs made a big bang and the Partizans believed they were valuable in demoralizing the enemy troops. Piats and bazookas were also very popular with the Partizans but it was almost impossible to get them to use these weapons for the specialized purpose for which they were intended. In one case a brigade commander was observed firing a piat by holding it between his knees and lobbing mines mortar-fashion into enemy personnel deployed on a mountain side. I repeatedly asked that these guns be used against locomotives as the wooded and mountainous terrain was well suited to such ambush operations. However, to my knowledge, this was never done.

The one 75 MM gun was often used in attacks on enemy garrisons to reduce buildings in which the enemy was barricaded. The usual range was fifty yards and never more than one hundred yards. The piece was laid by sighting along the barrel.

No standard anti-tank mines were delivered to the Partizans, but instead bulk explosive was used in locally made wooden mines. This had the advantage of reducing the weight of air-delivered stores. The wooden mine was essentially a box about eight by eight by six inches in which the fused and primed explosive was detonated by a standard pressure switch. The mine was tamper-proof and was extremely difficult to remove once it had been armed.

The Partizans also used made-up charges of ten to thirty pounds most effectively to demolish a wall of an enemy-held garrison. In the darkness a Partizan would creep up to the building and place his charge against the wall. A short delay would enable him to get under cover, and after the explosion Partizan machine gunners would get anyone who still wanted to fight. The usual effect of the charge was to drop the entire wall section and expose the interior to rifle and MG fire.

In rail operations explosives were used to cut rails, to destroy bridges, and to destroy retaining walls and embankments. Often every rail in a section two to three kilometers would be cut. At various times the Germans were so short of rails that they were forced to trim the blown sections with a cutting torch and weld the halves together.

In the operations which I observed, the use of explosive on bridges was primitive, but effective. The charges normally were not overloaded and were placed in effective positions. We repeatedly asked the base to send in beehives for bore-holing the stone and concrete bridges in our area. Their use would have considerably reduced the amount of explosive required. Although we were advised that beehives were available, none were ever delivered.

The double-track rail line between Zidani Most and Ljubljana followed the Sava through a deep gorge. There were many deep cuts alternating with embankments which the Partizans took advantage of to block the line.

Rock and earth on the sides of the cuts were blown onto the tracks to a height of thirty feet in many places. On adjacent sections retaining walls were blown and the road bed was dropped into the river.

AIR OPERATIONS

Combined air-ground operations in this area almost never came off. Our occasional requests for air support were in some cases not even acknowledged. In general, it is my belief that air support of Partizan-type operations are seldom successful due to the difficulty in timing and in predicting Partizan movements.

SUPPLY

During the summer months air supply was very difficult due to the uncertainty of the Partizans being able to control the drop areas. This situation was covered in a report made in September to Brigadier McLean and Colonel Huntington. The following factors determined the volume of supplies we were able to deliver:

a. *Weather.* During the summer months less than fifty per cent of the nights were suitable for flying.

b. *Communications with base.* Communications were intermittant as a result of our constant moving and because we were out of petrol most of the time. In spite of our most violent pleas for petrol several sorties came in with none aboard.

c. *Inexperience of drop area crews.* In order to be sure that we would always have one drop point free, we established four separate points. This necessitated using Partizans for crews and on at least two occasions sorties failed because of Partizan incompetence and irresponsibility.

d. *Communications between Mission and drop area.* Initially no internal radio communication existed and the only link with the drop points was by courier. Consequently we never knew whether or not these points were open.

e. *Constant changing of recognition signals.* Signal plans were repeatedly changed by the base, often on less than twenty four-hour notice. As we were unable to advise the drop areas in time, we lost several sorties.

As previously reported the loading of planes was often not according to our requests. Many items were requested and which the base advised were available and would be delivered were never dropped. After a few months the Partizans began to feel that the Allies had little real interest in helping them and were only interested in delivering tonnage. This was not altogether unjustified.

On several occasions brigades went to the drop areas to receive supplies which we had requested several days in advance. In most cases either the supplies never came or the wrong supplies were dropped. Had we been advised by the base that our requests could not be filled we could have advised the Partizans who would have altered their plans accordingly.

In many cases there undoubtedly was a reason why the particular items did not arrive. However, we were never advised of these reasons and consequently came to the conclusion that the base organization was indifferent and inefficient. In November the loading improved considerably and nearly all of our requests were promptly delivered.

In October a load of explosives was requested for Laze (Jurcloster) for use against the Zagreb-Zidani Most line. As it was impossible to transport explosives to this area from the main drop point, the operations against this rail line were absolutely dependent upon air delivery. This request was repeated several times but no sorties had been sent there up to our departure in December. During the same period approximately eighty loads were flown to the main drop point.

The subject of quantity of or classes of material delivered cannot be covered here as for security reasons all lists of material received were not kept but immediately forwarded to the base. It is estimated that approximately fifty tons of explosives and weapons for four thousand men were delivered during the seven month period.

Although several messages were sent advising that Rogla, and later Okonina, were the only drop points safe for bodies, the RAF dropped Major Matthews to a point definitely reported as unsafe. Captain Owen advised that Air Operations had pin pointed another drop point on top of a rocky mountain as safe for bodies contrary to our messages.

GERMAN OPERATIONS

The entire territory of the Fourth Zone was incorporated into the German Reich after the capitulation of Jugoslavia. Intensive efforts were made to completely Germanize the land and the people. All place names were Germanized as well as all family names. In every respect the territory has been treated as an integral part of the Reich. Consequently the defense of this area has been and will continue to be more determined than in the territories controlled by the "Quisling" governments. In 1942 and 1942 approximately thirty per cent of the Slovenes, including ninety per cent of the intellectuals, were deported to Silesia, to concentration camps, and to industrial centers. Large numbers of Germans were brought in to staff the local governmental offices. German teachers were used exclusively in the schools. Every effort was made to eliminate all elements of Slovene culture and replace them with German culture. All this was in response to Hitler's order to make lower Styria German.

Many of the best farms were left uncultivated as a result of deportations. It was announced that these would be given to the veterans of the Wehrmacht when the war was over.

Up until September 1944 no Yugoslav Quisling troops were used in the area. A home guard caled the "Wehrmannschaft" composed of Slovenes who had not been mobilized into the Wehrmacht was established to fight the then weak Partizans. This organization was directly under the Gauleiter of Steyermark.

German battle border for garrison troops in the area was in November as follows:

184 Landeschutz Regiment
   517 Battalion, HQ Kamnik
   921 Battalion, HQ Kranj
   927 Battalion, HQ Jesenice
18 Landeschutz Regiment, HQ Celje
   611 Battalion, HQ Sostanj

649 Battalion, HQ Brezice
922 Battalion, HQ Trebovlje
Grenzwacht Abschnitt XVIII/D
 Grenzwacht Kompanie 19/XVIII, HQ Mislinje
 " " 20/XVIII, HQ Dravograd
 " " 16/XVIII, HQ Marenburg [sic]
Grenzwacht Abschnitt XVIII/F, HQ Zidani Most
 Grenzwacht Kompanie XVIII/15, HQ Zagorje (on Sava river)
 " " XVIII/14, HQ Sevnice (" ")
 " " XVIII/21, HQ Litija (" ")
Landschutz Kompanie 1/802, HQ Zidani Most
Landschutz Kompanie 2/937, HQ Hrastnik (on Sava River)
Regiment Brandenburg, HQ Bled
 1st Battalion, HQ Bled
 2nd Battalion, HQ St Vid (near Ljubljana)
 3rd Battalion, HQ Kamnik
 4th Battalion, HQ Domjale.

In addition, approximately thirty Wehrmannschaft Companies and several hundred Gendarmes were mixed in with German troops in Garrisons.

In addition to these static troops additional German units were brought into the area from time to time to carry out offensives against Partisan units. In May approximately ten thousand troops were used in an offensive lasting a week. In October sixteen hundred troops were sent to Ljubljana in an unsuccessful attempt to reoccupy Gorni Grad. In December at least four SS Regiments (unidentified) completely recaptured all liberated territory and drove Partisan units into the mountains.

In August the German command was apparently so short of men for garrison duty that they brought in about five hundred metropolitan policemen from Vienna to strengthen their stations.

The objectives of the occupation troops were (a) to guard the mines in the Crna area (b) to guard the vital railway lines in the area (c) to occupy all villages and undertake offensive actions to deny the use of the valleys to the Partisans.

In September units of the Slovene White Guard were first employed in Stajersko and in November Ustase and Domobran troops appeared. About this time the Germans began a program of burning whole towns and of taking all food and livestock available.

Air operations carried out by the Germans against the Partisans were annoying but in no way affected the Partisan fighting strength.

INTELLIGENCE

(The problem of intelligence in respect to Austria is covered separately.)

It is estimated that the intelligence obtained in this area was about ten per cent of that potentially available. The Allied personnel were permitted no independent action of any sort in the collection of intelligence. The only intelligence available was that contained in the official handout of the Partisan staff. The Partisan intelligence staff was poorly trained and far too small to do an effective job. Had full co-operation been possible between Alled Intelligence officers and Partisan intelligence officers the coverage and the quality of the information could have been improved tremendously.

In the entire seven months not more than half a dozen German pay books were made available to us. We were never permitted to interrogate prisoners, deserters, refugees, and similar persons who had come out of German-held territory.

The original enemy battle order produced by the Partisans gave no unit identifications and contained only a numerical estimate of the number of troops in each garrison. It took us several months to get identification of these static units. Fourth Zone was astride the main rail lines connecting Italy, the Balkans, and Germany. Troop movements were taking place almost constantly over these lines but not once were the Partisans able to provide us with the identifications of such units.

Rail reports were first produced in September although we had been promised them repeatedly since June. The rail reports which were submitted were on the whole excellent. They were usually provided by a station master who had access to the bills of lading so that the origin, destination, and contents of each car was provided.

At the time of my departure I was permitted to make copies of sketches and plans of most of the main road and railroad bridges in the area; also the plans of many of the cities and towns, and of the entrances to the new Lobel Pass Tunnel. This material has already gone to Bari and should be made available to OSS and Force 399.[169]

On many occasions we happened onto information of considerable interest and military significance which had been deliberately witheld from us by the Staff and I feel certain that much more was witheld of which we never learned.

AUSTRIAN PENETRATION

It is most difficult to write a factual and objective report on our operations in connection with getting intelligence out of Austria and infiltrating Allied personnel into Austria. All Partisan operations in these areas were surrounded with the utmost secrecy and accompanied by the maximum intrigue. However, I feel quite certain that the Partisans obstructed and sabotaged our efforts in this direction in every way possible.

On my arrival at Fourth Zone I found that a small group of Partisans had crossed the Drava between Maribor and Dravograd and were in the southern Koralpen. I proposed to the Partisans that supplies be sent to increase this group to a battalion with the purpose of establishing a relatively secure 'bridgehead' on the north side of the Drava for penetration further North. The Partisans agreed to this and I advised both OSS and Force 399 but no reply was received from either organisation. In August and September when the American Austrian Mission and the British Mission arrived the crossing of the river had become much more difficult and the Partisan attitude on aiding us had apparently crystallised.

I believe it quite certain that the Partisans have regular lines into Villach, Klagenfurt, Graz, and Wien, although they advised us they had lost their contacts and could not provide us with safe addresses.[169] American pilots reported contacting Partisan civilian organisers in the Graz area. The Partisans were most uncooperative with Austrian personnel and in August requested that all British Austrian personnel be evacuated. This was due in fact to the capture of ISLD agent "Dick Black" and his subsequent exposure of Allied and Partisan personnel to the Gestapo.

In September a party of Americans arrived to penetrate Austria. For two months every excuse and obstacle was given to their moving north. Finally in late October, three of these men were permitted to go on to the Korosko Odred near Solcava. Here the same line was given them that previously had been given the SOE party under Major Cahusac, "We would like to put you across the river, but we have no weapons. If you send a few plane loads of stores we will see that you cross." Unfortunately, this party agreed, and attempted to get stores sent in independent of the mission. For two months no effort was made to put this party across the Drava, while the Partisans waited for the stores to be delivered. Meanwhile couriers were crossing almost regularly to the battalion with Major Cahusac and in addition a group crossed in November [October] and liberated Russian prisoners in a mine near Sveti Andras [St. Andrä] and a second battalion crossed in late November. Obviously no effort was being made to get this party over the river.

We were further obstructed in learning of events in Austria by the refusal of the Partisans to permit us to see and question persons coming from Austria. This was true even in the case of Allied fliers and POWs who were brought out of Austria by the Partisans. Of over a hundred Allied fliers and POWs brought from Stajersko to Slovene HQ in November, we saw only eleven. We attempted for three months to get a blind mailing address in one of the German held towns through the Partisans but were unable to do so. At another time we requested a set of documents from a French worker for use of ISLD. Although many French workers escaped through Stajersko no documents were forthcoming. After several weeks a set was given to the ISLD officer secretly by a Partisan officer who asked that the Staff not be told that he had given us the documents.

It is my belief that both American and British efforts for penetration of Austria were less successful than they could have been had other methods been tried.

With the exception of one, all agents which were to be infiltrated into Austria arrived without documents, cover story, safe addresses, or civilian clothing. Under such conditions they were at the mercy of the Partisans in obtaining such material. Had they been sent to us completely prepared to assume their cover and go on immediately, the Partisans could have had no excuse for not permitting them to go on immediately to the nearest German held town and from there by train north into Austria.

From all information we were able to gather during seven months there was no evidence of any Austrian resistance of any sort to the German occupation. There possibly is an underground organization in the Floritzdorf [Floridsdorf] suburb of Vienna and another in Graz. There is believed to be a group of deserters from the military hospital at Graz living in the Koralpen. However, none of these groups have taken up arms offensively or undertaken any sabotage operations. The British SOE party which crossed the Drava with a Partisan battalion in October into the Saualpen reported in December that Austrian resistance was nil.

In September, following a speech by Tito, an intensive propaganda campaign was begun demanding the incorporation of Klagenfurt and Villach and all "Slovene" Styria and Carinthia into Slovenia. The Partisans admit privately that in neither city is the civilian population primarily Slovene, but defend their claims on the basis of the majority Slovene rural population in this area.

POLITICAL NOTES

It is impossible to give any complete report on the political situation because of the secrecy imposed and because the work of the mission was military and not political. A few notes, however, may be of interest. Essentially the Partisan organization in Stajersko was political and the military was subject to political decisions.

Officially the freedom front was a coalition of many political parties. Actually there was no evidence of the existence of any party except the Communist party. The Communist party, the civilian government, and the Army was so interwoven that individuals often held positions in two or three simultaneously. The secretary of the Communist party for Slovenia, Bebler, spent several months in Stajersko in the uniform of a Partisan full Colonel, and was occupied the whole time with organizing the civil government and building up the Communist party. In all the meetings I attended the basic line was essentially the same: (a) the origin and growth of the Partisan movement was accomplished by the Communist party, (b) the Partisans were being aided in the liberation of their country by their brother Slavs the Russians, (c) it is the duty of every person to support the Partisans to the limit in their fight to expel the enemy and to defeat the collaborationists.

The rank and file are pro-American and British and look forward to an Allied liberation of the area. The officers, civil and military, are pro-Russian and attempt to magnify Russian war efforts and minimise the Allied effort. They are particularly anti-British in that they read into every British move the determination to restore the King and to block their territorial expansion.

In September an amnesty was granted to all Jugoslavs in the Quisling armies to join the Partisans before 15 September. This was unsuccessful both in Stajersko and in Dolinska and netted only a few hundred men. Since that time the Partisans have lost the offensive and the collaborationist troops, chiefly the White Guard, have become more aggressive. It is quite possible that after the failure of the amnesty offer the Partisan high command realized that it did not have the upper hand completely and that there would be strong opposition from the right wing parties and troops when the Germans withdrew. In light of this the Partisans, thinking the Germans would be gone soon, may have decided to conserve their men and supplies to defeat all opposition when that day came.

RELATIONS BETWEEN MISSION AND PARTISANS

In general, relations between the Mission and the Partisan Staff were good before the middle of September and bad after. The examples of non-cooperation, bad faith, and obstructionism became so numerous that it is impossible to explain them as carelessness or ignorance on the part of the individual staff officers. During one period all Allied personnel were under informal arrest, and on several occasions Partisans, officers and soldiers, told us they had been forbidden to have any contact with us. Many times all Allied officers at Zone HQ came to the conclusion that events could only prove that the basic Partisan policy had become that of "all obstruction short of an open break and the stoppage of supplies." I feel almost certain that some secret instructions were issued which were behind this policy by Tito's headquarters. Many examples of non-cooperation have been given in other sections.

It is difficult to determine the causes underlying this anti-Allied policy, but the following points are suggested as possibilities.

a/ After the failure of large numbers of the opposition to come over during the September amnesty the Partisans may have realized that their post-war position was not as secure as they had thought. They were very anxious that the extent of the opposition and the anti-Partisan feeling not be known to us, hence the attempt to isolate us.

b/ The nearness of the Red Army after the fall of Belgrade may have mad ethem feel less dependent upon the Western Allies, and more willing to throw over the marriage of convenience.

c/ There appeared to be a growing distrust of the Allied post-war intentions in the internal affairs of Jugoslavia. The Subasic government was regarded more and more unfavourably, and probably it was feared by many that Britain would do everything possible to get the King back.

d/ The Partisans feared probably our efforts in Austria ultimately would conflict with their territorial claims of Klagenfurt and Villach.

e/ The Allied supplies were not as large as the Partisans had hoped for or expected.

f/ Possibly the more violent of the Communist leaders desired to undermine the British and American popularity with the rank and file, and adopted a policy of putting us in the most unfavourable light possible. This is substantiated by their removal of all persons attached to the Mission who became over friendly and who they thought had been penetrated by us.

g/ Their natural Balkan super-suspicion probably made them suspect us of all sorts of imaginary secret intrigues.

h/ Finally much of what went on has no possible logical reason, and can only be ascribed to "intrigue for the sake of intrigue."[170]

During the entire seven months our relations with Lieutenant Colonel Bogomolov, Russian Liaison Officer, were the best. We had no evidence that any of our difficulties with the Partisans had been promoted by him, and I do not believe that any were inspired by him secretly.

The morning we left Zone HQ the Zone Commissar came to say goodbye. Among other things he said that he fully realized that our relations had not been completely satisfactory and implied that the blame was with the Partisans. He further stated that although many Partisans were very pro-Russian, many others, including himself, were equally pro-Allies and pro-Russian.

AIRFIELD

The difficulties encountered in our attempts to establish an airfield are quite typical of the relations between Allied personnel and the Partisans. On 25 August I sent a memorandum to the Zone Commissar stating that we had inspected a site near Recica and had found it suitable for a landing strip. In September the area became secure enough to make possible landings and the site was tentatively approved by the RAF. Before landing planes, however, they desired to drop an officer to approve the strip. The Partisans, however, refused to accept the officer in spite of my guarantee that he had Tito's approval. I explained that the establishment of this field would facilitate the delivery of supplies and make possible the evacuation of Partisan wounded. Subsequently, I was told informally by a Partisan officer that the Staff did not want an airfield and that their inability to obtain permission for the RAF officer was simply an excuse. On learning this I dropped the project.

In November a Partisan Major arrived from Slovene HQ and after we had come to know him he told us he was now directing the construction of an airfield at the point we had selected in August, but that he had received strict orders from the Commissars of both Slovene HQ and Fourth Zone not to tell the Allied officers of this under any circumstances. His motive in telling us was that he personally felt friendly to the Americans and the British and that he did not approve of such double dealing. At first we believed that the field was being prepared at request of the Russians; however, a few days later the Russian Liaison Officer asked me if I had seen the field and was quite surprised that I knew nothing about it. I then saw the Commissar and asked for an explanation of the secrecy. He had no explanation at all except that (a) this was Partisan territory and they could build an airstrip if they wanted without telling us, and (b) the Russian officer had not been told officially of the airfield either (this was not true). He then said that he hoped Allied planes would land with supplies and evacuate wounded and that no permission was necessary for an RAF inspecting officer.

I am unable to suggest any rational reason for such intrigue. Unfortunately winter weather and a German offensive prevented the field from being used. Had the Partisans cooperated with us in September we would have been able to evacuate all their wounded before the bad weather began.

Appendix B
ALLIED PERSONNEL

The Allied personnal accredited to Fourth Zone found themselves in an embarrassing and difficult position resulting from the decisions of various independent organizations to send independent missions to Fourth Zone. In September the Allied personnel at Fourth Zone totalled twenty seven officers and men. This caused us difficulty in that (a) as we represented independent organizations we could not always present a single policy in relations with Partisan command (b) a very poor impression was made on the Partisans due to the large number of persons with little or nothing to do (c) the various missions often put requests for identical information to the Staff (d) we were so large that provision for food, housing, and guard was a real problem. In contrast, all Russian interests were handled by a single officer.

Before leaving for the field Force 399 agreed that no personnel would be sent in without advising us and permitting us to express an opinion on the advisability of sending additional personnel.[171] Had this been done we would certainly have recommended that certain missions not be sent. After arrival these missions agreed that there was little work for them.

In September "A" Force sent Major Matthews to the mission.[172] Since his arrival he has been unable to accomplish anything in the liberation and evacuation of prisoners and airmen which would not have been done otherwise by the Partisans or by the existing mission personnel. This is no way a reflection on Major Matthews or his ability, but is due entirely to the methods by which the Partisans operated.[172]

As mentioned in the section on Austria an American party of twelve arrived to penetrate Austria. Our first knowledge of this group was when it arrived at Zone HQ. Had we been asked for our comments before this mission left Italy we could have saved them considerable effort which had been wasted through a misunderstanding of both the Austrian situation and of our relations with the Partisans.

During this period we received requests for intelligence from OSS, ISLD, and Force 399. All intelligence was provided through the official Partisan handout. Nothing could be accomplished by sending this simultaneously through three agencies.

It had been our policy to keep Lieutenant Bush and Sergeant Welles with the brigades as much as possible so that we could gain first hand knowledge of Partisan operations. After September this was no longer possible and these men became more or less superfluous.

I believe that all Allied affairs could have been handled more efficiently and effectively by a single combined mission of two officers, two radio operators, and one cipher clerk.

NARRATIVE ACCOUNT

The Mission was scheduled to drop in the vicinity of Slovene HQ on or about 15 April and then proceed overland across the German Frontier and the Sava river to Fourth Zone HQ in Stajersko, (Steyermark). We were delayed some ten days in clearing the permits already issued by Partisan General Headquarters through Slovene HQ. Weather then held us up for a few days and in late April we finally took off from Brindisi. On our arrival over the target area the pilot was unable to pick up the proper signals although approximately at the target point other fire signals, it is probable that we were over signals put out by the White Guard in hope of receiving stores or Allied personnel. In early May we made a second try but this time the target area was completely blanketed with clouds and we again returned to Italy. A third attempt was made on May 14, this time in a Halifax. We arrived over the target at 2300 hrs. This time the fire signal and the recognition signal were correct. Cargo containers and the fuselage loads were dropped first in four runs. On the next run Lieutenant Schraeder, a weather observer, and I dropped and on our last run Lieutenant Bush and Corporal Fisher dropped. Although we had asked to drop at eight hundred feet, we went out at nearly three thousand. It seemed to each of us as though we hung motionless in the air for several minutes before touching ground. The fires were the only things visible in an otherwise completely black night, and they appeared to be suspended in the blackness. On the ground we separately made our way towards the fires, not quite sure whether we would meet Partisans, White Guards, or Germans. At the fires I waited until all four "checked in". Then we went with a Partisan guide to a nearby village, where after being generously supplied with local wine, we spent the remainder of the night. The next day we made a ten hour march to Slovene Headquarters. Here we met Captain Goodwin, OSS, chief of the Anglo-American Mission and Lieutenant Vuchinic, OSS-SI representative. I had intended to go on immediately to Stajersko but a German offensive in the area made it temporarily impossible to get through.

On 27 May Lieutenant Bush, Corporal Fisher and myself started north, arriving at Seventh Corps headquarters the first night. Next day we continued during daylight to the village of Stiona, the last Partisan held territory south of the German frontier. Here we had a most excellent dinner in the village inn, the last for several weeks. At seven in the evening the patrol which was to escort us over the frontier and across the railroad and the Sava was assembled and given their instructions. The patrol consisted of nearly a hundred men well armed with German rifles and Bren light machine guns. At eight we moved off The first hour took us up a wooded canyon in the summer twilight. Then we began the climb to the ridge on which was the border.

The frontier consisted of a double barbed wire fence behind which were anti-personnel mine fields. The border and the ten mile strip between it and the Sava were guarded by roving patrols of White Guard and German troops. At ten thirty the column moved across a grass covered ridge and a passage cut in the fence at the frontier. The lights of Ljubljana ten miles to the west were clearly visible. We all felt a thrill at being on German soil, probably the first Americans to cross into Germany in uniform. From here on the travelling became more difficult. We crossed several steep and wooded ridges and on each one we had to scramble over loose rocks and roots and through muddy streams. It was now completely dark and we were unable to see the next man in the column. The only way to keep in the column was to listen for the steps of the man ahead and walk blindly in that direction, hoping not to fall into an unseen hole or slip off the path down the mountain side. Our contact across the river was at three thirty. At two thirty we reached the last ridge south of the river. As we dropped down into the canyon we could hear the trains climbing up the steep river canyon. As we were about to cross the tracks a train moved onto the line immediately before us. We lay in the long grass a hundred yards away and watched a heavy freight train, the engine fire flickering in the early morning fog.

As soon as the train had passed we crossed the tracks and the paralleling road and pushed through the thick undergrowth to the river's edge. Morning light was just breaking and the far side was dimly visible. The crossing was made in small flat-bottomed boats carrying three men in addition to the boatman. The current was extremely swift and I was quite sure we would capsize before reaching the other side. As daylight broke we moved up the side of the mountains north of the river and after a two hour march we reached an Odred headquarters. Exhausted, we slept until noon when we were awakened and told a German column was a half hour away and headed in our direction. After another two hour march we arrived at a mountain farm house which the Partisans said was safe. The next morning, however, a German patrol on the next hill opened up on our "safe" farm house with machine gun and mortar fire. The Partisans panicked and ran into the forest leaving behind our radio and batteries.

We spent the day in the forest and that evening we received a report that the Germans were concentrating in the valley below and might have the mountain where we were hiding surrounded by morning. We therefore moved back across the river to a farm house on the south mountain side. Here we waited three days and again crossed the river. We then found the road to the north blockaded and had to wait three more days before pushing on.

The trip from here to Zone Headquarters was made entirely by night and along mountain trails as the entire area was firmly held by the Germans. In addition to holding all the villages the Germans put out ambushes at the points where the Partisans normally crossed the roads and rivers. On several occasions our patrol located these ambushes before we moved into their range of fire and we either moved around them or when that was impossible waited until the Germans moved. At one point we crossed the Dravograd-Celje road two hundred yards from an ambush of a hundred men without having a shot fired at us.

On the fifteenth of June we arrived at Zone headquarters which was then in the forests on the top of the Pohorje. Life for the next few weeks was quite primitive and we were usually on the run. Much of the time there were heavy rains and we stayed soaked as there was no shelter of any sort.

On the 25th we received our first drop from five Dakotas. The next day sixteen hundred SS troops moved up the mountain toward the drop point and a battle developed a few hundred yards from it. We were unable to advise the base and that night we watched several planes circle overhead looking for the fires we dared not light.

In early July the Headquarters moved to the Kamniske Alpen area. Drops were most difficult to arrange during this period as radio communications were very irregular and as we could never be sure of a drop point being free of Germans until a few hours before the drop.

One day we radioed for a drop to us on top of one of the higher mountains in the area for the following night. The next afternoon a German column came up the mountain after us and by night we were almost completely surrounded and on the run. While we were moving a Halifax came over looking for us and flashing its signal light. We attempted to signal it to another drop point we thought to be free but our signals were misunderstood and the load was dropped. Fortunately the Partizans were able to collect most of the material.

In early August the Germans were thrown out of the Gorni Savinska Dolina by the Partizans and the Headquarters was able to come down from the mountains and live a fairly respectable life in the farmhouses in the valley. We now had more frequent air attacks and to prevent our location from being known we moved every four to five days. With the exception of one German offensive when we moved back to the mountains we were able to remain in the valley until our Mission was withdrawn.

In the middle of August Sergeant Welles joined our mission and a British ISLD mission and a Special Force One mission arrived.[173] In

September an A Force officer arrrived.

During August and September Lieutenant Bush and Sergeant Welles spent most of the time on operations with the brigades. In early October Lieutenant Bush left for Seventh Corps from where he flew to Italy to report on Mission activities. As it was then decided that our mission would be withdrawn and replaced by British personnel, he did not return to Fourth Zone as originally planned.

As the German withdrawal from the Balkans progressed in October and November we expected a strong German attempt to clean out the Partizan resistance behind their lines of communication in Austria. The offensive did not develop until we had begun the march to Slovene HQ after our relief had arrived. Had we delayed our departure two or three days it is doubtful whether we would have been able to get out for some time. As it was we took ten days to go some thirty miles from Zone HQ to the south side of the Sava. Both the main Celje-Ljubljana road and the river had been blockaded.

After several unsuccessful attempts to cross the river we finally made a crossing several miles east of the area normally used. The river was so high that the boat was carried down stream several hundred yards on each crossing and had to be carried upstream each trip to the original point. The crossing was completed at three in the morning and the column moved up the mountains on the south side. White Guard patrols were very active and we heard machine gune fire several times. Fortunately we did not run into any of them. In the late afternoon we reached the semi-liberated territory of Seventh Corps. Here we joined a battalion which was moving to Corps HQ that night. The area surrounding Trebnje had been occupied by a German column that afternoon and a fight was expected. However the Partizans apparently outsmarted the Germans by going directly through the town of Trebnje, the reported enemy stronghold, thus bypassing the blockades in the surrounding area. At three the following morning we arrived at Corps HQ after a non-stop march of thirty three hours.

After a day's rest we moved on toward Croatian HQ. Here we met Lieutenant Colonel McFarland, chief of the American Mission and it was decided that Corporal Fisher and myself would remain at Croatian HQ while Colonel McFarland went to Italy to report. Sergeant Welles proceeded on the Split and from there to Italy by sea.

APPENDIX C

Clowder Mission Records

November-December 1944, [PRO WO 204/1953]

1/2017
TOP SECRET
Copy No: 3

NOTE BY CLOWDER MISSION ON SPECIAL OPERATIONS IN AUSTRIA FOR THE SECOND HALF OF NOV. 1944

CURRENT SITUATION

1. The first heavy snows are falling in AUSTRIA. Apart from discouraging recruitment, the winter weather makes it impossible to fly to CENTRAL EUROPE on nine days out of ten. So until next March the chances of any Mission receiving more than one sortie a month are remote.

2. It follows that, even if we flush some organized resistance movement at, we cannot now undertake to arm or to supply it till next Spring. It is, therefore, clear that our hope of using a small para-military group of British Officers at TRIGGER, as an operational nucleus, round which to form Austrian 'resistance' independently of the Partisans, is now vain; further, whoever remains at TRIGGER is inevitably condemned to winter with the Partisans, and if they move southwards, he must go with them. The seasonal limitations apply even more strongly to the blind dropping of Anglo-Austrian operational groups in uniform, and this plan must also be abandoned.

3. The passes in the REUS sector are now completely snowbound and determined attempts to cross the CARNARIC Alps on skis have had to be

abandoned. The Mission is, therefore, making its way back to South Italy via JUGOSLAVIA.

CONCLUSIONS

4. The following conclusions emerge:
   a) No attempt can be made to form Austrian resistance groups until the end of March. Assuming that the war in GERMANY is then drawing to a close, it seems unlikely that there will be sufficient time left to arm or organize any sufficient numbers.
   b) While it should be possible to maintain a British Officer at TRIGGER so long as the Partisans remain there, no advantage would be served by reinforcing this. It may, however, be necessary to relieve the present officer who has been in occupied territory for over a year, and nearly eight months within the Reich frontiers.
   c) There is no object in dropping further uniformed para-military parties into AUSTRIA except for those which have 'safe addresses' to go to, or unless they maintain themselves without air support.

RECOMMENDATIONS

5. We make the following recommendations:
   (a) We should try and maintain a British officer at TRIGGER.
   (b) We should aim at establishing in AUSTRIA small clandestine groups with W/T communication who, although their role would necessarily be passive throughout the winter, would both form a framework for any subsequent action in the Spring and constitute a valuable source of intelligence.
   (c) We should hold an adequate number of personnel, both British and Austrian, until the snows melt at the End of March in order to carry out any role which may be given us in the closing stages in the war.
   (d) A.F.H.Q. should be invited to give a clear directive what these roles (see para. (c) above) are likely to be, and what action we may be required to take if a Rankin 'B' or 'C' condition develops.[174]

AIR COMMITMENT

6. If the policy outlined above be approved, we shall require four sorties for dropping personnel, and there will be a maintenance commitment of not more than five tons (nett) of stores per month for the next three months.

1/2097 TOP SECRET

Copy No: 3

NOTE BY H.Q. CLOWDER MISSION ON SPECIAL OPERATIONS IN AUSTRIA FOR THE FIRST HALF OF DECEMBER 1944

CURRENT SITUATION

1. Steadily deteriorating weather conditions in AUSTRIA, heavy snowfalls throughout the SAUALPEN area and increased enemy activity in the KARAWANKEN sector, consequent on the advance of the Red Army through HUNGARY, make it clear that the maintenance of a British officer at TRIGGER is a proposition even more hazardous than was foreseen. Cahusac's present situation is obscure. There has been no W/T communication with him since 3rd December and an unconfirmed report from Partisan 4-Zone H.Q. states that the local Partisan Commander at TRIGGER has been killed. Owing to consistently unfavourable weather conditions, it has been impossible to drop either stores or a relieving officer and W.T.O. to Cahusac.

2. Further east, the Partisans are moving 14th Division into the area south east of MARIBOR and concurrently sending two Battalions north to attack the important MARIBOR-GRAZ railway. The Partisans hope that these forces will eventually link up with a Russian advance from the south east. Our officer at 4th Zone is seeking permission to accompany the two northern Battalions, so that he may be in a position to enter AUSTRIA at the earliest opportunity.

3. Bad flying weather has equally prevented any direct drops of clandestine parties. (See para. 5(c) of our 1/2017).

CONCLUSIONS

4. No material improvement in weather conditions can reasonably be anticipated over the next two months. We should, therefore, not be justified in hoping for any considerable operational preogress before the end of March.

5. In consequence, CLOWDER's main immediate task becomes the adjustment of the training of personnel already held, to equip them for the roles which they may be called upon to perform in the Spring. In particular, as the arming of any Austrian resistance which may emerge after the snows melt is unlikely to be on a scale sufficient to produce an effective military contribution and may well be undesirable on policy

grounds, emphasis should fall on training for the tasks which may be called for under RANKIN conditions as laid down in "Instructions governing employment of Special Operations Personnel in Occupied Countries under conditions of enemy withdrawal or collapse".

RECOMMENDATIONS

6. We make the following recommendations:
    (a) We should continue, as far as weather conditions permit, the policy put forward in our 1/2017 and approved in G.3 (Special Ops.) letter (RIMH/gn) of 8th Dec.
    (b) Our officer at Partisan 4th Zone should be instructed to accompany the two Partisan Battalions (mentioned in para. 2 above) in all observer role.
    (c) We should modify the training of personnel being held for operations in the Spring to equip them for the tasks in "Instructions governing employment of Special Operations Personnel in Occupied Countries under conditions of enemy withdrawal or collapse".

TOP SECRET   Copy No: 3
                                             Ref: 10/3015
                                             Date: 23rd Dec. '44

PROGRESS REPORT: 26th Nov. – 23rd Dec. 44

CLOWDER MISSION

POLICY

1. The following policy has been approved by A.F.H.Q.:
    (a) We should try and maintain a British officer at TRIGGER.
    (b) We should aim at establishing in Austria small clandestine groups with W/T communication who, although their role would necessarily be passive throughout the winter would form both a framework for any subsequent action in the Spring and would constitute a valuable source of intelligence.
    (c) We should hold an adequate number of personnel, both British and Austrian, until the snows melt at the end of March, in order to carry out any role which may be given us in the closing stages in the war.

2. Owing to the extreme difficulty of the supply problem, the most which can be hoped for at TRIGGER is the maintenance of a British Officer with the Slovene Partisans throughout the winter. The formation and arming of independent Austrian resistance groups is out of the question until the snows melt and flying conditions improve at the end of March.
3. The CANARIC sector has been closed down until the Spring and all Missions withdrawn.[175]
4. At BUTT it is proposed that [censored] should move east with Partisan 4th Zone forces and aim at reaching the area North of MARIBOR, to be in a position to enter AUSTRIA as soon as possible.[176]

INDIVIDUAL MISSIONS

5. There has been no W/T communication with [Major Cahusac] since 3rd December. His last message stated that he was being being continuously harried by the enemy. An unconfirmed report from 4th Zone states that MIRKO, the leader of the Partisans at TRIGGER has been killed. Continual bad weather during the earlier part of the month prevented the dropping of stores to [Major Cahusac]. Arrangements were made for daylight stores dropping operations by Mustang aircraft, but before those could be completed W/T contact was lost. Owing to the improbability of recruiting independent Austrian resistance groups at TRIGGER during the Winter months, it was decided to abandon operation ELSMERE which consisted of 6 British officers and 2 N.C.O. WTOs. As a replacement, it was however decided to drop a British Officer and W.T.O. to TRIGGER to relieve [Major Cahusac]. This operation has not been despatched during the last moon owing to weather conditions. If W/T contact is re-established with [Major Cahusac] this operation will be laid on for the next moon period. [176]
6. O.S.S. report that the projected DRAVA crossing by the MODRAS Partisan Group to reinforce TRIGGER has now been abandoned.
7. [Censored] has moved eastwards with Partisan 14th Division. A signal received over I.S.L.D. link states that [censored] crystals and codes have been captured by the enemy.
It was originally intended to withdraw [censored] and his WTO (reference Monthly Report 10/1971 of 25th Nov:). In view of 4th Zone's projected attacks on railways in the PTUJ area and North of MARIBOR [censored] and his WTO will now be instructed to take part in those attacks in the role of an observer.
[8. and 9. were entirely excised by the censor.]

APPENDIX D

REPORT ON SLOVENIA

Peter N.M. Moore

[PRO FO 371/48811, R5717/6/92]
REPORT BY LT COL PNM MOORE, DSO, MC, RE
ON SLOVENIA
DATED 14 FEBRUARY 44

TOP SECRET
Ref Map 1/250,000 series – UDINE, TRIESTE AND LJUBLJANA sheets

PART I

1. INTRODUCTION

In the period under review [October 1944-February 1945] the JANL authorities took the most elaborate steps to ensure that no British personnel should have access to the ordinary peasant or soldier in the absence of a politically reliable Pzn observer. Information supplied by the staff about their own operations dispositions and intentions was the absolute minimum compatible with the very extensive support by air attack and supply dropping they were receiving.

Owing however to the extraordinary breaches of normal security rules and close cooperation with American missions and questioning of evaders and escapees passing through, a good deal of information was collected.

2. NARRATIVE

16 Oct. Landed Piccadilly Hope.
16 Oct – 13 Nov At HQ SLOVENIA, CRNOMELJ area.

13 Nov-16 Nov On move with HQ SLOVENIA during short enemy raid into CRNOMELJ area.
18 Nov-20 Nov Watched abortive attack on MOCEVJE.
21 Nov- 2 Feb At HQ SLOVENIA.
3 Feb- 8 Feb On march from HQ SLOVENIA-HQ CROATIA.
9 Feb-10 Feb Travelled by lorry from HQ CROATIA to ZARA.
11 Feb By air from ZARA-BARI.

3. TOPOPGRAPHY

See previous report dated Jul 44.

From 16 Oct-9 Jan the weather was exceptionally warm and wet.

On 5 Jan 45 exceptionally heavy falls of snow commenced with temperatures ranging down to $0°$ Fahrenheit at CRNOMELJ and 2 ft of snow lay in the lowest ground, at a height of 600 ft 'till 2 Feb 45.

All transport was then by sledge and few roads which had been cleared were only passable by jeeps with chains and a great deal of difficulty.

4. PARTISAN ORDER OF BATTLE

See Appx A [not included here].

5. PARTISAN FORMATION STRENGTHS AND FIGHTING ABILITIES

For 7 Comps only Bdes average between 300 and 800 strong 10th Bde seen at VIVODINA RK 0876 on 3 Feb 45 returning from KORDUN after carrying wounded was only 300 strong. Well clothed and well equipped but standard rank and file very low, majority being under 17 or over 35. Looked a very dispirited lot. Extraordinary difference in comparson same bde seen in June 44.

Only time troops seen in action was at KOCEVJE 18-20 Nov. Infantry fought with tenacity but little dash. Whole operation was abortive owing inability 7 Corps Adv HQ and 18 Div Staff to control a battle of such magnitude.

6. EQUIPMENT

Only units of 7 Corps were seen.

The very considerable quantities of clothing, small arms, and automatic weapons, delivered during the period have made an enormous difference.

Bdes are now 75% equipped with boots battle dress and great coats, and the proportion of automatic weapons particularly sten guns is extraordinarily high.

There is in addition an Artillery Bde comprising:
  One 100/17mm Italian Howitzer
  One 75/13 Mod MS Italian Howitzer
  One 75/27 Italian Mtn Field Gun
  One 50 mm P2 GR PAK 42

It is believed that three additional guns each of the first 3 types are hidden in woods owing to lack of transport.

Ammunition is practically exhausted and the guns in use are worn out.

7. PAST OPERATIONS

(a) 7 Corps

An attempt to capture RIBNICA on 4 Nov failed in spite of exceedingly accurate and destructive air attacks, particularly on RIBNICA. The bde containing KOCEVJE being surprised and dispersed at it's assembly area with the loss of it's Commander and the assault by two bdes on RIBNICA failing.

On 13 Nov a large force moved SOUTH from NOVO MESTO and while the Pzn main forces were engaged in heavy fighting a small force of some 300 men made a daring raid S from KOCEVJE and a party of 60 penetrated CERNO MELJ the administrative centre, securing a complete surprise, causing a considerable panic, and burning a building with considerable quantities of battle dress before withdrawing.

This force was however ambused on its return and suffered heavy casualties.

For 24 hrs the position was critical and the main enemy force from NOVO MESTO reached SEMIC but was finally driven back after 2 days fierce fighting.

The Pzns followed this up with an attack on KOCEVJE with effective air support from BAF – 18th and 20th Nov. This failed largely due to the inability of the Pzn HQ Command to control the battle. It did however temporarily regain the initiative and keep the Germans guessing.

This was the last serious Pzn attempt to take the offensive. A lull then followed while the enemy completed repairs to the Rly LJUBLJANA-KOCEVJE and his patrols became steadily bolder securing control of the area enclosed by KOCEVJE-GROSUPLJE- and ZUZEMBERK.

Early in December the enemy decided to reopen the road LJUBLJANA-NOVO MESTO. This he accomplished without difficulty establishing garrisons at OBCINA RD 7403 and near PONIKVE and, dominates the AJDOVEC area with fighting patrols.

On the promise of air support the Pzns decided to attempt to halt the process by recapturing OBCINA the attack begin planned for 1st January. Bad weather delayed the air attack until 4th when a destructive air attack killed or wounded some 40 of the garrison, but by this time surprise had been lost, the garrison reinforced and the Pzns after a half hearted attack on 1st, were forced to withdraw.

An inevitable sequel was the enemy capture of ZUZEMBERK during the second fortnight of January.

A White Guard fighting patrol penetrating towards LIPJE south of ZUZEMBERK was however threwn back with heavy casualties.

As a result of the massive attitude adopted by the Pzns the have now lost control of all the territory lying between the Rivers KRKA and SAVA and nearly all the territory NW of the rd KOCEVJE-STARI LOG-ZUZEMBERK.

(b) 9 Corps

For a short period during December the Pzns occupied
unopposed the garrisons of AIDUSSINA and VIPACCIO in the VIPAVA valley, due to a hitch in the enemy relief arrangements.

An enemy offensive however drove them out a fortnight later and and also drove off the high ground of the TARNOVO plateau their previous stronghold forcing the Pzns to retire to CERKNO. A counter offensive by the Pzns regained the TARNOVO plateau during January but they were again driven Northwards at the beginning of February. Th enemy now controls the road AIDUSSINA-ZOLLA-IDRIA, as well as the whole of the VIPAVA valley.

(c) 4 Zone

After the liberation of the upper SAVINJA valley in September, a passive attitude by the Pzns permitted the enemy to mount an offensive at his leisure which, starting in the first week of December, rapidly overran all the liberated territory and dispersed the brigades of 14 Div with heavy losses and cut all the overland communications between 7 Corps and 4 Zone. 6th and 11th Bdess of 7th Corps were sent to assist but failed to influence the situation. and were isolated after crossing the Sava.

(d) Attacks on Railways

After the magnificent efforts of the SLOVENE Pzns against the railways during the summer culminating in the destruction of the LITIJA bridge, there has been a great falling off in Pzn attacks against railways, and many lines now run uninterruptedly at night.

By allowing the enemy to economise in railway guards this has permitted the enemy to concentrate for offensive action against the Pzns and has proved as fatal for the Pzns as it is objectionable to us.

The strongest possible representations at HQ SLOVENIA have produced many promises but no improvement.

The increasing range, accuracy and striking power of our air forces have however produced successes against enemy road and rail transport by day far in excess of anything the Pzns have ever achieved. The Pzn failure to complete the task by permitting uninterrupted repairs and traffic by night is therefore all the more deplorable.

8. FUTURE OPERATIONS

HQ SLOVENIA have been particularly incommunicative about these but the following can be deduced from the present trend of Pzn and enemy operations, and from Pzn propaganda.

(a) The Slovene Pzns have lost interest in fighting the Germans as Germans as such and are conserving their forces for:

(1) The capture of Ljubljana and the liquidation of the White Guard after the defeat of Germany. Task 7 Corps.

(11) The occupation of TRIESTE and all NE Italy up to the TAGLIAMENTO to permit a "fait accompli at the peace conference. Task, 9 Corps.

(111) The occupation of KLAGENFURT and VILLACH. Task 4 Zone.

The irony of the situation is that had the SLOVENE Pzns continued their whole hearted co operation with the allies of last summer, they would have been far better placed to carry out their aims. Their military situation has now deteriorated to such an extent that only the occupation of TRIESTE seems possible without outside assistance.

The morale and backing of the White Guard although they are 100% collaborationist has paradoxically improved out of all knowledge in the past 6 months and it is now unlikely that after the withdrawal of the main German forces 7 Corps will be able to take LJUBLJANA and put down the White Guard without considerable assistance from CROAT JANL formations, whih would however be decisive.

The serious set back in 4 Zone has also made it unlikely that the Pzns can occupy by force KLAGENFURT and VILLACH without Russian assistance or persuading the German population of this area to accept their rule. A great increase in Pzn propaganda directed at Austrians and the formation of an Austrian battalion of the SLOVENE JANL has been noted.

9. PARTISAN TACTICS

No developments from previous reports. To prevent themselves from being surprised again as on the 14 Nov, a system of OPs on the high ground has been evolved.

10. PARTISAN INTELLIGENCE SERVICES

In addition to the normal intelligence duties at formation HQ there are a series of intelligence posts which collect information from agents who visit occupied territory.

Co operation by the Pzns has been very poor and in particular they will never indicate the source of their information.

A notable exception are railway traffic reports which are as a rule received without alteration in their original form, although frequently very late.

The Pzns still do not realize the importance of intelligence to the Allies as a whole in spite of repeated representation.

Although they are in correspondence with the Bishop of LJUBIJANA by underground channels at least 4 enemy divisions passed through SLOVENIA during the period under review without a single reliable identification being obtained.

The head of the Soviet Mission was during December equally disgusted with Pzn inability to produce intelligence network but hinted that the SLOVENES would not allow this.

In this connection an intelligence school in MOSCOW with instruction in SERBO CROAT was reported to have started it's first course for SLOVENES on 25th January.

11. ENEMY ORDER OF BATTLE

The only German troops in 7 Corps area up to the end of December were 3 Bns of 14 Police Regt. During January at least two Bns of 13 Police Regt were identified in the operations to clear the Rd LJUBLJANA – NOVO MESTO.

The White Guard have formed 4 "POKRETNE" or Mobile Battalions whose speciality is fighting patrols in the woods.

12. ENEMY MORALE AND DESERTIONS

(a) German

Amongst the German units there has been no evidence of failing morale.

A small number of Austrians have deserted and about 40 Alsatians deserted to the Pzns from the 10th Police Regt at POSTUMIA, on 2nd December.

(b) White Guard

The morale of the White Guard has risen remarkably in spite of their apparently hopeless position as 100% collaborationist.

The personnel of at any rate the POKRETNE [mobile] Battalions who are all volunteers are man for man of higher morale than the Pzns. Reasons are, bad Pzn food, Pzns resigning the initiative, and the high standard of training in Pzn warfare which the Germans have taught them, including the use of strong ski patrols.

The POKRETNE Battalions have definitely established an ascendancy over the Pzns in large areas of wooded country previously considered Pzn preserves.

The amnesty of 15 Jan did not secure a single desertion and the SLOVENE Pzns admit that the White Guard are as tough a proposition or even tougher than the Ustashi. White Guard troops fought stubbornly in defence of RIBNICA and KOCEVJE and are capable of bold offensive action as shown by this raid on CRNOMELJ in November.

13. DROPPING ZONES AND LGs

(a) DZs

VOJNA outside CRNOMELJ good for stores but unsafe for bodies owing to a railway embankment and many smashed railway wagons. Good approaches. Subject to ground mist at night and in the early morning.

PAKA RJ 8358. Good for stores and bodies much less subject to mist but practically inacessible during January owing to snow.

(b) LGs

NADLESK- Piccadillly "Club". Frequently visited by White Guard patrols.

OTOK – Piccadilly "Hope". Good LG but undrained and unserviceable for weeks on end after rain.

GRIBLJE – Piccadilly "Hope A". Separate landing and take off strips. Extensive drainage scheme carrked out by Pzns at instigation of and under supervision of F/Lt WYLIE has been a great success and LG dries off within 2 days after all but the heaviest rain.

An exceptionally heavy fall of snow 2 ft closed GRIBLJE for 5 weeks after the 5th January.

14. SUPPLY SITUATION.

(a) 7 Corps

Well supplied with weapons and and clothing is nearly 75% complete. Food situation is however becoming increasingly difficult.

(b) 9 Corps

A very large tonnage in January has considerably eased the situation.

(c) 4 Zone

Although 71 a/c were received in November, these were largely arms ammunition and explosives. A start could not be made in clothing requirements before the enemy offensive suspended all air supply. The troops suffered considerably in consequence, there were many desertions and some at least appear to have thrown away their arms. The ammunition situation is now becoming difficult.

(d) Air Supply

No report on supplies is complete without a tribute to the pilots and aircrews engaged in dropping operations over SLOVENIA.

On 2nd December 11 Liberators came down through 10/10 cloud which was below the tops of the surrounding mountains to drop their loads at VOJNA in a visibility of less than 4 miles. This was most favourably commented on by the head of the Russian Mission. On one day early in January two HALIFAXES came down through 10/10 loud and dropped their loads at VOJNA in a light snow storm with visibility about one mile. The Pzns appear to take this sort of flying for granted. It is suggested that some high Pzn officer be invited to try a journey as passenger in Supply Dropping a/c under doubtful weather conditions, to see what it is really like.

(e) Overland Supply

The SLOVENE Pzns are now getting supplies from the coast. Route is:
By MT Convoy from ZARA or SPLIT to the TOPUSK area.
By cart from PLSAROVINA across Rd ZAGREB KARLOVAC.
By night along the Southern edge of the ZUMBERAK hills and thence to METLIKA.

A column of 60 sledges with a bde as escort was seen at KRASIC on 6 Feb. About 200 wounded have already been evacuated by this route.

Appendix D

PART II

1. ECONOMIC SITUATION

These notes refer only to 7 Corps area where first hand information could be obtained.

(a) Food

A serious food shortage in liberated territory will arise in March. This territory at present has to feed 10,000 army at a maximum, and 60,000 civil population at a minimum. Reasons are:

(1) Area previously controlled by both sides which the partisans used used to draw on heavily for food supplies are now completely controlled by the enemy.

(11) The peasants are holding out on the Partisans over food supplies. A natural reaction after four years of war.

(b) Clothing

This is very seriously felt already. While the Army is well clothed in battledress, the peasants are very badly off. This is illustrated by the universal use of linen parachute cloth as currency. The peasants having little confidence in either Partizan requisition slips or the Partisan currency.

(c) Transport

Owing to the killing of draught animals for food, plundering by the enemy, and overworking the remainder, General KVEDER has estimated that 7 Corps liberated territory has only 20% of its previous stock of draught animals.

2. POLITICAL SITUATION

With the fall of BELGRADE a very marked change came over the Movement in SLOVENIA. The Communist Party whose influence had always been predominant in the Freedom Front now assumed complete control. Many changes in the staff were made which could not be explained on the grounds of military necessity. The OZNA or Security Police, a direct descendant of the previously unpopular "VOD" became extremely active. Most significant, KIDRIC the Secretary of the KPS (Slovene Communist Party) who was also Secretary of SNOS (Freedom Front Committee) left the committee and came down to take up the duties of Political Commissar HQ SLOVENIA some 4 hours ride from the committee. It was given out that he was going to do both jobs, an obvious impossibility, but reference to SNOs over matters of principle affecting Anglo-Partisan relations was discontinued.

While the change-over was carried out without difficulty, it was undoubtedly unpopular, and it is significant that I did not hear a single expression of pride or affection by a private individual for the National Liberation Movement during my whole stay. This was all the more extraordinary in that such expressions had been a feature of my previous stays in SLOVENIA.

While this change is entirely an affair for the Slovenes themselves, it has had a most unfortunate military effect.

Morale of the rank and file is considerably lower than in the Summer. The peasants outside liberated areas who hate and fear any form of practical communism have been an easy prey to German and White Guard propaganda. Support for the White Guard and the morale of the White Guard themselves have been greatly increased. A party member from LJUBLJANA was reported to have publicly admitted that the City which had previously been claimed as 75% for the Partisans was now only 25% pro-Partisan, 20% for the White Guard and 55% apathetic.

While there is no reason whatever to doubt the ability of the Partisans ultimately to establish themselves and rule SLOVENIA when the Germans go, the White Guard will almost certainly fight on with clandestine German support, and their ability to beat the Partisans at their own game is likely to leave SLOVENIA disturbed for some time after liberation, unless a more conciliatory policy is adopted by the Partisans in their hour of victory than their present temper indicates. An indication of their temper is that the Slovene Crimes Commission is reported to have been closed down, which seems extraordinary at this stage of the war.

3. PERSONALITIES

President VIDMAR

Titular head of the New SLOVENIA. Not a political figure before the war. An honest and sincere man. Looks ill and gives the impression of being a mere cipher. Very definitely Anglophile.

B KIDRIC

Political Commissar HQ SLOVENIA and Secretary KPS. Is quite clearly the supreme authority in SLOVENIA. Extremely able, a skilled negotiator and a forceful speaker. Very correct and friendly in his official relations with us but is definitely not to be trusted. Will say one thing and do another. On 5 Jan denied the existance of any organization such as OZNA and claimed that all unfavourable reactions to events in GREECE was spontaneous, both of which were manifestly untrue.

Major-General KVEDER

GOC SLOVENIA. A disciplinarian and a good organiser. A lawyer before the war. Age about 28. Made many speeches and wrote several sensible articles, including one attacking red tape in the staff. Completely subserviant to political requirements of Commissar which must at times have run counter to his military judgement, which is sound. Conceited at first, but this has worn off. A competent but uninspiring leader who does not visit his troops often enough.

4. PARTISAN PRESS ACTIVITIES

The entire Partisan press has been hostile by implications to BRITAIN and the US. Rigid adherance to Party line, even by SLOVENSKA PORCEVALEC, the official OF newspaper, was most noticeable.

Much unfavourable comment and misrepresentation of facts over GREECE.

War effort of USA and BRITAIN is either ignored or given negligible space. No single mention has ever been made of the extensive Allied help to Slovene Partisans.

5. PARTISAN REACTION TO ALLIES

The Red Army, by its successes in the field, has the unbounded and well deserved admiration of all Slovenes. The fullest possible use of this is made to convince the people that the SOVIET UNION is a heaven on earth and can do no wrong, and the MOSCOW line is faithfully followed in every matter under discussion however little it may concern SLOVENIA.

The Slovene Partisan authorities cannot dispense with British and American help, but are most uncomfortable at being under an obligation to us. The very real gratitude felt by the villager and the rank and file towards AMERICA and BRITAIN is also a source of great embarrassment to them, and every petty humiliation to British and American personnel, and discreditable story is employed to combat this, so far unsuccessfully. This gratitude is however entirely confined to the humbler members of the

community who know on which side their bread is buttered and their feelings are only expressed in private for fear of denunciation by OZNA. E.g. If British or American personnel in SLOVENIA while travelling want a good meal and a comfortable bed, it is necessary first to give one's courier the slip.
This does NOT however apply to CROATIA, where the interpretation of the Party line is clearly far more friendly.

6. RELATIONS WITH SOVIET MISSION

In pleasing contrast to the Partisans these have been most frank and cordial. Every effort was made however by the Partisans to listen in on all discussions I had with the Chief of the Russian Mission. While naturally politics was never discussed by me with them, Col PADRANALCEV volunteered a very realistic view f the Partisan military capabilities and limitations. In particular he was far from satisfied with Partisan activity against the railways and with their intelligence services. He also expressed his appreciation of the aid the Western Allies were given to the Partisans.

Lt Col BOGOMOLOV who was withdrawn from 4 Zone to take over the Soviet Mission at HQ SLOVENIA was less forthcoming, although obviously disatisfied with intelligence and under no illusions. There is now no Soviet Mission at HQ 4 Zone.

Other members of the Soviet Mission at HQ SLOVENIA were:
  Lt Col NAUMOV: Medical
  Major SARAKOUMOV: Infantry
  Major ZAVORONKOV: Infantry
  Capt BORIS: Infantry. Signal Officer.

Relations with these were purely social except Capt BORIS who expressed his disapproval to me of the Partisan handling of the KOCEVJE battle while we were watching it together.

The Russians have sent no supplies since early December, possibly on account of the weather.

PART III
CONCLUSION AND RECOMMENDATIONS

1. CONCLUSION – POLITICAL

75% of the population in liberated territory and the Army in SLOVENIA are war weary. The remaining 25% can think cf little but the jobs they are going to get after the war.

The KPS after 20 years of persecution are preparing to enjoy the sweets of office permanently, as is only natural. Soviet influence is and will remain predominant. Territorial claims will be secured by presenting a fait accompli to the peace conference.

Britain is regarded with intense dislike and suspicion by the Partisan authorities, who fear we may oppose their territorial claims or try and force them to moderate their internal policy. This is however likely to pass with time.

The present attitude of the Partisans should not however blind us to the fact that their regime is the only possible solution for SLOVENIA. However, a civil war of short duration and some discreditable excesses by the Partisans, are unfortunately only too likely after the departure of the Germans.

2. CONCLUSION – MILITARY

The JANL SLOVENIA has paid a magnificent dividend, but has now ceased to be an asset to the war effort and has become a liability.

In the event of our forces requiring the free use of the port of TRIESTE thay may well become a serious embarrassment, unless a clear understanding is reached with TITO and more important, underwritten by the Slovene Partisan authorities.

3. RECOMMENDATIONS

(a) Allied supplies to SLOVENIA should be in future confined to food, clothing, maintenance requirements of ammunition, and relief supplies.

(b) If it is decided to continue sending arms, they should all be British or American to give us some control over ammunition supply.

(c) Missions from all organisations in SLOVENIA should be reduced to an absolute minimum, and in particular the number of senior officers should be reduced. Otherwise the goodwill we have earned with the civil population will be lost, by our being identified with possible excesses by the Partisans over whom we have no control whatever.

(d) The Partisans should be encouraged to develop overland supplies to enable us to further reduce our personnel and to use bomber aircraft for bombing.

[signed]
P.N.M. Moore

APPENDIX E

SUB-SOURCE'S IMPRESSION OF PARTISAN ACTIVITIES IN SLOVENIA

[PRO WO 202/309]

SOURCE SHEET

No. 1 I(U) SECTION. C.M.F.

SECRET

Date: 28 Mar 45

YUGOSLAVIA – POLITICAL

Rept. No: YO 884

Subject: Subsource's impression of Partisan activities in SLOVENIA
Source: LUTE from Czech surgeon with Yugoslav Army
Remarks: rel believed good

LONDON
A.F.H.Q.
Rr. H.Q. 37 Military Mission
B.A.F. (INT.)
Coy. B. 2677 Regt.
A.2, 15 A.A.F.
FILE
HQ 2677 Regt
Main HQ 37 M.M.
PWE
SILO
Military HQ (Balkans)

NOTE: Subsource is Left Wing and naturally has a bias towards the Partisans. His observations are nevertheless considered of value in view of his excellent opportunities for obtaining first-hand information. His remarks on the atrocities committed by the "Whites" are borne out by another subsource who joined the Partisans, fought in their ranks and is now wounded.

Appendix E

Major D. Walker)
Mr Stevenson   )
[Document is stamped "Ref G(I), 30 MAR 1945 37 MILITARY MISSION"]

COMMENT SHEET

SECRET
Please detach and return completed to No. 1 I (U) Section, C.M.F.

FROM:_____

Date:
Rept. No.: YO 884

Please note below whether the information contained in this report is:
    (a) of considerable value
    (b) of value.
    (c) no value.
                                           soon
    (d) further information (please specify) required
                                           later
(e) Remarks:

SECRET

Y.O.884
29.3.45

YUGOSLAVIA – POLITICAL

Sub-Source's impressions of Partisan activities in Slovenia

Meine Erfahrungen beziehen sich auf die Zeit vom Mai 1944 bis März 1945.

Politische Linie

Die Führung der ganzen Freitheitsbewegung hat die K.P.S, welche vereinigt die Demokratischen Komponenten der Nation im Kampfe gegen den Okkupator und seine Helfershelfer. In Slovenien gibt es in der NOV keine andere politische Partei, die irgend eine Rolle spielt, obzwar behauptet wird, daß in der NOV auch andere Parteien vertreten sind. Die K.P.S. stellt heute den unerbittlichen Kampf gegen die Deutsche, Italiener und Landesverräterische Reaktion bis zur Verteibung des Okkupators und Vernichtung der Landesverräter, und damit bis zur Erringung der Freiheit. Dem ganzen Kampf wird betont und bewußt die Preägung [sic] eines Freiheitskampfes gegeben. Erst auf der zweiten Stelle steht die Lösung der Sozialen Fragen im Sinne der kommunistischen Doktrine. Die Führung der KPS ist sicher allerdings vollkommen dessen bewußt, daß Slovenien nur wenig Industrie hat, also das Industrie-Proletariat, das eine größere Rolle in der Sozialisierung spielen würde, ist hier nicht vorhanden. Großgüter sind auch nicht vorhanden. In der Industrie wird es also nichts geben, was mann verstatlichen könnte. Kolchosen-Sovchosen nach dem SSSR Mußter kommen also keinesfalls in Frage. Es wird behauptet, daß das Privateigentum unangetastet bleiben wird; nur größere Unternehmungen, es heißt Industrie und Landgüter von größeren Dimensionen, sollen zweckmäßig verstatlicht werden. Die Distribution der Güter und Nähmittel [sic] soll durch sogenannte Zadruge erfolgen. Es sind Genoßenschaften, die es ermöglichen, damit der Weg vom Produzenten zum Konsumenten verkürtzt wäre, und durch Ausschalten der Spekulation und Kettenhandels soll einerseits dem Bauer, anderseits dem Verbraucher Nutzen gebracht werden. Eine Frage No. 1 der Normalen Distribution der Güter und Nähmittel ist die schnellste Instandsetzung der Verkehrsverbindungen, die größtenteils zerstört sind.

Das Eigentum aller Kriegsverbrecher wird vom State beschlagnahmt. Also das Eigentum aller Reichsangehöriger, mit Ausnahme von denjenigen, die in den Reihen der NOV kämpfen, das Eigentum aller Angehöriger der Slovenischen Landwehr (Domobranci), die sich bis den 15 Januar nicht ergeben haben. Man glaubt, daß es sich um große Werte handelt.

Die K.P.S. ist in der NOV (heute Jugoslawische Armee) sonst im Hinterlande gut organisiert. Sie betont, daß ihre erste Aufgabe sei die Befreiung des Vaterlandes, aber auch noch im Verlaufe des Kampfes eine Lösung der Sozialen Fragen. Ich schätze die Zahl der organisierten Mitglieder der K.P.S. in der Armee auf dem Territorium Sloveniens auf Zirka. 15%.

VERHÄLTNIS ZU DEN ALLIIERTEN

Zu den Russen ist das Verhältnis herzlich. Es wird nicht nur die politische und wirtschaftliche, aber vor allen politische Hilfe erwartet. Als das größte Nachkriegsprogram wird das Wirtschaftliche betrachtet, und man sagt, daß nach dem militärischen und politischen Sieg noch die wirtschaftliche Schlacht errungen werden muß. Ohne Hilfe von Aussen sei es unmöglich, weil das Land größtenteils vernichtet und erschöpft ist. Die Beziehung zu England und U.S.A. ist zurückhaltender, besonders nach der Ereignissen in Griechenland. Es herrscht aber eine allgemeine Überzeugung, daß eine Analogie der Ereigniße in Jugoslavien, also in Raum von TRIESTE, ISTRIA unmöglich sei, sollte es zur eine [sic] Landung der Alliierten in diesen Raume kommen.

DIE GRENZZIEHUNG

Die Slovenien glauben und hoffen, daß Trieste, Istria, Gorizia, Fiume und Klagenfurt zu Slovenien angeschlossen werden. Sie sind der Meinung, daß England bereit sei, die Frage Trieste für Slowenien positiv zu lösen, dagegen USA seien nicht dazu geneigt. Man sagt, es wäre allerdings ein "D'Annunzio Streich" am besten, und sich der Hafen Trieste mit der Waffe in der Hand zu holen. Dies ist nach Konzentration der Cetniki-ROF (Gen. VLASOV) und anderen Bänden in diesem raume sehr schwierig und in gegenener Lage militärisch schwierige Aufgabe.

Slov. Heimatwehr (Domobranci-die Weissen)

Ich schätze die Stärke der Truppe auf zirka 25 bis 30,000 Man unter den Waffen auf dem Territorium Sloveniens. Nach den Information von Deserteren sei die Truppe stark demoralisiert, schlecht genähert und bekleidet, im Kampf im betrunkenen Zustand geschickt, fast immer von den Deutschen von hinten bewacht und ohne Rücksicht in Kampf getrieben. Es gibt unter Ihnen noch Fanatiker genug und alter mit Blut besudelten Verbrecher, die sich dessen bewußt sind, daß für sie keine Rettung geben wird. Diese Behaupten, daß sie bis zum Lezten kämpfen werden, bzw. glauben, daß im Falle einer Landung, sich den englischen Truppen übergeben würden, um ihr Leben auf diese Weise zu retten. Die Gefangenen und verwundeten Partisanen werden von den Weissen rücksichtslos massakriert und Bestialisch gemartet, sie erschlagen auch die Alliierten Flieger, die Ihnen in die Hände fallen. Die NOV, sowie ich mich selbst überzeugen konnte, erschießt weder die Gefangenen Domobranci, noch die Verwundeten. Es wird auch kein Gebrauch von dum-dum und explosiv Munition gemacht. Auf der seite der Deutschen und Weissen habe ich fast bei jedem Zusammenstoß den Gebrauch von d.d. und explosiv Infanteriemunition feststellen können. Ein großer Teil der Weissen ist gewaltsam mobilisiert worden. Aus diesem Grunde sollen nach dem Kriege nur nachgewiesene Kriegsverbrecher mit dem Tode bestraft werden. Der verführten Masse soll es nach angemessener Strafe die Möglichkeit der Wiedergutmachung durch Arbeit gegeben werden. [177]

KPS = Kommunistische Partei Slovenien
NOV = Partisan Bewegung [*Narodna Osvobodilna Vojska*]
ROF = Russische (Weiss) Freiheits Front.

APPENDIX F

MEMORANDUM: SLOVENE CLAIMS TO CARINTHIA 1919–1945

William Deakin

[PRO FO 371/48826, R8182/24/92]
28 April 1945

The purpose of this paper is to compare the background and history of Slovene claims to Carinthia in 1919-1920 with the development of a similar situation in the same area during the present war.

(A) Slovene Activities in Carinthia (to May 1929)

With the collapse of the Austro-Hungarian administration in the winter of 1918, a Slovene government was set up in Ljubljana (October 19-31) on instructions from the Yugoslav National Council in Zagreb. The immediate problem of law and order in an area of main communications with the battle fronts was serious.

National Guards were organised, and Serb prisoners of war, released from prison camps in Austria, were hastily formed into units to protect munition dumps, store depots, and the railways.

The boundaries of the new independent unit of Slovenia were unchartered. Troops of the new administration occupied at an early stage Maribor and the Drava valley, including the Slovene hills as far as Ljutomer. On November 5th, 1918 a Slovene delegation from Carinthia arrived in Ljubljana asking for military support to secure the union of that province with the new Slovenia. The Slovene military command possessed the most inadequate resources for such an enterprise, and could only send a certain Captain Lavric on a recruiting mission in the province. This mission failed to gather support and Lavric returned to Upper Carniola with 7 officers and 58 men. On November 30th the Austrian Government, however, approached the Ljubljana administration with a view to settling the disputed frontier by direct negotiation: these talks led nowhere, and according to the Slovenes, [were] only instituted to give the Austrians time to organise Home Defence units in Carinthia. In the following days small Slovene forces, including those of Lavric, now appointed "Commander for Carinthia", occupied most of the province. By February, however, Austrian troops had cleared the whole area with the exception of Völkermarkt, Unterdrauburg, and Miesstal.

It was clear that Allied intervention would sooner or later be necessary to settle this frontier conflict. Negotiations between the Austrians and Slovenes were opened at Graz, and the local Allied mission played a mediatory role in drawing a temporary line of demarcation until the whole question could be settled in Paris.

In January, an American commission headed by Professor Coolidge and a Lieut. Colonel Miles was sent from Paris to survey the position.

Lieut. Colonel Miles was largely instrumental in the drawing of the line which ran roughly along the Karawanken range to Freibach and then to the north and west of Völkermarkt.

The Slovenes remained highly dissatisfied with this arrangement and at the end of April, 1919 attempted to launch a military offensive in Carinthia. They appealed to Belgrade for help, and Serb troops were dispatched to Slovenia to take part.

Such was the general situation in the area when in May 1919 the question of Carinthia came up before the Allies in Paris.

(B) The Carinthian dispute before the Peace Conference

The first reaction of the Allied Powers to events in Carinthia was that of disapproval at the Yugoslav attempt to settle the affair on their own by force of arms. This attitude on the part of the Allied statesmen certainly prejudiced the case of the Slovene delegation which reached Paris on May 27th, 1919.

Furthermore, the Austrian Chancellor Dr. Renner, had arrived earlier in the month to save what territory still remained to his country. Southern Tyrol had already been lost to Italy. The Great Powers vetoed any union between Austria and Germany. Dr. Renner pointed out that both in Munich and Budapest "Red" governments had appeared in the chaos of post-war conditions. Any further territorial weakening of Austria might well lead to the emergence of a "Red" Vienna. Such a situation could surely not be in the interests of the Allies!

Appendix F

President Wilson consulted his experts, who recommended that:
  (a) Carinthia north of the Karawanken should generally be left to Austria.
  (b) An internationally controlled plesbiscite should be held in certain disputed areas. (A mission under Mr. Coolidge had already been sent to Austria in January 1919 to go into this matter.)

With these points in mind, Wilson received the Slovene delegation on June 5th. They warned him that unless Slovene claims were considered there would be disturbances in the country: they emphasised the injustice of handing Venezia Giulia to Italy (a decision for which Wilson was in great part responsible), and they spoke bitterly against the project of a plebiscite. Wilson's reactions to this meeting were not favourable.

The following day the news reached Paris that Serb troops had occupied Klagenfurt. Rail communications between Italy and Vienna were threatened. The Italians took prompt action. The whole of the 22nd Army Corps (six regiments with artillery) under General De Bono immediately occupied the line Villach-Feldkirchen-St. Veit.

The Italian attitude to the whole future of the Yugoslav state was clear from the beginning. The Italian Government was consistently in favour of weakening as far as possible the position of such a state. Italy therefore was the most determined supporter among the Big Powers of the Austrian position in Carinthia.

The military occupation by Serb troops of Klagenfurt also alienated both the British and American delegations in Paris. The Slovenes themselves showed their lack of experience in the way in which they handled the situation. Their delegation apparently advised Ljubljana that the Allies would accept a fait accompli in Carinthia. In fact, Clemenceau did support their claims, and they may have been misled by the high reputation among the Allied leaders of the Serb Minister in Paris, Monsieur Vesnic. But the Serbs were regarded by these leaders in a somewhat different light to the Slovenes and Croats, until so recently enemy subjects.

The united decision, therefore, taken at Paris was that a plebiscite should be held, and that Yugoslav troops should immediately withdrew from Klagenfurt and into certain defined areas only of the region in dispute.

Owing to the intervention of Monsieur Vesnic, a general plebiscite in Carinthia was not held, but the disputed area was divided into two zones. Zone "A" comprised 1,705 square kilometres and contained 22,800 Germans and 49,000 Slovenes. Zone "B" comprised 365 square kilometres and contained 49,000 Germans and 4,500 Slovenes. The former zone was to be temporarily garrisoned by Yugoslav and the latter by Austrian troops. The demarcation line between the two zones was to be regulated by Allied negotiation in Klagenfurt. Only if the plebiscite went in favour of Yugoslavia in Zone "A" would a further plebiscite be held in Zone "B". On June 12th the Yugoslavs were ordered to evacuate Klagenfurt. This was not carried out until July 31st.

The Italians in the meantime occupied the heights of Petelinegg, whence their artillery dominated the larger part of Zone "A".

(C) The organisation of the Carinthian Plebiscite

A year passed before the Inter-Allied Commission, deputed to organise the plebiscite, started work. This body held its first sitting in Klagenfurt on July 16th, 1920. The British representatives were Colonel Peck (Chairman) and Roland Brice. France was represented by the Comte de Chambrun, Italy by Prince Livio Borghese, Austria by Captain Peter-Pirkheim, and Yugoslavia by Professor Jovan Cvijic.

The first serious action of the Commission was to abolish the temporary demarcation line drawn up the previous year and to demand the withdrawal of Yugoslav troops from Zone "A" prior to the plebiscite. The Yugoslav delegate on the Commission, Professor Cvijic, resigned immediately, and was replaced by Jovan Jovanovic.

On September 13th, Yugoslav troops were withdrawn from Zone "A" and the Slovene administration in Ljubljana resigned.

Preparations for the holding of the plebiscite meanwhile proceeded on the general lines laid down in Paris.

On October 10th the plebiscite was held in Zone "A" with the following results: Out of 37,304 valid votes (94-94% of those entitled to vote), 22,025 voted for Austria and 15,279 for Yugoslavia. The area had been divided into 51 districts, in 33 of which there was a majority vote for Austria.

Roughly 10,000 of the votes for Austria were cast by people of Slovene speech.

These results were announced on October 14th. On the following day Jovan Jovanovic resigned from the Commission. Simultaneously with the announcement of the results. Yugoslav troops re-entered Zone "A".

The Allies reacted swiftly to this defiance of their decision, and the Allied ministers in Belgrade on October 18th made a joint demarche to the Yugoslav Government demanding an immediate withdrawal of their troops from the area. The following day these forces were recalled.

On November 18th, 1920 Zones "A" and "B" were handed over by the Plebiscite Commission to the Austrian authorities.

(D) Consideration of the 1920 Plebiscite, and of the Slovene case against the affair

The work of the Plebiscite Commission has been obscured in succeeding years by polemics from both the Austrian and Slovene side – particularly the latter. It is with the charges made by the Slovenes that this paper is concerned. They may be listed as follows:

- (a) The Yugoslav delegate on the Commission was not allowed to vote.
- (b) The British and Italian delegates connived at the entry of names into the Klagenfurt voting registered given to them by the Austrian *Heimatdienst*. It is claimed that between October 7th and 9th, 4,000 such entries were made of people who were not domiciled in the Zone.
- (c) The ballot urns were left unsupervised under the guard of Italian soldiers from October 10th to 13th. Austrians could obtain voting slips illegally from these soldiers.
- (d) Incorrect conduct of Italians, who held numerous conversations with the *Heimatdienst*. An Italian officer was sent from Vienna to Kranj during the talks between the Slovenes and Austrians in June 1919 to warn the latter against signing an armistice as the Peace Delegation in Paris had already given orders for the Yugoslav troops to fall back to the Karawanken.
- (e) The Italian delegate, Prince Borghese, later received a villa on the Wörthersee from a grateful Austrian government.
- (f) The reports of American officers on the Coolidge Commission in Vienna formed the basis for the unfavourable attitude of President Wilson towards Slovene claims. These reports were biased and inaccurate.

These accusations are listed only to show the feeling of the Slovenes on these events. Their bitterness at their failure to gain this territory was further accentuated by the following facts:

- (a) For nearly two years the disputed area had been occupied by Slovene or Serb troops, given ample time for propaganda in favour of annexation to Slovenia.
- (b) The demarcation line was constantly patrolled by Yugoslav troops, thus preventing a mass movement of pro-Austrian voters into Zone "A".

(c) 10,000 Slovene-speaking voters had decided in favour of Austria. Against this background, it is profitable to consider the representation of the Slovene case for Carinthia as expounded since 1941.[178]

PART II
SLOVENE CLAIMS FOR CARINTHIA 1941 - 1945

(A) The building up of the case 1920 - 1940

Slovene propagana during these years concentrated tirelessly on certain points:

(a) Census returns

The Austrian census of 1880 showed 100,000 Slovenes and 240,000 Germans in Carinthia, i.e. a 38% Slovene population. By 1910 the population was 18%. After the plebiscite of 1920 a census was taken in 1923 and in 1934. These returns showed a Slovene population of some 37,000 or 10% of the total.

These figures are hotly contested by the Slovenes. They attribute the decline of the Slovene population to:

(1) the method of taking the census on the basis of *sprachliche Zugehörigkeit*. The 1934 census was, according to Slovene pamphlets, conducted in the districts by renegade Germanized Slovene schoolmasters appointed by the Austrian Government as census commissioners, and largely executed on the basis of pro-Yugoslav as opposed to pro-Austrian sentiments of the population;

(ii) the intensive Germanization policy of the Austrian Government since the 1880's.

The Slovenes claim that between 70-80,000 of the Carinthian population are still properly of their race.

(b) Violation of Slovene minority rights

According to Slovene propagandists, the minority rights granted under the Treay of St. Germain (Article 69) have been systematically violated by the Austrian Government.

Slovenes have been removed from all public offices, Slovene schools have been closed, and Slovenie cultural activities barred.

Attention was in particular drawn to these charges in a speech in the Belgrade Senate by Dr. Valentin Rozic on March 26th, 1933.

There is no doubt that every effort was made during these years by the Austrian administration to assimilate this "troublesome" element in their midst and to emphasise the Teutonic character of the Carinthian March. The German minority in Slovenia could similarly appreciate such tactics.

There is no doubt that the failure of 1919-1920 has been carefully studied, both in regard to military action and propaganda, and in relations with outside Powers.

During the early months of the Partisan resistance in Slovenia, little opportunity arose to bring forward post-war claims.

(B) Partisan military activity along the Carinthian frontier (1942-1944)

In 1942 the first Slovene Partisans entered Carinthia from the direction of Venezia Giulia (Primorsko). At the beginning of 1943 the first Partisan detachment was formed upon the northern slopes of the Karawanken mountains. At the end of the year a British officer visited this detachment, which appeared to number about 120 men, and known as the West Carinthian detachment.

At the beginning of 1944 the Germans reduced the activity of this group to the small area between Jesenice and the Loibl pass.

In April, however, about 150 men crossed the Austrian frontier and established themselves in the neighbourhood of Eisenkappel. This became the East Carinthian detachment.

The following month an independent Carinthian command was set up directly responsible to Partisan Headquarters Slovenia, with the principal role of crossing the Drava river in force. By October about 1,000 men had been recruited in South East Carinthia.

The senior leaders of Slovene resistance in Venezia Giulia, Franc Leskovsek and Alex Bebler, were sent to organise both the crossing of the Drava and the recruitment of Carinthian Slovenes.

In all, four small parties had crossed by September when the Carinthian command was abolished. A Carinthian odred (detachment) was then formed of about 400 men operating in the area Solcava-Eisenkappel-Dravograd (the south side of the frontier). The railway unit operating in Austrian territory at this date was a small group of 100 men in the Saualpen.

This restriction of military activity was probably dictated by (i) the approach of winter, (2) the advance of the Red Army towards Slovenia, and (3) the failure to gain a sufficient footing to enable Partisan forces to exist on Austrian territory.

Slovene Claims to Carinthia

(C) Revival of the Slovene case for Carinthia.

The opening of the propaganda campaign coincides with the lessening of military activity.

Marshal Tito's speech on Vis on September 12th, 1944 made the first public mention of the Yugoslav claim to Carinthia. This speech was followed by "Free Yugoslav" broadcasts during the following month.

(It is interesting to note that "Free Austria" – a *Russian* station – broadcast on October 11th that the Austrian people endorsed the Yugoslav claim to territory in Carinthia.)

The campaign has also been developed in the Partisan press in Slovenia, though in more general terms than in the case of the claims to Italian territory.

(D) Slovene Partisans and Austria.

Mindful of their failure in face of Austrian action in 1919-1920, the Slovenes are concentrating on:

(a) The establishment of an Austrian Government, which would endorse Yugoslav frontier claims.

(b)The creation of an independent Austria too weak to oppose by military action any such frontier revision.

Intensive political activity has been organised in two directions:

(1) The creation of the Österreichische Freiheitsfront *on Slovene territory*

This body is ostensibly the core of an Austrian resistance movement representing all Austrian democratic elements for the liberation of that country. The degree of control exercised by the Slovene Freedom Front over the Ö.F.F. and the precise relations between the Slovene Communist Party and the Austrian Communists with the Ö.F.F. are not clearly distinguished.

Some reports indicate that most of the members of the Ö.F.F. are Carinthian Slovenes and that the Communist elements of the Ö.F.F. dominate that body under the direct supervision of the Communist party of Slovenia.

Although positive evidence is slight, the Ö.F.F. seems to have but nebulous contacts with resistance inside Austria.,

In all probability, the future role of the Ö.F.F. will be to set up liberation committees in Carinthia at the moment of general collapse, and to organise a plebiscite in favour of annexation to Slovenia before the major Allies have time to intervene. The deciding factor in such a move would be the attitude of the Russians and a Russian-controlled administration in Vienna.

(*Note*: On April 16th, Boris Kidric, Secretary of the Slovene Communist party, in a speech at Crnomelj voiced categorically the claim for Klagenfurt, and asserted that this was now assured by virtue of Russian support).

(2) The formation of Austrian battalions

On November 4th, 1944 the Ö.F.F. formed an Austrian battalion on Slovene soil to operate under Slovene command. The recruits were drawn largely from the frontier areas with a thin sprinkling of German deserters.

Increasing publicity in the Slovene press has been given to this unit (probably not more than 60 strong), and in April 1945 a second battalion was formed.

These troops might well suffice to occupy the disputed frontier areas under Slovene command, at a moment of general confusion, and to help in the organisation of a plebiscite.

(*Note*: The small party sent into the Saualpen in February were drawn from the Austrian battalion.)

Throughout March 1945 the Slovene leaders have shown a renewed interest in the activities of these Austrians.

A delegation from the provincial committee of the Ö.F.F. for Carinthia and Styria, purporting to come from across the border arrived in Crnomelj with letters addressed to the Allied leaders.

It seems that the Slovene intend to make full use of the O.F.F. in furthering their frontier claims.[179]

(E) The Federal Government of Yugoslavia and the claims to Carinthia

One of the main values of the federal connexion in the eyes of the Slovene leaders is the added weight which can be given to Slovene claims for territorial revision by the official demands of the central administration to the Allied Powers.

In his speeches and interviews to the Press, Marshal Tito has recently, in referring to the revision of frontiers, always included Carinthia, and in is latest and somewhat naive move, has asked for an occupation zone in Austria which corresponds precisely with the disputed area.

This area has been defined in recent months in conversation with Allied officers at the Slovene Headquarters (please see attached map). [Not reproduced]

The stage is now set for a full dress presentation of these claims simultaneously with local action in the area concerned, possibly with the connivance of the Russian occupation authorities in Austria.

Carinthia will fall into the occupation zone of Anglo-American forces. These forces may well find Slovene and Slovene-controlled Austrian forces already in possession.

CONCLUSIONS

(1) There is no satisfactory evidence that an articulate majority in favour of Slovenia exists in the disputed areas of Carinthia. The Slovene-speaking population of Carinthia has, on the whole, remained passive in face of the recruiting and propaganda efforts of the Slovene Partisans. There is no reason to believe that the situation whereby nearly 10,000 Slovene-speaking Carinthians voted for Austria in 1920 has materially altered by 1945.

(2) The present Slovene leaders have inherited from the days of 1919-1920 a deep distrust of Allied "mediation" and of Inter-Allied commissions. This explains, in part, their suspicion of the activities of British and American officers sent into the frontier areas.

(3) The Slovene leaders probably intend to occupy the disputed territory by force, organise their own plebiscite, possibly in conjunction with the Austrian Freedom Front and with the tacit connivance of the Russians in Vienna.

(4) Every effort has been made by the Slovene leaders to prevent a similar alignment of forces in post-war Austria to that which thwarted the realisation of their aspirations in 1919-20. The formation of the *Österreichische Freiheitsfront* and the Austrian battalions in the Slovene Liberation Forces is part of a coherent plan to establish, possibly with Russian assistance, a like-minded regime in Austria which would not oppose Slovene claims.

(5) Unless the Russians agree to support the British and American intention to preserve the 1937 frontiers of Austria, at least during the period of military occupation, the Slovenes will probably be able to settle the question without difficulty or delay in their own favour.[180]

APPENDIX G

MAIN 5 CORPS PERSONAL DIRECTIVE OF 6 MAY 1945

Charles F. Keightley

[PRO WO 170/4241]

TOP SECRET AND PERSONAL
(Not to be passed on in writing)

MAIN 5 CORPS
07/2/G
May 1945

PERSONAL DIRECTIVE
from
Lt. Gen. C.F. Keightley CB DSO OBE

To: Maj. Gen H. Murray DSO Commander 6 BRIT ARMD DIV
Maj Gen. R.K. Arbuthnot CBE DSO MC Commander 78 DIV
Maj. Gen C.E. Weir CBE DSO Commander 46 DIV

INTERNAL SECURITY SITUATION WITHIN 5 CORPS AREA

1. OBJECT

Our object is to maintain a secure base and L of C for our operations in AUSTRIA. Our immediate objectives are VILLACH and KLAGENFURT.

2. SITUATION

(a) The present position within the CORPS area is that the area is administered mostly by local partisans and in some cases in collaboration with men from Marshal TITO's Army and in other cases solely by men from Marshal TITO's Army.

(b) The Field Marshal is at present in consultation with Marshal TITO with a view to determining a military boundary between the two armies. Until such a decision is reached it is clearly of the greatest importance that NO hostile act should occur between British troops and Marshal Tito's forces which might prejudice the issue.

(c) Marshal TITO has not yet declared his hand, and it is therefore not clear what he wants or how far he intends to go. It was originally believed that once he got to the R. ISONZO and up to the pre-war Austrian border he would be satisfied, but he has already instituted a certain administrative control in villages and towns WEST of the River. It is also believed that he has directed certain elements towards KLAGENFURT and VILLACH.

(d) A further complication consists of the fact that there are a number of semi-organised units indirectly under Marshal TITO who had been living in this area for some years. These are now banded together into battalions more on the partisan principles and their "objective" is mainly pro-Slovenian propaganda in this area. They are part of Marshal TITO's 9 Corps and are commanded by an officer who is in touch with me and lives in UDINE. 9 Yugoslav Corps is not in such direct touch with Marshal TITO as other Yugoslav troops, and to some extend independent of direct command. However, they get their general directions from Marshal TITO's HQ.

(e) As the most certain way to maintain order in the area is to run the local administration under a British military adm officer, I have adopted the policy of putting in as many British troops as possible and as quickly as possible in the hope that where he finds strong British forces he will be reluctant to take any very decisive action and in any case to exert any force over the local inhabitants.

It is not believed that he is either willing or able to take any form of organised action against the British troops, but as is always the case under these conditions local commanders may easily start large scale hostilities by a local shooting episode which will spread rapidly and cause fighting over a very wide area. The form of this fighting would be purely guerilla and no formed bodies of Marshal TITO's forces would be found to deal with. It would in fact be very difficult to find out who our enemies were.

Appendix G

3. PRESENT POLICY

(a) The policy at the moment must therefore be to maintain the most friendly relations with all local forces, whether they are [Italian] partisans or wear Marshal TITO's red star.

Hostile acts must be avoided at all costs unless Marshal TITO's men open fire first on our troops or the situation in the view of the local commander becomes unsafe for British troops.

It is believed that Marshal TITO would welcome some
ill-considered act of aggression by British troops which he could turn into propaganda and use as a bargaining counter to move his troops deeper and take over more control.

(b) Within the next three days I hope that orders will come from the Field Marshal which will enable us to take a stronger line, but in the meantime situations will be dealt with as far as possible on the following lines:

    (1) Where we wish to go through villages which have been previously reached by Marshal TITO's forces along the roads toward VILLACH and KLAGENFURT we can take any steps such as driving tanks through road blocks if any attempt is made to stop us. Such action will be preceded by every possible attempt to get on by other means but if these fail it must be made clear that we have a job of work to do to finish off the Germans and that we will not be prevented from carrying this out. If our troops are fired at then we must fire back and we must then assumne that those who fired on us are against us, and that those who fire at us could not possibly be members of Marshal TITO's Army but must be under the orders of some German commander.

    (ii) It is undesirable that large forces of Marshal TITO's should come into this area. Until a firm directive from higher authority is received, this is however difficult to prevent.

I am arranging a number of road blocks which will be manned by both British and Yugoslav troops; this will be a check on movement to some extent.

Further orders on this will be issued separately.

Local commanders may block roads where this is operationally necessary and the nearer the Austrian border we get the stricter must this control become.

(c) When units move into towns their general directive should be on the following lines:

    (i) The local commander should choose a locality consisting of certain houses or areas in which in the event of real trouble his

troops can dispose themselves tactically and are able to prevent any movement through this area and safeguard all vehs and eqpt.
(ii) If shooting breaks out between the [Italian] partisans and Marshal TITO's men, British troops will avoid becoming involved in the trouble. They should picqut cross-roads near the scene and endeavour to seal it off and prevent other troops – of whichever side – from joining in. If the situation becomes out of hand then the local commander may at his discretion withdraw to his "keep" and confine hiomself to protecting his men, vehs and eqpt.

4. CONCLUSION

It is very important that all officers and NCOs, and especially those on detachment, should realise the repercussions of hasty and ill-advised action at the present time.

I do not believe that the present situation will deteriorate if all British soldiers act with the common-sense, thought and sense of humour for which we are renowned.

When the situation is clarified between the Field Marshal and Marshal TITO, probably in a few days' time, we shall be able to take a really firm line.

[signed]
C.F. Keightley
Lieut. General
LFC

Copy to: DGS
DA & QMG
CCRA
CE
CSO [181]

APPENDIX H

NUMBER SIX SPECIAL FORCE STAFF SECTION (CLOWDER MISSION)

i.

[PRO FO 371/46610, C3103/141/3]

ARCHIVES[182]

THIS DOCUMENT IS THE PROPERTY OF HIS BRITANNIC MAJESTY'S GOVERNMENT

[Number Six Special Force]

AUSTRIA
June 13, 1945

CONFIDENTIAL SECTION 1.

D

[C 3102/141/3]
Copy No. 8

Notes on the Political Situation in Carinthia and Western Styria
May 1945.--
(*Communicated by Mr. Mack, 13th June, 1945*)

A. The Background

1. Pre-Anschluss (see Appendix "A.")

The Marchland mentality has always stimulated in Styria and Carinthia strong German and anti-Slav feeling. This was already so under the

Habsburg Empire and was intensified by the fight against Yugoslav claims after the last war, which culminated in the activity of the Heimschutz in 1919-20 and the plebiscite of 1920.

In Carinthia the bulk of popular support was distributed equally between the Social Democrats, who then belonged to the moderate wing of the party but had a slightly Pan-German tinge, the Landbund which was definitely Pan-German and the Christian Social party, which was in Carinthia largely free from the taint of "green" fascism.

In Styria the situation was somewhat different. The industrial areas in Graz and, above all, in the towns in the Mur valley remained up till 1934 strongholds of Social Democracy. The Landbund was weak, but the Styrian Heimwehr, closely associated with the Right Wing of the Christian Social party, developed early Pan-German leanings and in the early '30's went over *en bloc* to the Nazis. The Heimatblock, a straight clerico-Fascist party, gained the third largest representation in the last free elections in 1931.

2. The Anschluss

The Social Democrat organisations had already been destroyed by the Dollfuss Government in 1934. The Styrian Heimwehr, the Landbund, the Pan-Germans went solidly Nazi. The remaining Christian Socials, who in 1931 had represented well over 25 per cent of the population, were swamped and either forced out of office or, in the case of a few officeholders, joined the Nazi party in self-defence.

Almost immediately came the first wave of disillusion. The new régime flooded the country with officials from Germany, who shut out the local Nazis from the best appointments and were bitterly resented by the local patriotism of the conservative peasants.

3. 1938-44

In the first years after the *Anschluss*, economic advantages were undeniable. The gearing of Austria into the German war economy eliminated unemployment. Greater Germany provided Austrian agriculture with both a wide market and a cheap and abundant source of artificial fertilisers. Forestry also benefited from the new market. At the same time, credit facilities and new social services made a strong selling point with the peasants.

These advantages were short-lived. The maze of controls and regulations, becoming more stringent as the war progressed, and the steadily decreasing purchasing range of the mark were regarded as the precursors of an economic collapse, which could not indefinitely be delayed.

The direct impact of the war on the population had two main effects. It denuded the country of all its young men with the exception of party officials. As a result, both agriculture and industry became dependent on conscripted foreign labour and, at the same time, the bulk of the most solidly Nazi age-groups were removed to the front.

Secondly, the extreme youth, so far from being presented with new opportunities, which had been the chief Nazi bait to the young Austrian from 1933 to 1939, could only look forward to early conscription and probably the horrors of the Eastern front.

In spite of the growing disillusion, no significant Austrian resistance emerged. Gestapo control, popular reaction against the Tito "bandits," the absence of the young, and, above all, the naturally lethargic characteristics of the population and the failure of the inter-war Austrian Republic to produce a strong national consciousness, all combined to render abortive the numerous small attempts to organise anti-Nazi feeling into open resistance. Right up to the immediate pre-collapse period the only known openly active anti-Nazi elements were the Slovene partisans in the Sau- and Kor-Alpen and a small group operating with the Italian partisans in the Tarvisio area.

B. The Collapse

4. *The Defeat of the German Armies*

The first months of 1945 made it finally clear that the German armies were facing total defeat and that eleventh hour rescue with the aid of v-weapons was a vain hope. This produced a catastrophic loss of morale within the party itself, which gave birth to the so-called "surrender group", which in Carinthia had at least the conditional support of Gauleiter Rainer.

5. *Economic Collapse*

The disorganisation of German economy produced by military defeat and the disruption of communications was intensified by financial chaos, finanlly resulting in a currency famine which forced the provincial Governent to resort, in Carinthia, to the printing of local promissory notes, and in Styria and other provinces to the fantastic resort of issuing photostaic reproductions of existing Reichsbank notes.

6. *The Overthrow of the Régime*

With the last disappearance of hope which the Vittighof [Viettinghoff] surrender [in northern Italy] represented, the pressure of the "surrender group" became overwhelming, the submerged pre-*Anschluss* figures began to reappear, and such underground resistance as had existed came to the surface. The Gauleiter Rainer endeavoured to procrastinate, or at least to ensure that the retreat routes for the German armies in Yugoslavia were kept open, and that General Loehr's surrender to Anglo-American forces and not to Tito be agreed. But pressure was too great. Before Loehr's advances were rejected, the basis of a new Carinthia Provisional Government had emerged on the 3rd May, although it was not fully consituted till the 5th May, and finally achieved executive control on the [evening of the] seventh. By the time British troops crossed the frontier in Styria, the underground organisation of Knittelfeld had liberated the town and the Zeltweg airfield had been cleared of mines and held for the Allies by the local Hungarian troops, and, in the Carinthian villages, Nazi local authorities had been replaced, in most cases by their pre-*Anschluss* predecessors.

7. *The New Carinthian Government (see Appendix "B")*

The composition of the new Government corresponded roughly to the political complexion of the 1933 Diet, except for the absence of the Slovene Catholics and the presence of Communist members (one of whom has since resigned), who demanded seats on the model of the Renner Government in Vienna. The personalities concerned are chiefly pre-*Anschluss* officials and are said to be, in so far as they are at all representative, second strings of the groups involved, the more able and ambitious standing aside to await developments.

Both the old and the new Governments found themselves faced with a dual problem: surrender to the Allies and the prevention of encroachment in Carinthia by Tito forces. Even the Communist members initially supported a resolution in favour of the territorial integrity of Carinthia. A surrender mission to the Allied forces in Italy was prepared, on whose orders it is not clear. This mission, owing to the refusal of co-operation by the SS troops in the Val Canale, the impossibility of passing through Tito territory and the report of Italian partisan control in Carnia, was constrained to secure indirect contact via the American commander in Salzburg, whence a message was transmitted to A.F.H.Q.

By the time the mission returned to Klagenfurt, 5th Corps troops had entered Austria.

8. *Nazi Resistance*

There is evidence that plans had been made for a Werwolf organisation the Niedere-Tauern. Local Nazis state that these were called off by Dönitz, but that they still intended to function in Russian occupied territory.

Various attempts by individual Nazis to reinsure and at least one attempt to drive a wedge between the Western Allies and Russia by the formation of a rival to the Renner Government have been noted. There is also some evidence that elements of the "surrender group" will endeavour to reinfiltrate into public affairs in due course.

C. Current and Future Trends

9. The dominant and unifying factor is the fear of the Russians and Tito. This is likely to transcend all divergent tendencies for some time to come and makes the presence of British forces very popular.

10. The Human Material

This falls roughly into three classes:

The over-40's who are tending, so far as they ever abandoned them to return to their pre-Nazi loyalties.

The class of 25-35. Almost soldidly Nazi but largely absent, prisoners or dead.

The very young, who have gained nothing from the Nazi régime, are disillusioned, but possibly amenable to re-education, and already show signs of developing an Austrian national consciousness.

11. Communism

Apart from Tito adherents, communism is virtually non-existent. The impact of the Russians and Tito forces is acting as a powerful prophylactic. Only after this threat has been removed and in the event of a catastrophic economic depression coupled with the general disillusionment produced by defeat could there be a fruitful soil for this development. Even then it is considered that the natural peasant resistance is too strong.

12. Legitimism

Legitimism in Carinthia was, before the *Anschluss*, virtually non-existent, and there is no evidence of its presence now. In the present British zone in Styria, on the other hand, a large proportion of the older peasantry is looking back to the "happy days of the Habsburgs," and there are indications that a certain amount of discreet legitmist propaganda is being put out, including even some for the Austro-Bavarian Union.

13. The Nazi Revival

An early Nazi revival is unlikely. There are, however, factors which might lead to its emergence later, when Allied control is relaxed, and eventually removed. There is a strong possibility that the recollection of the present Tito encroachments may lead to a recrudescence of the Pan-Germanism and the Marchland mentality. The present reaction to the Russian occupation, which is to blame it on the Nazi régime, may later give way to the belief that the Nazi attitude to "bolshevism" was justified. There can be little doubt that there will be an attempt on the part of some Nazis to retire to their farms to await the day when a new depression will provide the necessary economic basis for radical political developments.

14. The Influence of the Church

The influence of the Catholic Church in Southern Austria has, on the whole, been consistently anti-Nazi. The southern dioceses are not under the aegis of Vienna and hence not tainted with Innitzer collaborationism. The Styrian Bishop Palikowsky has come out openly against the régime throughout.

Unlike the indigenous Protestant pockets in Styria, the Reformed Church in Carinthia is purely artificial and finds its adherents solely amongst the German settlers introduced by the Carinthian Government in 1919 to offset the Slav threat. These Protestant settlers became Nazi to a man.

15. The Economic Factor

The great bulk of the Carinthian population consists of peasants and railway workers. On the prosperity of these more than anything else depend the prospects of political peace. The food situation was well in hand. The new authorities, in response to Field-Marshal Alexander's appeal, took steps to safeguard food dumps. Subsequently, as a result of wholesale requisitioning by Tito and Russian forces, this situation has deteriorated rapidly.

D. Conclusions

16. (a) Political unity is likely to remain as long as the Tito (and to a lesser degree the Russian) threat is present.

(b) A satisfactory solution of the economic problem is the main guarantee against the re-emergence of extreme political creeds with their consequent disturbances.

(c) This entails in Carinthia support to agriculture and the re-establishment of railway traffic.

(d) Amongst the peasants, the Catholic Church is likely to play a large part in assuaging the disillusionment of defeat.

(e) The main factor productive of stability will always be the natural lethargy and laziness of the Austrians, which will tend to make them particularly amenable to occupation by the Western Allies.

Appendix "A"

The Pre-Anschluss Political Parties in Carinthia and Styria

A. Carinthia

1. Social Democrats

The strongest party up till 1934. Polled about 30 per cent. of the votes in the last free elections in 1931. The Carinthian faction belonged to the right wing of the party and was slightly tinged with Pan-German leanings. It found its support in the railway Trades Union which comprised the only large group of workers in the province.

Suppressed in 1934 by Dollfuss. Went underground but remained active until 1938, since when it has remained largely a dormant loyalty.

2. Christian Social Party

Polled 25 per cent. votes in 1931. In Carinthia the democratic wing of the party was dominant and although membership of the Heimwehr was widespread in Carinthia, its formations and leaders were anti-Nazi, rather than anti-Socialist and largely free from the Fascist tendencies of Styria.

3. Landbund

Once the largest party in Carinthia. In complexion originally agrarian-democratic but being the party par excellence of the Marchland mentality, always Pan-German. Its following declined after the middle twenties and eventually went over *en masse* to the Nazis.

4. Pan-German Party (Gross-Deutsche)

10 per cent. votes in 1931. A middle-class party with the main plank of union with the Reich. Went Nazi *en bloc*.

5. N.S.D.A.P.

5 per cent. votes in 1931. Went underground in 1933 and gradually drew to itself most of the Landbund and the whole of the Pan-German party.

6. Slovene Catholic Party

5 per cent. votes in 1931. Represented the Slovene rural minority in the area south of the Drau.

7. Communist Party

Negligible following, mostly of disappointed office-seekers from the Social Democrats.

B. Styria

8. Social Democrats

About 35 per cent. of electorate in 1933. Styrian Social Democracy was more radical but less Pan-German than in Carinthia, the industrial towns in the Mur valley being the last strongholds of fighting in February, 1934. After 1934 the most active "underground" section of the Party.

9. Christian Social Party

45 per cent. of the electorate in 19333. The right wing of this party had strong Fascist tendencies. The Syrian Heimwehr, formerly under Starhemberg's influence, was later closely associated with Rintelen and was already virtually Nazi at the time of the Dollfuss assassination.

10. Heimatblock

A straight clerico-Fascist party with strong ties with Mussolini, Later became largely Nazi. 10 per cent. of the electorate 1933.

11. Landbund and Pan-German Party

Very weak in Styria.

12 N.S.D.A.P.

Never secured a seat in free elections, but gained an immense following in its "underground" period after 1934.

13. Communist Party

Appendix "B"

Notes on the New Carinthian Government
(N.B.: Evidence on this subject is incomplete.)

A. The Formation of the Government

(For personalities see B below.)

1. There are indications that over the last two years certain preparations were being made by groups and individuals of the pre-*Anschluss* parties for the time when Germany would be defeated and the Nazi régime destroyed. It should be emphasised that these preparations were in no way connected with actively attacking the régime, nor associated with any active resistance movement. On the contrary, their declared tactics were to take no premature action and so to avoid destruction. There is little doubt that they must have been known to the very efficient Gestapo and allowed to continue as constituting no serious danger to the régime. It is certain that no closely organised movement was allowed to exist. Consequently, only the most cautious groups survived, and these were necessarily largely out of touch with each other. It is not without significance that in Klagenfurt it was the Nazi [Meinrad] Nadmesnig [Natmeßnig] who knew and eventually summoned the leaders of the two main groups to form the executive committee which selected the new Government.

2. The development up to the end of April is obscure. It is alleged that some time before the arrival of the British, Tito partisans endeavoured to contact the Wehrmacht and elements of the new régime. The position of the Wehrmacht and the date of the partisan approach have not yet been established. In any event, Oberst-Lt. [Josef] Stossier, who was acting as liaison, managed to stall the partisan approaches until British troops arrived.

3. The final initiative was taken by the Church, whether independently or at whose instance is not known. On the 2nd May Mgr. [Josef] Kadras and Mgr. Unterluggauer called on Rainer and asked him to surrender or resign in order to save Carinthia from becoming a battlefield. Rainer answered that he considered himself bound by his allegiance to Dönitz, and his responsibility to keep open Loehr's escape routes. he would, however, be willing to resign if he lost contact with the Führer or if Allied troops were actually marching in, provided that Loehr's surrender to the Anglo-Americans and not to Tito had been agreed.

4. On the 3rd May Kadras got in touch with the Gauhauptmann Nadmesnig and demanded that he form an executive committee.

Nadmesnig invited [Franz] Krasnig [Kraßnig] of the Christian Socials and [Julius] Lukas of the Social Democrats to form as committee with two members from each of their groups. Arrangements were made to secure Wehrmacht assistance should a "Putsch" be necessary to remove Rainer. Names mentioned in this connection are Oberst Ming [Meng] and Hptm. [Hans] Mayer and a Major Bleich [Blaich], a contact of Krasnig, who declared that he had 300 men of the Luftwaffe prepared to dispose of Rainer if he persisted in his refusal to resign.

5. At 1000 hours on the 4th May the Executive Committee met in the Landhaus. Members: [Sylvester] Leer, Krasnig, [Hermann] Grossauer (Christian Socials), Lukas, [Friedrich] Schatzmayer, [Hans] Herke (Social Democrats).

At 1200 hours Rainer received the committee and reiterated his former conditions. At 1400 hours he delivered a broadcast appeal to the Carinthians to make a last-ditch stand and accused the committee of treachery.

At 1500 hours Bleich's men were prepared.

At 1700 hours the committee was informed that Rainer had lost touch with Dönitz and would resign that night.

At 1800 hours the committee prepared to take over control; Nadmesnig was told that his membership was unacceptable.

At 2000 hours Rainer reestablished contact with Dönitz and refused to resign, and at 2200 hours delivered an even more uncompromising broadcast speech.

6. On the 5th May it was rumoured that SS-General Rösener was coming to the aid of Rainer with SS troops. Dr. [Hans] Tschurtschenthaler, who now appeared openly associated with the committee for the first time delivered, pressed for immediate action, but by this time Bleich's force had been dispersed.

In the evening the committee asked [Hans] Piesch to form a new provincial Government. It is not clear how far the committee controlled the composition of the Government, but both Krasnig and Tschurtschenthaler opposed the inclusion of [Stefan] Tauschitz. The Communists claimed two seats on the precedent of the Renner Government in Vienna, but were persuaded to support a resolution in favour of the territorial integrity of Carinthia in the face of the Tito threat.

7. On the 6th May negotiations continued with Rainer, who adopted stalling tactics, perhaps in the hope that the popular rumours of Rösener's aid were well-founded.

Some time during the day two emissaries left Klagenfurt in company with an O.S.S. officer who had been released from imprisonment. They have stated that contact was made with the American headquarterd in

Salzburg, whence a signal was sent to A.F.H.Q. explaining the position in Klagenfurt and urging the speedy arrival of Allied troops. Under whose orders these emissaries were acting has not been satisfactorily established. The composition of the mission – one a member of the "surrender group," an ex-SS officer, and the other a non-party business man, not a Carinthian – does not at first sight suggest that they were chosen by the new Government, especially as at least one member of the party appears to have been under the impression that the Government as such was formed on the 3rd May. It would seem possible that the mission was despatched by Nadmesnig, with or without the knowledge of Rainer, in order to force the latter's hand or save his face by ensuring the early arrival of Allied troops.

8. On the 7th May, the police and gendarmerie declared in favour of the new Government. Rainer continued to resist all day. At 2300 hours, the Government went in a body to Rainer and were able to inform him that that they were in control of the executive power. thus at 2304 hours Rainer was finally forced to resign.

Early the next morning 5 Corps troops crossed the frontier near Tarvisio.

B. Personalities

9. *The New Government*

(i) Landeshauptmann u. Schulreferent Hans Piesch (Social Democrat). Former director of Bürgerschule in Villach. Reported honest and reliable and consistently anti-Nazi. [183]

(ii) Stellv. des Landeshauptmanns u. Finanz Ing. Tauschitz (Landbund). Former Landbund Member of Parliament, served several times in Austrian cabinet. Before 1933 was closely associated with Landeshauptmann Kernmaier who later went over to the Nazis. In 1933 member of the group which attempted to form a Pan-German counter-organisation to the Dollfuss Vaterländische Front, but on the failure of this sworn allegiance to Dollfuss. Secured his appointment as Minister in Berlin, who was the Nazi nominee for Chancellor in the "Putsch" which resulted in the assassination of Dollfuss. Tauschitz, on his appointment to Berlin, secured the unheard-of guarantee of a ten-years' appointment, which made his dismissal impossible. Adopted a consistently accomodating attitude toward the German Government, and is believed to have sabotaged any attempt to form an Austrian political intelligence section in Berlin.

On the day of the *Anschluss*, abruptly cut short the British Ambassador's formal visit of condolence in order to attend the Nazi *Anschluss* celebrations in the Berlin Stadium (cf. Nevile Henderson: "The Failure of a Mission"). Disappeared from public life after the *Anschluss*.

(iii) Gesundheitswesen: Sylvester Leer (Christian Socialist). Strong Catholic and pre-*Anschluss* member of the Provincial Diet. Has been described as the Nazis' worst hated enemy in Carinthia. Personal reliabilty uncertain.

(iv) Bauwesen: Ferdinand Wedenig (Social Democrat). Has a general reputation as a moderate and reliable member of the old Social Democrat organisation.

(v) Wohn- und Siedlungswesen: [Albin] Tschofenig (Communist). Merchant in Villach. Young and said to be mild Communist.

(vi) Sicherheitswesen: Julius Santer (Independent). Business man: quiet, honest, not highly intelligent.

(vii) Landwirtschaft: [Hans] Ferlitsch (Landbund). Peasant. Honest but politically inexperienced.

(viii) Wirtschaft: [Franz] Ritscher (Christian Socialist). Little known politically. Former adherent of Schuschnigg.

(ix) Soziale Fürsorge: Josef Hanni (Communist). Unknown hitherto. Resigned from the government the 16th may and openly associated himself with the Tito partisans.

(x) Gemeinden: Hans Herke (Social Democrat). Former railway official. The outstanding Social Democrat member of the Government and one of the committee which originally took the initiative in its formation.

10. Other Officials.

Landesbauernführer: Hermann Gruber. Always an influential figure among the peasantry. Strong sense of Austrian patriotism. With his whole family, consistently and openly anti-Nazi, but his outstanding reputation saved him from arrest. held his present office before 1938.

Sicherheitsdirektor: Obst. Lt. Stossier. Said to have been liaison between Pzn. delegates and members of new Government before the arrival of British troops, and to have successfully carried out stalling tactics.

11. Church Dignitaries

Mgr. Kadras. Vicar General of the Diocese of Gurk, in charge of diocese since the Prince Bishop [Adam] Hefter's resignation. A schoolmaster before the *Anschluss*, but sacked by the Nazis.

Mgr. Unterluggauer, Dean of Cathedral Chapter. Member of one of leading Catholic families of Carinthia. An old man of extensive political experience.

12. Miscellaneous

Nadmesnig. Gauhauptmann, *i.e.*, senior administrative official of the Gauleitung. A Nazi of long standing, active during the underground period from 1933 to 1938. Nevertheless, even his opponents state that his behaviour as an official was correct and not radically Nazi. On very bad terms with Rainer. Leader of the "surrender group" among the local Nazis.

Krasnig (Christian Socialist). Formerly a Catholic journalist. Barred by Nazis and forced to earn his living as clerk and shop assistant. Said to have been preparing a resistance movement, and appears to have had contacts with anti-Nazi elements in the Wehrmacht. A member of the original committee.

Grossauer (Christian Socialist). A former Under-Secretary of State. Consistently anti-Nazi. A member of the original committee. Believed to be able and tipped for future prominence but at present standing aside.

Dr. Tschurtschenthaler (Christian Socialist). Former member of Provincial Diet. Not a member of the original committee, but believed to have been one of the powers behind it. Like Grossauer at present standing aside and tipped for future prominence.

Lukas and Schatzmayer (Social Democrat). Social Democrat leaders pre-1934. No details known. [184]

ii.
Letter of Finlay Lockhead to Brigadier Anthony Cowgill, 27 September 1987

We were sent to Venice with a jeep & a Dingo armoured car with instructions to contact the S.O.E. officer with the Partisans there, to contact personnel in Belluno and keep in touch with 8th Army HQ. by radio. Radio contact from the top of the car park at Venice didn't work.

We made contact with the S.O.E. (M?) officer and the Partisan leader Milo? who had just accepted the surrender in Venice. We were there for a week & went to Belluno having managed to contact them on an Electricity Board telephone. At the end of the period Chas. Villiers arrived and proceeded at the head of a column into Austria to Klagenfurt and settled in what had been German Air Force HQ. After a short period we moved to Viktring. I was attached as liaison officer to the Jugo. 4th Army 11th Brigade at Rosenbach.

My duties were those of an observer & to liase with 5 Corps. At this time the Jugoslavs had town majors in most Carinthian towns and the first objective was to confine all Jugoslav personnel to the South bank of the river Drau. This took place and I reported to 5 Corps. Von Paulus? [Löhr] had surrendered to Tito and as a result the Jugoslavs claimed the German arm[our]ed vehicles etc. These were to be removed to Jugoslavia and I spent a considerable amount of time taking Major Dubaics to 5 Corps HQ. in order to obtain permission for the to bring their transporters across the Drau to remove the abandoned tanks. The Guards were on duty at the bridges and delaying tactics were employed until such time as the tanks had been made inoperable. The Jugoslavs were busy taking photographs of the engineers' activities and were far from pleased. In due course permission was granted. At this time I did a regular run as far as Bleiburg, south to Eisenkappel collecting general information.

From memory I was the only member of 6 SFSS south of the Drau. I may have had a driver from time to time although I don't remember this. I acted purely as a liaison link with Major Dubaics. I have no recollection of Capt. Dominko. Dubaics was 22 years old. Most of the unit were in their mid-teens.

At no time during the movement of the Chetniks [Serbian Volunteer Corps] was I envoled in removing personnel or unloading bodies from the train. I was at Maria Elend in a liaison capacity. The trains were loaded by the units escorting the prisoners & handed over to the Yugoslavs by them. Once the trains left Maria Elend they were not seen by myself or any other 6 S.F.S.S. personnel and I was certainly unaware at that time of the massacres.

As far as Todorovics' [Lieutenant Branislav Todorović] account is concerned – he did appear to wish to leave the [Yugoslav Army] unit at Rosenbach. One of his reasons was that he had a sister in the West, I think U.S.A., & he wished to join her. My recollection of him was that he was not very reliable and that he would probably sympathise with whatever party suited him at any particular time. I have no recollection of him supplying any information on Partisan troop movements. In fact I have no recollection of there being any Jugoslav troop movements in the Maria Elend-Rosenbach area during my duties as a liaison officer. Apart from reporting the withdrawal of the town majors the one other duty I performed for 5 Corps was to inform Popski that he was to withdraw his unit from Austria.

I was interested to read the account by Todorivics of the supper which a Capt. Brown, 2 other officers, myself and Galbraith attended. I have no recollection of this although it may have taken place. I don't now remember Galbraith although he may well have been there to "engineer" Todorovics' passage to a "safe house".

I hope that the above will tie up with your information & be of use somehow. The passage of time certainly removes the sharp edges of one's memory.

Yours

Finlay [185]

[N.B.: the text has been transcribed from the handwritten original.]

APPENDIX I

The Interrogation of Erwin Rösener

[PRO WO 170/4241]

SUBJECT: Interrogation Report.

Main 5 Corps,
4/1/GSI.
18 May 45.

To: ALL CONCERNED

Below is a preliminary interrogation, by CSDIC 78 Div, of SS General Erwin RÖSENER.

[signed]
J.C. Crawley
for Lieut-General,
Commander

Interrogation Report of SS General Rösener, Erwin

1. Circumstances of Capture

On 17 May a German officer in the German PW hospital at SPITTAL informed the British medical authorities that SS General RÖSENER was in the hospital masquerading as a private soldier. FSS were informed and when the General was questioned in the hospital he admitted his real identity after first attempting to conceal it.

2. Recent History and Movements

SS General RÖSENER was the senior SS Commander in Army Gp 'E', under Col Gen LOEHR. His normal function was to command the Army Rear Areas and to safeguard them from partisan attacks. Some six weeks ago he formed KORPSGRUPPE RÖSENER, which was employed in an anti-partisan role. Tps under his command included:

    438 Landesschützen Div (Railway Security)
    17 Police Regt
    19 Police Regt
    Unspecified Serbian, Slovene and Russian Royalist tps incl a Cossack Regt., and some German base and L of C Units. The approximate strength was 50,000

The General brought a majority of these troops back into CARINTHIA, but refused to surrender to TITO. He despatched his G(Ops), Maj. SCHOLZ, to 61 Bde, and his group surrendered to the British and was subsequently disarmed. He then considered the moment opportune to disappear, and leaving Col. [VON] SEELE[R] in command, the general doffed his SS uniform and badges of rank, assumed the pose of a private soldier and took to the road. His intention was to make his way to SALZBURG where his wife and four children were living. He said he had had no leave for three years and wanted to see his wife and children before giving himself up to the Allied Authorities. Having hitch-hiked as far as SPITTAL the general began to suffer from chest trouble and a skin complaint and consequently entered the military hospital in that area. He had been there for some five or six days when removed by the FSS.

3. Conclusion

Asked why he had acted in such a manner the General replied that German propaganda had continually stressed the fact that high ranking SS officers would be shot by the Allies. When told that nobody with a clear conscience would be dealt with in that manner the General did not reply. He appears to be in a very emotional if not neurotic frame of mind and broke into tears once during the interrogation.

APPENDIX J

Conclusion and Security Implications

[PRO FO 371/46612, C5832/141/3]

[Report]

Intelligence Branch, Ad. Hq., BFA, Army Div, Austria

TOP SECRET

CONCLUSION AND SECURITY IMPLICATIONS

Since the Jugoslavs had collaborated as the Allies of the British in the defeat of the Germans, reports that they were engaged in clandestine activity against the British forces of occupation in CARINTHIA and STYRIA were at first treated as malicious gossip. It was recognised that the large number of Slovenes living in the southern portion of CARINTHIA could reasonably claim some consideration from the Austrian Government, and their close ties with JUGOSLAVIA during the war, when a number of them fought with the Jugoslav army as partisans, made some support of their claims by the Jugoslav Government comprehensible enough. Provided that this support consisted only in overt encouragement by ordinary straightforward means, it would have caused little anxiety to the British occupational authorities, who indeed have been scrupulously careful not to prejudice by undue interference what is after all essentially an Austrian rather than a British problem.

Nevertheless, the contemporaneous activities of the Jugoslavs in VENEZIA GIULIA were interpreted as a warning that the situation might develope unfavourably, and the position was accordingly observed with close attention as a precautionary measure. As will be evident from

Appendix J

the foregoing pages, it has become increasingly clear that the activities of the Jugoslavs in CARINTHIA are going far beyond legitimate and friendly encouragement to former comrades-in-arms. Not only have they deliberately falsified the true facts about British administration, but have committed flagrant violations of British regulations, and have introduced into CARINTHIA all the apparatus of secret agents, subversion, assassination and propaganda which finds an analogy in the Nazi organisation amongst the Sudeten Germans opn the borders of CZECHOSLOVAKIA in 1937-38. Finally, they direct their agents to obtain information about the British Order of Battle, and point to the British as the origin of the "oppressed" Slovenes unhappy existence.

Until this final stage, however troublesome their activities might be, they could have been regarded without due concern. The direction of military espionage agents against the British forces, however, reported plans to kidnap British soldiers, and incitement against the British Occupation, have marked a new turn of events, which must be taken more seriously.

The actual danger from leakage of information, in the absence of any attempt to use it for military operations against British-occupied territory, is admittedly not serious. The details required are now largely public property, the agents sent to obtain them are of a low calibre, and in any event it is hard to see why they could not be better obtained by such Jugoslav missions as are from time to time attached to British headquarters.

On the other hand, the investigation of large numbers of allegations which invariably prove false necessitate the diversion of security personnel from their many important and pressing tasks of detecting and arresting members of the former Nazi machine, and similarly the deliberate refusal to respect frontier regulations is a drain on Field Security resources which are already strained to the utmost.

Finally, the incitement of the local population against the British forces and Military Government may well lead to hostile acts and disturbances. This danger is admittedly not great at present, but soon materialize if present agitation is carried on during a winter when lack of food and fuel is likely in any event to cause an unstable and inflammable situation.

[signed]
W.D. Davies
Colonel,
11th September 1945   GSI (b).

APPENDIX K

Report on Yugoslav Deportations

[PRO FO 371/51243]

Report of 8 October, 1945,
British Military Government, Carinthia,
on Yugoslav Deportations

HEADQUARTERS
MILITARY GOVERNMENT, KÄRNTEN

8th October, 1945

Ref. No.: MGK/2840/PS
Subject: Report on deportation of Austrian Nationals during the period May/June 1945 from the area of Southern Carinthia by the Jugoslavs
Top Military Government Branch
H.Q. B.T.A.

1. Investigations carried out by Captain Hayden temporarily att. to Public Safety M.G. Land Kärnten, provide the following information.
2. Information was obtained from relatives of deported people and of individuals who had returned as well as from the Local Police.
3. It was not possible to interview every returned individual or every relative of deported individuals, but a selection was taken.
4. The main points brought out following interrogations at the following places:

(1) a. KLAGENFURT Area: People deported include some of the local leading National Socialists or individuals known to be staunch National Socialists. In the case of girls detained for the greater part it was on account of overstaying the curfew hour, in some cases no reason for the detention was known.

b. BLEIBURG Area: Again very much the same reasons applied as for the KLAGENFURT Area, personal enmity accounted for certain individuals being deported.

c. EISENKAPPEL Area: In this area it appears two Austrian girls prepared a list of individuals known to be staunch National Socialists as well as others.

d. VÖLKERMARKT Area: The deported individuals were mostly holding official positions in the Nazi party.

e. EBERNDORF Area: Mostly Nazi Party officials.

Most of the individuals deported from the BLEIBURG Area have returned and were imprisoned in the STERNTAL camp, in some cases they were also taken to the PRÄVALI camp. Individuals deported from the EISENKAPPEL Area were taken to the two already mentioned camps or were in the MARBURG prison.

Of the individuals returned, most of them had only been interrogated twice, they had been asked questions about English troops in their area and whether they themselves were Carinthians or not.

(ii) Conditions in this camp were reported to be very bad up to mid August when a Civilian Administration took over the guarding of the camp. It was rumoured in the camp that the improvement in conditions was also due to British intervention.

At the same time it appears that the camp was partly closed down, the persons being asked whether they were Carinthians, in which case they were not allowed to go, being told that the Jugoslavs would return with them to Carinthia.

4. As will be seen, most of the individuals were deported by the Jugoslavs on account of their political status or position or on account of personal enmities existing within their respective communities.

The feeling against the Jugoslavs in the areas visited appears to be strong, mostly on the ground of the treatment received during the Jugoslav occupation of these areas, and many times the investigator was asked whether the Jugoslavs would return.

5. In view of the above information, it would be appreciated if the matter could be taken up as a certain amount of uneasiness is being caused to the civilian population in these areas, and Military Government is receiving frequent applications from relatives concerning the welfare and possible return of the persons who are still missing.

(Sgd.) A.H. Parker (Lt. Col.)

for Colonel
Senior Military Government Officer
H.Q. Mil. Govt. Kärnten

Copies to:
"A" Area Security Office
PWB D Sec.

Appendix A
List of individual deported by Jugoslavs [211 names]

Appendix B
List of individuals who were deported by the Jugoslavs and have now returned [33 names][186]

Notes

1. The topic was treated superficially by the author in his study, *The Slovene Minority of Carinthia* (Boulder and New York: East European Monographs and Columbia University Press, 1984), pp. 192-202.
2. *Pregnanstvo in upor. Vertreibung und Widerstand. Ob 40. obletnici pregnanstva koroških Slovencev in njihove vključitve v boj proti nazifažizmu. Zum 40. Jahrestag der Vertreibung der Kämtner Slowenen und ihrer Eingliederung in den Kampf gegen den Nazifaschismus* (Celovec/Klagenfurt: Zveza slovenskih izseljencev/Verband ausgesiedelter Slowenen), 1982.
3. This phenomenon can also be regarded as a natural reaction to the solicitously nourished German nationalist cult of the so-called "Self-Defense Struggle" (*Abwehrkampf*) of 1918-1920.
4. Pp. 82-83. Published as Heft 39-4 "Militärhistorische Schriftenreihe" (Vienna: Heeresgeschichtliches Museum/Militärhistorisches Institut, 1979).
5. Ljubljana: samozaložba [self-published], 1977.
6. Klagenfurt: Universitätsverlag Carinthia, 1985.
7. Other works dealing at least in part with this book's theme will be cited in succeeding notes.
8. The first Slovene edition was published in 1958 in Ljubljana (Glavni odbor Zveze borcev NOV Slovenije, Založba Borec), the second revised and expanded one in 1974 (also Borec). The first German edition (Drava Verlag) appeared in Klagenfurt in 1980 and the second, with slightly amplified notes, in 1984 (Drava Verlag, "Delavska enotnost Taschenbuch"). The German versions are definitive, the references in this volume being to the first one. "Gašper", like all partisan second last names, is a wartime pseudonym or nom de guerre. The author was also known locally (vulgo) as "Wölfel", the designation for the family farm.
9. Helena Kuchar, *Jelka, aus dem Leben einer Kämtner Partisanin Partisanin* (Eisenkappel: Longo-mai Kooperative, 1984). Tape-recorded memoirs edited by Thomas Busch and Brigitte Windhab.
10. Another first-hand account, thoroughly exploited by Rausch is Ladislav Grat-Kijev, *V metežu [In the Heat of Battle]* (Ljubljana: Zavod Borec, 1969). However, Grat-Kijev's activity, as an SNLA liaison officer with a tiny group of solidly Communist Austro-German partisans flown in from Moscow to act – probably unwittingly – as agents of Stalin's power-political objectives, had much more to do with southwestern Austro-Styria than Carinthia. Cf. Christian Fleck, *Koralmpartisanen: Über abweichende Motiven politisch motivierter Widerstandskämpfer*, No. 4 "Materialien zur Historischen Sozialwissenschaft" (Vienna: Ludwig-Boltzmann-Institut für Sozialwissenschaft and Böhlau Verlag, 1986); and the memoir by Walter Wachs, *Kampfgruppe Steiermark* (Vienna: Europa, Verlag 1968). The guerrillas, who almost certainly could not have survived without the direct support of the SNLA's 300 man-strong Lacko *Odred* operating in the pre-1933 border region of southwestern Styria (the Koralpen) and northern Slovenia, accomplished little of military value. They played only a transitory political role at the war's end, in fact were ousted in late July immediately after the British assumed control of a territory initially occupied by Bulgarian, Albanian, Yugoslav, and Soviet forces.

The hard nucleus of mainly Spanish Civil War veterans was able to recruit a very few German-Styrian rustics. However, the group did not count more than 40-50 fighters until the final weeks of the war. Strengthened by largely apolitical Wehrmacht deserters and aided willy-nilly by a small number of local inhabitants, it was then apparently several hundred men (and women) strong. The main point of Fleck's sociologically-oriented monograph is that the *Kampfgruppe* was a failure not so much because of the debility of Austrian patriotism but because its goals were both politically "deviant" and contravened behavioral norms that held good even under totalitarian Nazi rule. That is to say, its core was also made up of social revolutionaries – and mainly Viennese working class ones at that. It is ironic that persons who *were* Austrian patriots (as well as idealists) served as the tools of their own party leadership and of Moscow's interests. Equally incongruous is the fact that after 1945 on-the-spot adherents were persecuted by the Austrian authorities and scorned by the public at large. Only surviving nucleus figures like Wachs managed to get on unmolested as members of a foreign-sponsored political grouping. Fleck suggests further that Austro-Germans were prepared to tolerate resistance to Naziism only when it was mounted by prewar political elites (ibid., 281–282). See also notes 54 and 113.

11. Patrick Howarth (Wilkinson's assistant), *Undercover: The Men and Women of the Special Operations Executive* (London: Routledge and Kegan Paul, 1980), passim. The information in this book stemming from Peter Wilkinson is based upon extended conversations during three visits to his home in Charing (Kent), letters, tape recordings sent to the author, and telephone calls (August 1987–January 1989); further references to this material are phrased simply "In discussion with Wilkinson". Other studies of the SOE are: M.R.D. Foot, *SOE: The Special Operations Executive, 1940–1946* (Frederick, Md.: University Publications of America, 1986); and David Stafford, *Britain and European Resistance: A Survey of the Special Operations Executive, with Documents* (London:Macmillan for St. Anthony's College, 1980). Wilkinson's memorandum (Appendix A, 83–117), remarkable for its literary grace, quickly reached No. 10 Downing Street. A comprehensive, sober, and realistic assessment, it enabled British statesmen to weigh the risks they were taking in helping the Slovene partisans and make balanced judgments. Of course this was before Churchill began to mistrust Tito (cf. note 106). The memorandum has also been reproduced on pp. 727–747 of Vol. XXXV (No. 11-12) [1983] of the Slovene scholarly journal *Borec [The Fighter]*, published by the veterans' society of the same name, with an introduction by Dušan Biber (pp. 722–726). For the Dakota, see note 80. Maclean's representative was Captain D.E. Davies who had been ordered to replace another Allied liaison officer at Ninth Corps headquarters, the less than suitable Neville Darewski (note 36). Unfortunately, Davies, who was outranked by Wilkinson and Hesketh-Prichard, was a "pretty ineffectual officer", at least according to Wilkinson's recollection of him, and had a rough go during his stay in the region.

12. For the origin of the term "national liberation struggle in a non-Slovene, albeit entirely Communist framework, see Milovan Djilas, *Wartime: With Tito and the Partisans* (London:Secker and Warburg, 1977). Djilas is likewise useful (pp. 333–4) for understanding the intensely nationalist character of the OF. (The Communists were **allegedly** not as strongly involved in the quasi-parliamentary OF before Hitler's invasion of the USSR as they were afterward; Dmitrij Rupel, "The

Heresy of Edvard Kocbek", *Slovene Studies*, 10 [1988], No. 1, pp. 52-53.) The present writer's statement about the military character of the Slovene resistance is supported by the observations of wartime Allied liaison officers, the best analysis being Wilkinson's memorandum. Also see Djilas (pp. 338-9) for the strange dichotomy between the fervent nature of Slovene patriotism and the intelligentsia's enthusiasm for the anti-fascist war on the one hand and the SNLA's relatively weak numbers on the other. The standard history of the Slovene partisan host is *Narodnoosvobodilna vojna na Slovenskem* (Ljubljana: Vojaški zgodovinski Inštitut ljudske armade in Inštitut za zgodovino delavskega gibanja v Ljubljani, 1976). It should be noted that two officer-veterans of the Spanish Civil War, Franc Rozman-Stane (vide infra, p.? and note 43) and Aleš Bebler knew a great deal about guerrilla fighting and played crucial roles in organizing the SNLA. For the YNLA as a regular force, see Walter Laqueur, *Guerrilla* (London: Weidenfeld and Nicholson, 1977), pp. 214-220. The last quotation stems from a report of Wilkinson's adjutant, Sir Charles Villiers; see note 23.

13. The term "Gail valley" is sometimes used in the sole context of its strategically crucial lowermost segment, namely, the 18 kilometer stretch between Arnoldstein/Podkloster and the river's confluence with the Drau/Drava near Villach/Beljak. Andreas Moritsch reports mention of partisan activity in the gendarmerie records of his home community of St. Stefan an der Gail/ Sv. Štefan na Zili. This was doubtlessly tied to an attempt by the Carnian contingent of the Garibaldi-Natisone partisan division to establish contact with a minuscule group of Austro-German Wehrmacht deserters operating near Rattendorf (Walzl, 66). See also note 149.

14. Cf. T. Barker, 198-9, and notes 79 and 86.

15. Hanau, sometimes wrongly said to have used the British Legation as cover in Belgrade, was an agent of Section D of MI6, an organization which was set up just after the Anschluß. Together with the Royal Army General Staff's Section R, it provided the nucleus for the SOE, established for its part in the summer of 1940. Elizabeth Barker, *British Policy in South East Europe in the Second World War* (London: Macmillan, 1976), and Foot, 15-16. See also Tone Ferenc, *Akcije organizacije TIGR v Avstriji in Italiji spomladi 1940* (Ljubljana: Borec, 1977).

16. T. Barker, 195-8; *Pregnanstvo*, 18-40; Rausch, 11-12; and Stefan Karner, *Kärntens Wirtschaft 1938-1945 unter besonderer Berücksichtigung der Rüstungsindustrie mit einem Nachwort von Albert Speer*, No. 2, "Wissenschaftliche Veröffentlichungen der Landeshauptstadt Klagenfurt" (Klagenfurt: Magistrat der Landeshauptstadt, 1976), pp. 120-7.

17. John Shy and Thomas W. Collier, "Revolutionary War" in Peter Paret, *Makers of Modern Strategy* (Princeton: Princeton University Press, 1986), pp. 815-62, esp. 839-843.

18. Karner, 15-17, analyzes this on a documentary statistical basis and Kuchar, 15-16, from a subjective vantage.

19. For Prušnik-Gašper's comments on hunting, see op. cit., 14-15, 19, 34, 126-7, 204-06, and 285 (where the author remarks that captured Italian carbines and Mannlichers would make excellent poaching weapons). The question of the gamekeepers slain by the partisans remains highly controversial. The most interesting case is that of one Hugo Urbas, evidently an assimilated native Slovene-

speaker who was shot dead at home – the *Jagdhaus* of Ebriach/Obirsko – on 12 August 1942, apparently the first instance of a partisan execution. A devoted, industrious Thurn employee and not a Nazi, he is said to have behaved contemptuously toward nationalist Slovenes and to have worked as a Gestapo informant. Radomir Luža, *The Resistance in Austria, 1938-1945* (Minneapolis: University of Minnesota Press, 84), p. 139. Whatever the precise circumstances, local Slovenes certainly had a score to settle with Urbas, who like most of his colleagues was hated both as an outsider and a *nemčur*. Prušnik-Gašper's account of his demise (p. 204) may be compared with the German nationalist side of the story in Ingomar Pust, *Roter Stern über Kärnten, 1942-1945: totgeschwiegene Tragödien* (Klagenfurt: Abwehrkämpferbund, 1984), pp. 15-17. Pust, a Villach journalist, has interviewed surviving witnesses of partisan killings. However, he also relies heavily on hearsay evidence and twists his data to serve the political purposes of the volume's sponsors. Though significant, the material must be used cum grano salis. The *Nachwort* by Valentin Einspieler, an historically trained linguistic Slovene, is a trifle less emotive; see pp. 257-9, 264-5 for the Urbas affair. Einspieler would surely have ranked as a *nemčur* during the war, and evidently other members of his extensive clan were the targets of partisan bullets. For gamekeepers as mortal enemies of the partisans, see also Fleck, 121.

20. For the partisan-OF goals, see Appendix A, 83-84; Prušnik-Gašper, pp. 17-18, 99, 134-7, 160; and *Narodnoosvobodilna vojna*, 1029-1035. Prušnik-Gašper notes inter alia that some partisans, at least initially, disliked the Communist organizers' stress upon political lessons which were also hampered by an inadequate stock of literature, a problem later remedied (vide infra, p. ?). The Thurns should not be confused with other identically named noble families. Descendants of the Bleiburg branch of an aulic dynasty of purportedly thirteenth century Italian origin which began its East European career in late medieval Bohemia and was promoted to imperial comital status in 1541, they rendered frequent service in the K.K. army in the seventeenth, eighteenth, and and nineteenth centuries and belonged to the Habsburgs' innermost, the so-called "First Society". Constantin von Constantin von Wurzbach, *Biographisches Lexikon des Kaiserthums Österreich*, Vol. 45 (Vienna:?), pp. 93-125. For the Leitgebs, see Karner, p. 267. The family's activities, beginning in 1883, culminated in 1941 with the discovery of an answer to the problem of an effective utilization of timber residues. The Leitgeb particle board factory rapidly grew into an "economic bulwark of Lower Carinthia". Surely the aristocratic Thurns, owners of vast tracts of forest land, must have been more than pleased with the achievment of their upstart neighbors.

21. "Totalitarianism at the outset is enthusiasm and conviction, only, only later does it become organization, authority, careerism." Djilas, 341. The Communists' dexterity in exploiting Slovene patriotism is well described in a report submitted by Captain D.J. Reddiford on 29 March 1944 (PRO FO 371/44251, R4986/8/692): they were able to win over many persons opposed to their sectarian political aims. For the White Guard, see note 162.

22. Luža's judicious summary analysis (op. cit., 10-16) of the Austrian resistance underlines the fact that only "a tiny minority of people of conscience" did anything (p.10). To be sure, the strength of the native NSDAP, the draft, and the use of German as the common idiom facilitated the workings of Himmler's police apparatus (p. 11). In Carinthia the chief examples of renitency were: devoutly Catholic

Legitimists who were supported by a not inconsequential number of old-fashioned, Habsburg loyalists but were crushed by 1943; Jehovah's Witnesses who were decimated; and the KPÖ which survived the war, albeit in battered condition, its nation-wide organization having also been broken up in 1943. See also Walzl, 52–58. For Prušnik-Gašper's comments, see op. cit., 164–6, 174–6, 214, 244–7, 249. The Slovene Communist leader does acknowledge logistical assistance from left-wing Carinthian Socialists, people like like Ferdinand Wedenig (vide infra, p. and note 119). The excuse of the Germanophone Communists was that they could not risk their lives in combat because of the need to resurrect the Party after the war. See also p. 35 as well as notes 10, 120 and 184.

23. The other British observer was Villiers who wrote a detailed report over his clandestine visit to Carinthia while in the Ninety Eighth General Hospital (November 1944). The document has been excised without insertion of the legally required reader notification card from PRO file FO 371/44265, R16968/8/692. (It is described as "attached" in another of the file's memos.) However, the writer has had access to the information it contains through Professor Mark Wheeler who is writing a British government-authorized history of secret Allied operations in Yugoslavia. Wilkinson's late wife, Mary Theresa, was Sir Charles' sister. The Villiers are a very old, well-known English lineage.

24. In discussion with Wilkinson.

25. "Joint Weekly Intelligence Summary, No. 2, 13 July 1945", PRO FO 371/46610, C4258/141/63; Prušnik-Gašper, 107, 121, 128, 171; and Fleck, 73–74.

26. Strle, p. 205, describes Rösener as the "the greatest hangman of Slovene people". The source of most of the data in this and the next two paragraphs is the remarkable, politically a bit ambiguous study of the Friulian Pier Arrigo Carnier, *Lo sterminio mancato: la dominazione nazista nel Veneto orientale 1943–1945* (Milan: Mursia, 1982). See also, for Globocnik, Gerald Reitlinger, *The SS: Alibi of a Nation* (New York: Viking, 1968), passim. See also Walzl, 43–5.

27. On certain occasions, although not until just after the armistice in Carinthia (vide infra, p. 70–72), the SS Police collaborated with the Waffen SS. As noted, many of the rank-and-file were not pre-1939 German citizens but Alsatians, Lorrainers, other ethnic Germans (including the Seventeenth Regiment which was sent to Slovenia from Russia), and various non-European European collaborationists. The Nazi troops trained and worked in tandem not only with the *domobranci* but with all other quisling forces such as the Ustashi. François Duprat, *Histoire des SS* (Paris: Les Sept Couleurs, 1968), pp. 181–2. The best overall survey of Himmler's fiefdoms is Robert Lewis Koehl, *The Black Corps: The Structure and Power Struggles of the Nazi SS* (Madison: University of Wisconsin Press, 1983). A useful SS organizational chart will be found in Heinz Höhne's rather anecdotal volume, *The Order of the Death's Head* (London: Secker and Warburg, 1969). See also George Stein, *Geschichte der Waffen SS* (Göttingen: Musterschmidt Verlag, 1970), and W. Victor Madej, *Hitler's Elite Guards: Waffen SS, Parachutists, U-Boats* (Allentown, Pa: Game Publishing Co., 1985). The latter book, although intended for military history buffs and literally pasted together, reproduces rare, informative wartime handbooks and other materials collected just after hostilities had ended. For Globocnik's mélange of forces, cf. Walzl, 103–4.

28. Rausch, 15–27, passim. The Replacement Army, which had an important role in the abortive 20 July 1944 plot against Hitler's life and regime, was regularly

used to combat the European resistance as a form of on-the-job training. This was a dangerous apprenticeship for men who were not prime physical or intellectual specimens. See Madej, *German Army Order of Battle: the Replacement Army, 1935-1945* (Allentown, Pa: Game Publishing CO., 1984), esp. p.18.

29. Rausch, 15-27, passim, and Karner, 42-3. For the Loibl pass tunnel, see Walzl, 48-52.

30. France Škerl, "Koroška v borbi za svobodo", *Koroški Zbornik* (Ljubljana: Matica Slovenska, 1946), pp. 534-7 and Rausch, 102-3.

31. Ibid., 31; Pust, 241; and *Pregnanstvo*, 53, 59. For the *Jagdkommandos*, vide infra, p. 31, and note 142.

32. See Appendix A, 89.

33. *Pregnanstvo*, 53-4, 62; Rausch, 27-8; and Prušnik-Gašper, 45-6. Other organizers came from Upper Carniola in January of 1943 in order to assist Verdnik-Tomaž. The name Rosental does not derive from the words for "rose" or "flower" but, most likely from the medieval counts of Rosen.

34. *Pregnanstvo*, Rausch, idem; Prušnik-Gašper, 130; and Karner, 232-5. Karner, 106-111, also treats the relative status of the the slave-workers and the POW's. without whom Carinthia's wartime economy could not have functioned. The former were marginally better-off. See also note 156.

35. PRO FO 371/44251, R4834; cf. *Narodnoosvobodilna vojna*, 501-511.

36. Rausch, 9, 29, and Škerl, 523; PRO FO 371/44255, R7125/G/82; and in discussion with Wilkinson. Jones, an aficionado of the partisans' revolutionary schemes, hastened to write a gushing, self-justifying account of his experiences, *Twelve Months with Tito's Partisans* (Bedford [U.K.]: Bedford Books Ltd, 1946). His radiograms preserved in the PRO, though not to be taken at face value, are nevertheless revelatory. On 1 August 1943 he signalled his superiors that "you inspire us with no confidence; three old Liberators no damned use for this job; Partizan mentality not to be played with. We are pro-Partizan to the extent that we are pro-British; for God's sake be British" (PRO WO 202/436). His relationship with a fellow liaison officer, the Polish Jewish-descended Major Neville Darewski whose post at Cerkno with the Ninth Corps was called "Livingstone" (and later "Crayon"), was notably bad. The probable reason was that Darewski, who had been dropped into to contact local Chetniks (see note 162), did not share his zeal for Communist objectives. There is a documentary trail rendolent of intrigue in the PRO (WO 206/276). In all events, Jones had to be ordered not to meddle in politics: "HMG will not commit themselves in any way about frontiers. Yours 4 of 11. You should avoid all discussion of this subject and explain that you are simply concerned with military matters" (PRO WO 202/389). The difference in nationality and social outlook certainly also predisposed Wilkinson against Jones. The Slovene view has naturally been more positive; cf. *Narodnoosvobodilna vojna*, 485-6, 559. See also Dušan Biber, "Le missioni alleate nel Litorale Sloveno (1943-1945)", *Resistenza e questione nazionale, Atti del convegno "Problemi di storia della Resistenza in Friuli, 5-6-7 Novembre 1981"* (Udine: Del Bianco Editore [Istituto Friulano per la storia del Movimiento di Liberazione), pp. 303-19; and _____, "Zavezniške misije v Slovenskem Primorju", *Borec*, XXXV (1983), pp. 501-511. Jones was not the only left-winger in Yugoslavia, indeed he had been preceeded, at Lika in Croatia, by a group of Slavic Canadians with similar views. Cf. Hans Knoll, *Jugoslawien in Strategie und Politik der Alliierten 1940-1943*

(Munich: R. Oldenbourg Verlag, 1986), pp. 629-630.
37. Villiers, loc. cit. (note 23); Rausch, 29-30; and Dušan Pirjevec-Ahac, "Vojni napori koroških Slovencev v drugi svetovni vojni" in *Kolendar Osvobodilne Fronte Slovenije 1947* (Ljubljana: 1946), pp. 41-45.
38. Prušnik-Gašper, 46-54; Pust-Einspieler, 248-52, 259-69; *Fregnanstvo*, 52, 59-60; and Rausch, 30-1. Prušnik-Gašper had lost touch with the KPÖ which had left many of its followers disillusioned after the Nazi-Soviet Pact of 1939. The emergence of a Yugoslav alternative must have seemed a godserd to left-wing, nationalist Carinthian Slovenes. One of the first acts of Županc and Mrhar was the assassination of the Thurns' gamewarden, Urbas (note 19).
39. Prušnik-Gašper, 53-74; *Pregnanstvo*, 52, 60; Pust-Einspieler, 271-3; and Rausch, 31.
40. Idem and Prušnik-Gašper, 19, 58ff, 99.
41. Pust-Einspieler, 265-6, 270-1, and Prušnik-Gašper, 90-91 93. Only half of the victims were from Zell. One was a Ferlach gunsmith.
42. Ibid, 77, 106-107; Rausch, 31-2; and Pust, 17-19.
43. Prušnik-Gašper, 84-90; Pust, 19-21; Rausch, 32-3; and Kuchar, 26 ff. Rozman-Stane was killed in a firearms accident in November in November of 1944. Prušnik-Gašper, 215; see also note 12.
44. Rausch, 33. For the Leitgebs, see note 20.
45. Prušnik-Gašper, 93 ff; Rausch, 33-4; *Pregnanstvo*, 53, 61-2; and Pust-Einspieler, 283-4.
46. Cf. T. Barker, 150-3, 178 ff., and note 136. (The *Heimatdienst* was known as the *Heimatbund* as of 1924.)
47. Vide infra, note 19.
48. (Borovlje/Ferlach-Celovec/Klagenfurt: Založba Drava, 1981-1982). Polanšek, who weaves in much factual material and judges the the partisans harshly for their excesses manifests a strong revulsion for civil strife and a sense of humanity totally absent in Pust. (The critique has been proviced by Andreas Moritsch.)
49. Rausch, 34-5, and Karner, passim.
50. Rausch, 36, and Prušnik-Gašper, 109-24.
51. Rausch, 36-7, and Prušnik-Gašper, 138-9.
52. In discussion with Wilkinson. Although he lacked the technical expertise and backup facilities of the Clowder Mission, Jones notes on the first page of his book that "seeking cooperation in the destruction of military objects, such as railways, which would hinder the movement of enemy troops and supplies" was major feature of his work, a statement that is in accord with Yugoslav data on the subject. Wilkinson observes that interdiction of the rail route across the Karst would have been an equally appropriate and certainly more feasible enterprise although the dreamer Jones could not have helped the SNLA in any material way there either. See also note 36. Prušnik-Gašper, pp. 144-5, ignores the British role altogther.
53. *Narodnoosvobodilna vojna*, 687-98.
54. In discussion with Wilkinson. See also Howarth, 21-3. For the very limited armed resistance (three lesser exchanges of fire) of the left-wing German Styrian partisans - one of only two militarily active ÖFF groups in what was to be postwar Austria - see Max Muchitsch, *Die Partisanengruppe Leoben-Donawitz* (Vienna:

Europa Verlag, 1966). In this case the Gestapo and other Nazi agencies were even more effective in combatting the partisans, who barely survived the winter of 1944-45 hiding in the woods, than in Carinthia. The absence of the ethnic factor surely had much to do with this. See also notes 10 and 113. The only other case of an Austro-German group using guns against the Nazis inside the country (as opposed to having a direct, physical tie with the SNLA) was the largely ineffective "O.5" organization, a middle-class, Catholic-flavored group that operated mainly in Vienna and Innsbruck with the assistance of adherents inside the Wehrmacht (cf. Otto Molden, *Ruf des Gewissens: der österreichische Freheitskampf 1938-1945* [Vienna: Herold, 1958]). However, there was a third, unique case: Wilkinson assembled a yet another party of indigenous subversives who, penetrating a part of the country that was apparently not as pro-Nazi as Carinthia, were modestly successful. The Clowder Mission dropped Albrecht Gaiswinkler into the Salzkammergut on 8-9 April. With the help of a locally recruited band of supporters, he took over part of the Bad Aussee area as the war drew to a close. PRO FO 371/46611, C48833. With one other (unlucky) exception, Gaiswinkler was the only good "Austrian" agent Wilkinson disposed of; see p. 36. For the Carinthian German Communists, see Walzl, 59-65.

55. Rausch, 37-39, and Prušnik-Gašper, 151-161. For the *Kampfgruppe "Avantgarde" Steiermark*, which left Črnomelj on 7 August, see note 10. Wilkinson's view of the Eastern Carinthian *Odred* is less flattering than the author's. Clowder's ex-boss considers it to have been a band of "village boys" and "old men" following a "way of life"; since it was "not looking for trouble", it rarely engaged in combat.

56. Prušnik-Gašper, 145 (death of Verdnik-Tomaž); Rausch and Villiers, loc. cit.

57. Idem, both.

58. Villiers, loc. cit., and Prušnik-Gašper, 102-4, 141-3. See also note 142.

59. Prušnik-Gašper, note 45, pp. 307-8 (Ribičič's detailed report on the incident to his superiors); Villiers, loc. cit.; and Wilkinson in discussion. For the ISLD, see Nigel West, *MI-6: British Secret Intelligence Service Operations, 1909-1945* (London: Weidenfeld and Nicholson, 1983), passim. Ribičič's account mentions not only forthcoming supply drops but also plans, never apparently realized, for an RAF-assisted attack on a chemical plant in the western Carinthian sector.

60. Villiers, loc. cit.; Foot, 75-9; and Howarth, 2, 21, 24-5. Wilkinson doubts that the Clowder Mission supplied the Carinthian Slovene partisans with any of the superlative Bren light machine guns or trusty old Lee-Enfields (both .303 caliber) that were otherwise provided in liberal quantities to the SNLA.

61. Idem; Prušnik-Gašper, 191-2; and Rausch, 57-8. A total of 49,003 Sten guns was delivered to the YNLA (inventory of equipment of equipment delivered by the British in PRO FO WO/1357); see also note 80.

62. Prušnik-Gašper, 190-2; Howarth, 27; and Villiers, loc.

63. Luža, 197-8; Prušnik-Gašper, 255-655; Walzl, 58-65 and T. Barker, 227,229f, 232-5, 357n72, and 361n117. Walzl also gives a good account (pp. 52-55) of the fierce Nazi repression of **all** persons suspected of not sympathising with the régime (as opposed to resisting it actively) and believes that the exact number of executions, possibly as many as 1000, will never be known. For the KPÖ, see also notes 22 and 184.

64. Villiers, loc. cit., and according to Wilkinson. The BAF was "chagrined"

that Clowder did not discuss policy with them. See note 54 for agents and note 81 for aircraft.
  65. PRO FO 371/ 44264, R16049/8/92
  66. Idem; Jones, 57; and PRO FO 371/44265, R1753/8/92. For attitudes within the Slovene Communist Party leadership see Dušan Biber, "Jugoslovanska in britanska politika o koroškem uprašanju 1941 – 1945," *Zgodovinski Časopis,* XXXIII (1979), pp. 127 – 143. Although on balance the Foreign Office objected to the SOE's caper – even south of the Drau – Colonel Roger Thornley of the SOE's German Section managed to persuade Harrison that Wilkinson might be right after all. PRO FO 371/44265, R16968/8/92. Broad's chief informant, via Maclean, was Major Franklin A.Lindsay, U.S.A. (vide infra, 51 and 118 – 140)
  67. PRO FO 371/44265, R1753/8/92 and Villiers, loc. cit. See also Dušan Biber, "Britanske misije o slovenskih etničnih mejah", *Borec*, 1984, pp. 574 – 6, and (Villiers) "Spomenice o slovenskih manšinaj v Južni Avstriji in Severozahodni Italiji", ibid, 577 – 583.
  68. Stafford, 190 – 1, 195. See also pp. 8, 28, 74, and note 149.
  69. Appendix C, 141 – 145.
  70. In a memo dated 16 January 1945 (PRO WO/1953) Villiers sought to sought to redefine the Clowder Mission's goals. He refers to the flabbiness of "Austrian" resistance, the Communist effort to gain control of it, the SOE's accumulated expertise in frontier matters which would be useful at the war's end, and the probability that the SNLA would try to grab Carinthia then. He likewise points out the danger of a Carinthian Slovene EAM (*Ethnikon apeleftherotikon metopon* = National Liberation Front), obviously having been impressed by Britain's very recent military repression (December) of the Communist-dominated Greek guerrillas. This rethinking was preceded by a Wilkinson memo (idem) which discounted earlier plans to organize resistance in Austria prior to a putative German military defeat only on the Western Front and a consequent weakening or collapse of civil authority ("Rankin 'B' and 'C' Situations"). In the context of Hitler's Ardennes Offensive (Battle of the Bulge) this now appeared unlikely. Seasonal and aircraft limitations also made it impossible to stimulate resistance inside Austria even if there proved to be a genuine potential for it Aid to unorganized regime opponents in the last stage of the war under "Rankin 'B' or 'C'" conditions (taken as simultaneous, overall military defeat and civil collapse) would serve no purpose.
  71. PRO FO 371/44265, R1696/8/92, and Rausch, 43, 44 – 7.
  72. Prušnik-Gašper, 148 – 50. It is unclear whether the Germans were "Greens" as Prušnik-Gašper records or Territorial Riflemen as Pust argues (pp. 64 – 6). The Nazi column's failure to exercise the tactical security required by guerrilla operations suggests that the latter version is the correct one. Rausch's account of the July fighting in the High Obir area (p. 47) does not resolve the problem.
  73. Vide infra, p. 78.
  74. Rausch, 49 – 53.
  75. Ibid., 53 – 56.
  76. Ibid., 56 – 61, and Prušnik-Gašper, 186 – 9. For the White Guard, see note 162.
  77. Ibid., 192 – 193, and Rausch, 64 – 65. Rausch surmises that Slovene headquarters was unimpressed with the achievments of the now numerically much stronger

Carinthian *odredi* and/or believed that their prospects were no longer as good as they had been at the beginning of the summer. Villiers reported that the Saualpe detachment counted "about a 100 men". PRO WO 204/1953.

78. Kuchar, 51-65; *Ljudska Pravica* (Ljubljana), 20 July 1947; and indictment of Friedrich Rainer et alia, court-martial of the Fourth Yugoslav Army, archive of the *Institut za zgodovino delavskega gibanja* (Ljubljana), p.a., fasc. 924/I. I am endebted to Dušan Biber and Tone Ferenc for the provision of this material.

79. Cf. Malte Olschewski, "Die psychologische Kriegsführung und Propaganda der Titopartisanen in Kärnten und Slowenien", ph.d. dissertation, University of Vienna, 1966.

80. Rausch, 71-6.

81. In discussion with Wilkinson; Prušnik-Gašper, 170-1, 186; and Kuchar, 68-9. The problem of deliveries to smaller, more clandestine resistance groups was that there were not enough of the RAF Special Flight crews to go around. (Since they were so sophisticated, it was a shame, according to Wilkinson, to use them for mass supply drops to the regular units of the YNLA.) The difficulty was compounded after SOE activities in the Mediterranean came under AFHQ's command and hence under the Balkan Air Force in July of 1944. There was no longer any way of supervising custom packaging of stores for subversive missions; loads became standardized for the sorties to Bosnia. As noted on pp. 36-37, Clowder was also forced on occasion to rely upon regular BAF crews, untrained for the delicate job in question.

82. Prušnik-Gašper, 242-3; William Deakin, *The Embattled Mountain* (London: Oxford University Press, 1972), pp. 38-9; and Djilas, 402-3. The crypto-Nazi apologist Pust (op. cit., 112-17) alleges that in Carinthia crippled and captive guerrillas were well treated but that German wounded and prisoners were dispatched as a matter of course. Certainly, the Nazis, disposing of vastly superior medical facilities in Klagenfurt and Villach, could treat wounded foes much more readily than the partisans. Moreover, to save the lives of guerrillas who had fallen into their hands was an eminently rational thing to do from an intelligence-gathering perspective: heal the captives, and then let the Gestapo or the SD minister to them. However, there were also instances of the torture and killing of partisan wounded and prisoners. Cf. Prušnik-Gašper, 247-8, 267-9, and Kuhar, 66-7. Deakin notes that in Yugoslavia the partisans at least spared collaborationist women and children while Djilas (p. 285) suggests that German behavior, while barbarous overall as a policy matter, depended upon the individual officer's personality.

83. Prušnik-Gašper, 267. For atrocities see, note 143.

84. Stafford, 189; PRO FO 371/44264, R16049/8/92; and information from Lindsay.

85. Prušnik-Gašper, 222.

86. Ibid., 200; Foot, 108-111, 124-5; and Wilkinson in discussion.

87. Karner, 194-5; Prušnik-Gašper, 199ff, 218-9; Rausch, 67; Pust, 82-5; and Fleck, 288-90 (reprints contemporary, confidential Nazi report, emphasizing the gravity of the mine's destruction.) See note 10 for the *Kampfgruppe "Avantgarde" Steiermark.*

88. Ibid., 68, and Prušnik-Gašper, 205-7, 228-32.

89. PRO WO 204/1953.

90. Pust, 67-8; Prušnik-Gašper, 214-217, 222-227.
91. In a message dated 23 November Maclean reported that the order was based upon a misunderstanding probably due to Tito's momentary absence from headquarters. PRO FO 371/44266, R19143/8/92. See also PRO FO 371/44267, R19380/8/92. The real problem was the presence of the OSS McDowell Mission at Mihailović's headquarters. Cf. Dušan Biber, "The Yugoslav Partisans and the British in 1944" in: William Deakin, Elizabeth Barker, and Jonathan Chadwick, *British Political and Military Strategy in Central, Eastern and Southern Europe in 1944* (London: Macmillan Press, 1988), pp. 111-129, esp. 122.
92. Howarth, 26-8.
93. Ibid, 28. Rumors circulated in Ljubljana after the war that a particular individual, now dead, made the decision to do away with Hesketh-Prichard, but, as there is no hard evidence of any kind and probably never will be, the name cannot be given.
94. Pust, 79-80, and Rausch, note 189, pp. 98-9.
95. Prušnik-Gašper 233; Rausch, 68-71; and according to Wilkinson.
96. See Appendix B, 131-132. The United States National Archives contain certain materials about the OSS penetration of Carinthia and Austria. In the former instance, the effort does not appear to have had any practical effect other than the collection of not unduly important tactical intelligence, especially from the British vantage (see note 121). The writer seriously doubts the claim of the author of the May 1945 monthly report of Headquarters, Detachment A, 2677th Regiment (OSS) [NA Records Administration, Record Group 26, Entry 99, Box 25, File 121] that the Dillon Mission was "able to play a major role in the liberation of Klagenfurt from the Germans" in light of the lack of corroborating evidence from any other primary or secondary source. Cf. note 121. However, another document of considerable interest, if not for Carinthia at least for Slovenia proper, is the report of the later Minnesota Congressman, the Slovene-descended John Blatnik, who coordinated the evacuation of downed Allied fliers rescued by the SNLA (NARA, RG 226, Entry 154, Box 25, Folder 348). It has been published in Slovene translation by Dušan Biber: "Doslej neznani ameriški viri: Poročilo Kapetana Johna Blatnik o službovanju v Jugoslaviji (na Hrvatškem in v Sloveniji) od augusta do septembra in od novembra 1944 do maja 1945," *Borec*, XL (1988), pp. 199-211.
97. According to Peter Kuchar. See also note 155.
98. PRO WO 202/309. The author, who describes himself as an American of Serbian descent, was evidently George Vuchinich (a veritable disaster and a full-blown Communist according to Wilkinson and Lindsay) rather than Professor Wayne Vuchinich or his brother, Alex, both of whom also served with the OSS in Slovenia. Cf. Appendix B, 137. Three other reports, including one on Carinthia, are missing from the file.
99. PRO FO 371/48811, R5717/6/92, and Fitzroy Maclean, *Eastern Approaches* (London: Macmillan, 1949), pp. 425-6, 470-1, and 489-516.
100. PRO WO 202/520. Cf. *Narodnoosvobodilna vojna*, 728f. John Phillips of *Life Magazine* accompanied the partisans during an action at Litija on 19-23 September 1944, carried out with the assistance of Goodwin (who was wounded) and Allied tactical air support. For Phillip's overenthusiastic report, including vivid photographs, see *Life*, 6 November 1944. Cf. NARA, RG 226, E99, B, 21, F. ("Report of Capt. James M. Goodwin"). The raid in question, in which there

were numerous casualties on both sides, was only partly successful because the Yugoslav commander was killed at a critical juncture. See also note 168.
101. PRO FO 371/48811, R5717/G/92. The official Slovene history speaks of a "mobile defense (*manervska obramba*)" of liberated territory and treats the matter as the outstanding strategic problem of the war. *Narodnoosvobodilna vojna*, 771 ff, 1027-9; see also Appendix B, 120. Of course political considerations always underly strategy, and thus it might be appropriate to apply the more refined professional concept of "national strategy".
102. PRO FO 371/48823, R12899/6/92. The author has discussed this problem with Dušan Biber and Tone Ferenc. See also note 101.
103. PRO FO 371/48811, R5717 (a gloss on the back of the folder).
104. Deakin, esp.. p. 265; Basil Davidson, *Special Operations Europe: Scenes from the Anti-Nazi War* (London: Victor Gollancz, 1980), pp. 56, 57, 154, 155, and 166-7 (Grafton paperback edition); Howarth, 83-4, 90-1, 94-5, 109, 227, 236; and Biber, "Jugoslovanska in britanska politika". For the BAF, see Michael McConville, *A Small War in the Balkans British Military Involvement in Wartime Yugoslavia*, 1941-1945 (London: Macmillan, 1986), pp. 265-72; and note 80. For the ÖFF, Luža, 196-7, Prušnik-Gašper, 255 ff; and Wilkinson in discussion. See also note 113. One may safely posit that Tito's strong support of Slovene irredentism since September of 1944 was dictated by domestic political considerations: a united, federal Yugoslavia would surely require a Slovenia which believed that its particular aspirations had been met or at least that a major effort had been made on its behalf.
105. PRO FO 371/48813, R7964/6/92. The document was drafted by Mr. Hood of the Southern Department.
106. In a telegram to Secretary of State Edward R. Stettinius (PRO FO 371/48813, R5717/6/92). The prime minister, who added that he had never trusted Tito "since he levanted from [the island of] Vis [in September of 1944]", placed the matter in the hands of the chiefs of staff. On May 2 he had to insist that the aid "should dwindle and die without another moment's delay", but the corresponding instruction was transmitted to Eisenhower and Alexander only five days later. The truth of the matter was that the Mediterranean theater commander, not disillusioned by his supposed friend Tito until the Trieste crisis was actually underway, had been bucking the decision. PRO 371/48812, R6708/6/692 (minute of M. Addis, 19 April); and FO 371/48813, R7964/6/42, Annex (letter of Sir Orme Sargent 23 April). The many materials in PRO WO 204/1357 remove any doubt about Tito's absolutely desperate logistical straits. For Allied aid to the Slovenes, see *Narodnoosvobodilna vojna*, 929-923; and note 110. For the dealings between the British and Yugoslav leaders, see Dušan Biber (ed.), *Tito-Churchill, Strogo tajno* (Belgrade: Globus, 1981).
107. The standard works are: Karl Hnilička, *Das Ende auf dem Balkan: die militarische Räumung Jugoslawiens durch die Deutsche Wehrmacht* (Göttingen: Musterschmidt Verlag, 1970); and Erich Schmidt-Richberg, *Das Ende auf dem Balkan: die Operationen der Heeresgruppe E von Griechenland bis zu den Alpen* (Heidelberg: Kurt Vowinckel Verlag, 1955). Both authors barely conceal their emotions and justify the tenacious German effort in terms of saving Carinthia and the Western world from the Red menace. Hnilička is good for the harsh fate of the 150-175,000 German troops who had to surrender inside Yugoslavia. At least

a third of them perished in one way or another, 10,000 on a Bataan-style death march alone. Obviously, the Yugoslavs were ill-disposed to share their less than meager food stocks with individuals who so recently had been ravishing their homeland. For the Austrian flavor of the Army Group's staff, see Schmidt-Richberg, pp. 155 – 6. For Yugoslav literature, see Tone Ferenc, "Predaja nemške vojske iz jugovzhodne Evrope" in Dušan Biber (ed.), *Konec druge svetovne vojne v Jugoslavji (Četrta okrogla miza jugoslovanskih in britanskih zgodovenarjev, Brdo pri Kranju, 9. do 11. decembra 1985)*, special issue (38) of "Borec", 2 (XXXVIII [1986]), 38, p. 807.

108. Treated by Ferenc and others in idem.

109. Strle, 442 – 3. For the creation, by the Western Allies, of a modicum of Slovene and Yugoslav artillery, armored, and flying units, cf. *Narodnoosvobodilna vojna*, 799 – 815.

110. Troop strengths can only be estimated on the basis of the theoretical size of the contingents in question. The various unit war diaries in the PRO WO file series contain monthly figures which indicate that the flow of replacements at this time was quite steady. For the interrelationship of the Carinthian and Trieste crises, a topic which unfortunately cannot be treated in depth within the limits set for this study, see William Jackson and T.P. Gleave, *The Mediterranecn and Middle East*, Vol. VI, Pt. III, "History of the Second World War" (London: Her Majesty's Stationery Office, 1988), pp. 336 – 349. The Dalmatian operation, which began on 19 March, is treated in the preceeding section of the book.

111. Created in 1943 and manned with Polish Ruthenian volunteers, this division was pulverized in the battle of Brody (July 1944). A few survivors fled to remote terrain and broke out of Eastern Europe via Czechoslovakia as late as 1947. Other Ruthenes, drawn from SS police regiments, were used to reconstitute the original formation. Not having been used against the Soviets and at full strength, it was sent to Lower Styria to fight the SNLA in April of 1945. After withdrawing to Austrian Styria and Carinthia – a few of of its soldiers deserted to the partisans in order to save their skins – it surrendered to the British. The latter, encouraged by General Wladyslaw Anders, commander of the Polish Corps serving with the Allies in Italy, accepted the providential argument that their prisoners were Polish citizens and did not repatriate them. The bulk of the unit ended up emigrating to Great Britain and the United States. Roger James Bender, *Uniforms, Organization and History of the Waffen SS*, Vol. 4 (San Jose: R.J. Bender Publishing Co., 1975), pp, 6 – 52; Duprat, 355 – 7; Rausch, 71; Walzl, 185; and PRO FO 371/48818, R9137 (size of contingent captured in Carinthia; reunion with the other detachments, some of which had been fighting the Koralpen partisans [note 10], doubled the number of surrendered personnel).

112. For the *Alpenfestung*, see Manfred Rauchensteiner, *Krieg in Österreich* (Wien: Österreichischer Bundesverlag, 1970), Vol. 5, "Schriften des Heeresgeschichtlichen Museums in Wien", pp. 239 – 44; and Walzl, 93 – 96. To say that the *Alpenfestung* was illusory and that the barriers in Carinthia were makeshift does not mean that substantial effort was not expended on the project of regional defenses, especially if one takes Istria, the Littoral, and Friulia into account.

113. Rausch, 71, 76 – 7, and Appendix F, 172. One of the two Austrian battalions serving in Slovenia suffered heavy battle casualties and was riven by dissention between Communists and non-Communists. The SNLA refused to

provide replacements, kept a close watch on the survivors, and valued the unit mainly for propaganda purposes. Report of W.S. Pears, RA, April 4, 1945 (PRO WO 202/309). Altogther there were five such contingents in Yugoslavia. Some of their members ended up in the Vienna police force and constituted a potential Soviet fifth column. Cf. Willibald Ingo Holzer, *Die Kommunistische Partei Österreichs im militanten politischen Widerstand: die österreichischen Bataillone im Verband der NOV i POJ, die Kampfgruppe Avantgarde/Steiermark, die Partisanengruppe Leoben-Donawitz*, University of Vienna Ph.D. thesis, 1972.

114. See note 82. There were 3700 ex-German-led Hungrian troops in Carinthia after the armistice. Under the command of a Lieutenant General Imre Kálmán, they had been largely disarmed by the Germans after their transfer from Hungary. Another 10,000, who did have weapons, were said to have just entered or to be on their way. PRO WO 202/387. The author's good friend, the eminent Hungarian historian Géza Perjés, was one of them. Many brought their families, some returned to their homes, and others were allowed to emigrate abroad.

115. Rausch, 77-8; Prušnik-Gašper, 265-7, 278-80; and Instituto Croata de Cultura, *La Tragedia de Bleiburg: documentos sobre las matanzas de los croatas en Yugoslavia comunista en 1945. Suplementos: La Tragedia del pueblo esloveno, Exterminio y expulsión de la minoría alemana de Yugoslavia* (Buenos Aires: "Studia Croatica", 1963), p. 180. "Rupnik fue depuesto y despojado de todos los cargos, inclusive del mando militar; con ello se echó por tierra todos los planes para ofrecer la última resistencia con el fin de conseguir la intervención de los Aliados occidentales." The quisling leader was later executed by the Communist régime, having been handed over by the British.

116. Claudia Fräss-Ehrfeld, "Kärnten 1945 – vor Neubeginn und Bewältigung", *Österreich in Geschichte und Literatur*, 20 (1976), pp. 100-9, esp. 100-2; and Walzl, 127-8, 132-3. Walzl questions whether the bluff was really effective and suggests that a mutual desire to avoid further bloodshed was the chief factor. In all events, Noedelchen's forces, concentrated at Maria Saal were among the last (June 6) to be disbanded and sent home to Germany by the British. War Diary, Sixth Armored Division, June 1945 (PRO WO 170/4337). See also Luža, 264-5.

117. Rausch, 70, 78-9, and Prušnik-Gašper, 278. Accounts of the massacre conflict. Cf. Prušnik-Gašper, 271-7, and Pust, 107-11. Both seem tendentious.

118. In discussion with Wilkinson; Strle, 86-111; PRO WO 204/1358 (Eighth Army to Fifteenth Army Group 8 May). The British furnished the Yugoslavs altogether 103 light Stuart tanks, 26 armored cars and 525 miscellaneous vehicles. FO WO 204/1357. This was of course a mere drop in the bucket with respect to developing an effective armored force.

119. In discussion with Wilkinson; PRO FO 371/4611, C48833; Fräß-Ehrfeld, 101-2; Wilhelm Wadl, *Das Jahr 1945 in Kärnten: Ein Überblick* (Klagenfurt: Verlag des Kärntner Landesarchivs, 1985) [especially given to terminological hyperbole]; and Walzl, 125-151. For the Miles Mission, see T. Barker, passim. For Piesch, ibid., 208, and Robert Edward Herzstein, *Waldheim: The Missing Years* (New York: Morrow, 1988), 178-80. Walzl (p. 135) maintains that it was Noedelchen who pressured Rainer into empowering Natmeßnig to commence discussions with the "democratic" faction, whereas Special Force Six reported that the Church was the prime mover (see Appendix H, 186): neither possibility of course excludes the

other. Three other points made by Walzl (loc. cit.) should also be noted: (1) the non-Nazi German nationalists were the first to discuss taking steps in order to adjust to changing circumstances; (2) the first five persons ("die Fünf der ersten Stunde", i.e., Schatzmayer, Herke, Grossauer, Leer, and Santer) who dealt with Rainer did undergo a certain personal risk even though they were accompanied by Natmeßnig; and (3) the Socialist Karl Newole, a decent and principled individual whom the present author met years ago, played an important behind-the-scenes role. It should also be observed that the chief dilemma of the Germanophone leftists including certain Communists (whom Newole insisted upon adding to the new government, presumably as a necessary window dressing) was that they were one with the Nazis and other Carinthian political groupings in opposing the cession of the southeastern part of the province to Yugoslavia. Prušnik-Gašper's remarks about the inefficacy of the non-Slovene Marxist opposition and the implied charge that it was pusillanimous (op. cit., 176, 214) ought to be viewed against this background as he himself indirectly recognized. For direct collaboration with the partisans, Luža, 196; and for the KPÖ, p. 35 as well as notes 22 and 184. For the non-Communist politicians, see the Appendix H, 188-190.

120. Walzl, 118, 281 (for Globocnik). Though Walzl, has done much to clarify the day-to-day course of events in Carinthia in the period 1944-1945, he often lets himself be carried away by a rigid anti-Communist or "Tolstoyan" (note 149) mind-set. Totally misconstruing a British account (Frank Donnison, *Civil Affairs and Military Government in North-West Europe, 1944-1946* [London: Hasso, 1961], p. 287 ff), he asserts (p. 97) that the Fifth Corps worked hand in glove with the Yugoslavs as it pushed northward from Udine. This flatly contradicts the war diaries and all other files in the PRO which leave not the slightest doubt that the relationship was extremely tense and required the Tommies to combine firmness with the maximum degree of tact. (Cf. Appendix G, 174-7.) Further on (p. 109) Walzl alleges that the the British "hesitated exclusively in order to accommodate their Yugoslav ally". The charge is repeated on pages 168-9 and 173, albeit a bit equivocally since he now says (p. 173) that one may "surely *assume*" (author's Italics) that the advance was deliberately delayed to suit Tito's interests. A related, also documentarily groundless claim (pp. 114, 174, 321-2), although Walzl is perhaps less categorical about it than Wadl (op. cit., pp. 26-28), has to do with the delegation of civilians dispatched to Mauthen and the adjacent Plöcken pass by the would-be government in Klagenfurt. It is said to have been responsible for persuading a supposedly cataleptic Fifth Corps to resume its stalled march to Klagenfurt. Blithely ignoring fundamental strategic and geographic logic, Walzl also declares (p. 174) Major General Robert K. Arbuthnot's Seventy Eighth "Battle-Axe" Divsion (a mechanized infantry formation!), rather than Major General Horatius Murray's Sixth Armoured at Tarvisio, to have been the "point of gravity" in Keightley's dispositions. At yet another juncture (p. 192) Walz. maintains that the British could easily have occupied southeastern, trans-Dravan Carinthia, had they so desired. This too reflects total unawareness of basic military realities. The nasty repatriation business (vide infra, 72-76) likewise offers Walzl an opportunity for rash, ideologically tinted asseverations. The Allied commanders, above all a supposedly anxiety-stricken and fainthearted Keightley, suffered from an "overfulfillment complex" (p. 222); they were in fact guilty altogether of "total observance of Soviet wishes" (p. 232). Revisionism of this sort will simply not

wash. The overall military situation from the beginning of Operation Grapeshot on 9 April must be taken into account. Moreover, the war diaries, with their huge mass of evidence, cannot be cavalierly dismissed as containing "only vague formulations" (p. 321). Two summary points may be made. Except for aircraft and matèriel, the nationally quite heterogenous Allied contingents in Italy were not especially strong, at least compared to the gigantic host on the western front, in the interests of which they had been systematically bled during late 1944 and early 1945. The regrouping and resupply necessary after crossing the Po along with acceptance of the separate surrender (29 April) of the approximately 425,000 enemy troops belonging to General Heinrich von Vietinghoff's Army Group Southwest imposed tremendous strains upon the Eighth Army and the rest of Alexander's forces. It is elemental that an advance of any kind requires prior assurance of the line of communications. As Jackson (p. 326) puts it, "bridging and logistics became the limiting factors in the final phase of the Italian campaign"; the advance was in doubt as late as 2 May because "the British were still operationally and logistically overstretched" (ibid, 339). The delay in getting to Austria, not to mention Trieste, is thus entirely comprehensible. It should be added that Wadl's claim (p. 27) that the Fifth Corps was blocked for an extended period by stubborn Nazi resistance at Gemona is errant nonsense; "the very presence of our approaching tanks caused the Germans to withdraw" (entry of 2 May, War Diary, First Derbyshire Yeomanry [PRO WO 170/4631]). The drive through Friulia was marked principally by a series of white-flag parleys, on-the-spot armistices, and voluntary pullbacks by Globocnik's and Harmel's troops, who were part of Löhr's non-capitulating Army Group E. The chief obstacle facing the Fifth Corps, which also moved up along the second axis of the Isonzo valley, were "blows", craters in the road that had to be filled in or bypassed before vehicles could proceed. The British unquestionably proceeded as rapidly as military prudence allowed them to. All that Walzl has to add to this sub-chapter of World War Two history is the fact that Löhr himself, though he was evidently aware of and tolerated the goings-on in Klagenfurt (which he permitted to be declared an open city), sought to assure continuing resistance on his far right flank until 7 May and the signing of the overall surrender (pp. 108, 117,118). This explains the behavior of the Nazi forces in Friulia which so puzzled local British intelligence officers at the time. Walzl has also illuminated other, albeit equally inconsequential Carinthian German attempts to contact the Allies (pp. 130, 132, 146, 147, and 173–4). See also notes 106 and 110. The author has discussed the Wadl-Walzl Friulian-Carnian thesis with eyewitness Wilkinson who agrees that it is inane.

121. The author has also consulted the ex-Clowder Mission's chief about Walzl's portrayal of the events of 8 May (op. cit., 181 ff). While it is true that there were various Allied agents and parachutists to be picked up in Carinthia and Styria, there is no basis at all for the German Carinthian scholar's assertion (op. cit, 109) that any of them had been acting in Yugoslavia's interest. The Crayon Mission may well have had links with left-wing Austro-German groups in Villach toward the end of the war, but there were no longer any SOE personnel with the SNLA Ninth Corps as Walzl alleges elsewhere (p. 231). Nor was there any particular need for information "since we had more material than we could use from ULTRA and other high grade sources; there was no need for agent intelligence". The course of events was "dictated by the [separate] armistice negotiations with SS

General [Karl] Wolff [speaking for Vietinghoff] and Kesselring's and Löhr's surrender [1:00 a.m. 9 May]". Wilkinson's own people, now mainly Jewish Social Democrats, were at Murau, the Zeltweg airdrome, and Mürzzuschlag. Among the other private armies" messing about at the time were "Major Popski's" crew of genial Saharan buccaneers known as the Long Range Desert Group, as well as, probably, the SAS (Special Air Service) and SIS (MI6) outfits. Cf. Vladimir Peniakoff (Popski), *Private Army* (London: Johnathon Cape, 1950). Wilkinson does not believe that his men, some of whom had radios, sent back any data of value to Renton at the Clowder Mission's base in Siena. Dropped in only several weeks earlier near Muchitsch's vestigial partisan group (note 54), they "contributed to the general confusion" but achieved little of military value". (For yet another group of not especially significant Allied agents, cf. note 96.) Finally, it may be noted that Walzl is entirely unaware of the immense importance of ULTRA, the originally Polish-conceived system of devices for deciphering messages sent via Nazi "Enigma" coding machines, in the planning of the Western Allies' military actions. His fixation upon spies sending purportedly crucial messages to AHFQ thus seems all the more simplistic.

122. In discussion with Wilkinson; PRO FO 371/48813, R8128/6/92 (Macmillan to FO 9 May); and PRO FO 371/48827, R8586/24/92 (posters). With regard to the minority's momentary sentiments, the British soon deduced that the main reason for favoring Tito had been a common hatred of Naziism. However, this element of the population was ignorant of the Communist leader's true political views, and a majority among it was averse to union with Yugoslavia. PRO FO 371/146610, C3243/141/6 (report of 18 June from Klagenfurt). The authors evidently confused linguistic and ethnic minorities and may have been influenced by semi-assimilated bilingual informants (such as Wedenig). The strongly Catholic component among the ethnic Slovenes, or at least certain individuals within it, had probably not yet quite given up the idea of joining a Communist Yugoslavia.

123. PRO FO 371/48813, R8129/6/92. The SNLA unit was the Fourteenth Shock Division's "Miloš Zidanšek" Brigade which had penetrated the Klagenfurt basin from northwest of Celje (Cilli) in Lower Styria.

124. Brigadier Anthony Cowgill, Christopher Booker, Lord Thomas Brimelow, and Brigadier Teddy Tryon-Wilson, *Interim Report on an Enquiry into the Repatriation of Surrendered Enemy Personnel to the Soviet Union and Yugoslavia from Austria in May 1945 and the Alleged "Klagenfurt Conspiracy"* (London: Royal United Service Institute for Defence Studies, 1988), pp. 8, 69. The privately funded volume, the heart of which is a selection of crucial documents based upon a massive combing of PRO files with the assistance of the Defense Ministry, removes any doubt about a "culpability" of Harold Macmillan and presents the clearest picture to date of what happened in Carinthia in May of 1945. Tryon-Wilson was a Senior Administrative Officer at Fifth Corps at the time in question.

125. PRO WO 202/319, pp. 67,69, 88; Jackson, 337, 342; Cowgill et al, 9, 71; and discussion of other documentation in ibid with Lord Brimelow, who, as Second Secretary at the Foreign Office, was concerned with the execution of the Yalta Repatriation Agreement and is now engaged in a comprehensive scholarly study of the subject.

126. PRO FO 371/48814, R8235/6/92; Tito had expressed the wish as early as February 21 to assist in the conquest of Austria with 200,000 men (PRO WO

204/1357); PRO FO 371/48814, R8290/6/92.
127. PRO FO 371/48815, R8320/6/92; and R8322/6/92. The looting of civilian property, especially cars and bicycles, was a: much a manifestation of logistical inadequacies as it was of soldiers' acquisitive greed. Another facet of the partisans' military organizational debility was a widespreasd need for medical care and the immediate utilization of civilian medical facilities (Walzl, p. 203). See also note 139. To be sure, disciplined behavior has never been a strong point of guerrilla armies, and SNLA officers, without the professional military tradition of the British army, had their hands full.
128. Loc. cit., R8354/6/92
129. Loc. cit., R8405/6/92.
130. Loc. cit., R8472/6/92; and Cowgill, 11-13.
131. Loc. cit., R8418/6/92. The total number of Axis prisoners was 278,800 (130,000 Germans [Wehrmacht], 9200 SS, 23,800 Hungarians, 72,800 Russians, and 43,000 Yugoslavs). PRO FO 371/48818, R9137/6/92. The figure does not include the 5000 Ruthenes of the Waffen SS Division "Gallizien" (note 111). The Yugoslav total evidently incorporates not only the forces that had fled from the Ljubljana basin but also the smaller proportion of Croatian collaborationists who did manage to cross the restored Austrian frontier (and were in fact more than twice as numerous than the hodge-podge of quislings from Slovenia). See also note 147.
132. Loc. cit., R8428/6/92.
133. Loc. cit., R8225/6/92; and Jackson, 345. Also personal discussion with Deakin and Maclean.
134. Loc. cit., R8358/6/92; R8548/6/92; R8656/6/92; PRO FO 371/48817, R8733/6/92; WO 204/621, and 67339 (18 May AFHQ memo stressing, in particular, the linkage of the Trieste and Carinthian situations and the urgent need for corps commands to be rid of the logistical burden of surrendered personnel and refugees); and Cowgill et al, 78-9 (summary of signal NAF 974 [17 May] of Alexander to Eisenhower, in which SHAEF is requested to accept transfer of the Wehrmacht personnel [less Austrians] and the Cossacks).
135. Loc. cit., R8751/6/92, and PRO WO 204/6870.
136. PRO FO 371/48817, R8770/6/92.
137. Read by Wilkinson to the author. Pust, pp. 147-178, provides a lurid, hyperaffective, journalistic account of the abductions. Walzl (pp. 204-170) is more thorough and balanced. He emphasizes that there was a multiplicity of reasons: Marxist ideology, personal grudges (some held by German Carinthian stoolpigeons), revenge for opposing annexation to Yugoslavia in the fighting and plebsicite campaign just after World War One [*der Abwehrkampf*], as well as the settling of scores deriving from the savage civil strife of the preceding partisan campaign. The British were generally hoodwinked although they were several instances of successful military intervention and many others by Carinthian civilians with partisan contacts. The arrests were especially numerous south of the Drau. Of the 263 individuals apprehended, 98 were shot (mainly in the Meža valley where another 700 persons were done in by the victors); the others were ultimately allowed to return. See also T. Barker, 201-2. The writer has spoken with the kinsmen of one of the mortal victims, a well-to-do, right-wing, but non-Nazi landowner. The family's bitterness over its loss was enhanced by the fact that only a few weeks earlier the *Grossgrundbesitzer* had been carted off by the Gestapo

on suspicion of disloyalty to the Third Reich. Having managed to extricate himself, he was then snatched by the partisans. Apparently, his crime, apart from his wealth, was that he had played a prominent role in the *Abwehrkampf*. For the abducted NSDAP members, see the Appendix J, 195–6: they were believed to have constituted the majority of the deportees. (The author is indebted to Dušan Biber for pointing to the existence of this material.) Kidnappings of "traitors to the partisan cause" continued well into the second half of June. Two-to-three, sometime uniformed squads sneaked back and forth across the border from Slovenia: "none of the cases reported so far have been in arrestable /Nazi/ categories". PRO FO 371/46610, C5832/141/3 (British Army intelligence report of 11 September 1945).

138. Cowgill, 14–15, 71 (for McCreery); PRO WO 204/1358A, xc/A51348 (AFHQ document of 18 May recognizing the error over the Bleiburg Croats); PRO WO 202/319, pp. 84, 95–96, 107 (Lee); PRO FO 371/48817, 8/6/92 (Macmillan, etc.); PRO FO 371/48828. R10003/24/92 (Yugoslav guarantee of fair treatment, the giving of which has been orally confirmed to the author by Hočevar); PRO FO 371/48819, R9315/6/92 (Yugoslav troop strength) and PRO WO 170/4241 (notes on verbal agreements with Ivanovic and Hočevar); and discussions with Deakin, Lindsay, and Maclean. The Fifth Corps' plan to eject the Yugoslavs ("Operation Beehive", Operational Instruction No. 24 dated 18 May, PRO WO 170/4241): "Military control will be secured by capturing or destroying all Tito tps in the CORPS area". (Hočevar recalls that Low went so far as to inform him in a general way, of the British intention to use force if necessary.) See also PRO WO 204/621, 67339 (note 134). The sequence of actions by Keightley and Low leading to the return of the quislings may also be roughly traced by comparing the War Diary of Fifth Corps Headquarters (PRO WO 170/4241) with the situation reports ("sitreps") of the intelligence officer Nige Nicolson (PRO WO 170/4404). The idea (in regard to Cossack forces) was apparently being bruited about already on 13 May, the day of Macmillan's visit. (Nicolson). A representative of the Yugoslav Fourth Army – i.e., Hočevar – (re)arrived for discussions, rather sharp in tone, with Low on 15 May, the day the Thirty Eighth Brigade closed the frontier at Bleiburg to the Ustashi. (War Diary). Specific instructions, distinguishing between the Croats and other repatriable Yugoslav prisoners, were issued at 12:50 hours on 17 May (Nicolson, War Diary), and on 19 May, before the first of the two formal agreements was signed, 2500 Croats were sent back (Nicolson). See also p. 69 and note 147. For the total number of repatriates, which evidently included the Croats sent before the 19–20 May agreement, see note 147. Wadl, p. 42, also alleges that the Soviets ordered the Yugoslavs, who were technically subject to Marshal Tolbukhin's Third Ukrainian Front, to leave on 16 May, but British records make it clear that the evacuation began only upon Tito's explicit instructions. The interpretation presented here may have to be revised when all Yugoslav archival evidence becomes available. One thing is, of course, already sufficiently clear (cf. pp. 68–9) the continuing collaborationist resistance, above that of the Croatians, prevented the Yugoslav Army from getting as firm a hold in Carinthia as it had secured in Trieste and environs and thus averted what would have been an international crisis of even greater magnitude. However, to imply that Carinthia escaped Yugoslav annexation because of the post-armistice fighting, as Walzl (p. 193) does, is to enter the realm

of the purely hypothetical. It may be noted Walzl's claim (p. 237) that the quislings were sacrificed more to save Trieste than Carinthia is not only totally irrelevant – as they were not the victims of an appeasement policy – but also overlooks the elemental fact that both places were essential to maintaining the Allied line of communications into the center of Austria (note 134).

139. PRO FO 371/48817, R9137/6/92; R9153/6/92; 371/48817, R8957/6/92; PRO WO 170/4352; and PRO WO 202/319, pp. 139 – 141. See also note 127.

140. PRO WO 170/4465 (entry of May 20). The phrasing of the May 15 entry is rather oblique and could also be construed to cast doubt upon Schmidt-Richberg's generally accepted assertion (op. cit., pp. 155 – 6) that Löhr returned voluntarily to Yugoslav captivity. It states that he was "ordered to report to Yugoslavs at 17:00 hours for disposal instructions". Cf. Biber, *Konec*, passim. The greatly overextended Thirty Eighth Brigade was also charged with guarding, either as "surrendered enemy troops" or as outright POW's, the Hungarians (note 114), Ruthenes (note 111), the vestiges of the SS Police, the vestiges of Waffen SS "Prince Eugene" and "Handžar" Divisions (notes 143 and 147), other of Himmler's hooligans, Croats, plus fragments of the Wehrmacht and even of the navy! The War Diary of the Forty Sixth Infantry Division (Major General C.E. Weir), the last major contingent of the Fifth Corps to reach Carinthia, also contains some piquant details abbout the SNLA's withdrawal: "The Jugoslavs will retain all German eqpt captured by them and incredible scenes are witnessed as their tps withdraw taking much tpt crammed with every conceivable object from sewing machines to tommy guns; the Jugoslav partisan occupation of Cartinthia appears to have solved sundry shortages of eqpt in the Jugoslav army". WO 170/4352 (entry of 20 May).

141. Pirjevec-Ahac returned to Slovenia to enjoy the fruits of office, but Prušnik-Gašper and Primošič, aided by their wartime "legal" collaborator, the eminent Völkermarkt physician, Dr. Franc Petek (one of the Catholic-oriented Carinthian Slovenes whom the Communists genuinely respected), remained behind in order to supervise, surreptitiously, the activities of the OF. (From the British army intelligence report excerpted on pp. 195 – 196 [Appendix J].) The summer of 1945 and the next several years, a period which exceeds the parameters of this book, were a time of tremendous tension between the British and the leftwing Carinthian Slovenes. Cf. Kuchar, pp. 102 – 6. See also Robert Knight, "British Policy Toward Occupied Austria, 1945 – 1950", London University (London School of Economics and Political Science) ph.d dissertation, 1986.

142. Walzl, 59, 148 – 50. It is ironical that, had Hesketh-Prichard not pushed on to the Saualpe, he might well have touched base with the Social Democrats who took to the woods in the Ferlach area at the end of 1944 – although this too would surely not have been to the SNLA's taste. Where the "German Battalion" got its weapons is another open question. It may also be noted that Stossier and Wedenig showed considerable personal courage in visiting Ferlach on 7 May in an attempt to prevent further bloodshed in a tense situation involving the Social Demoratic "German Battalion", the Slovene partisans, and German forces: they barely escaped being killed by SS men.

143. The Prince Eugene Division, which included both Yugoslav and Rumanian subjects technically speaking but was officered mainly by Reich and Austro-Germans, was set up in 1942 for counterinsurgency use in Yugoslavia. Because the

Danube Swabians were at first reluctant to volunteer, Gottlob Berger, Himmler's Waffen SS organizer, had to fall back upon local militia (*Selbstschutz*) and *Einsatzstaffel* as a cadre for the formation. It was involved in unrelenting combat from its inception to its demise and earned one of the worst reputations for the commission of atrocities of any body of troops during World War Two. Its behavior was surely a principle reason for Yugoslavia's postwar expulsion of some 250,000 remaining Banat Swabians (cf. Djilas, p. 423). However, from a strictly military viewpoint "Prince Eugene" was was extraordinarily effective. In combination with "Handžar" (note 147), SS police regiments, and collaborationist contingents, it specialized in hunt and kill missions (*Jagdkommandos*). Instead of hunkering down in fortified posts, it aggressively chased the partisans – a style of fighting to which Deakin was immediately introduced upon parachuting into Montenegro. Split into small groups and backed by artillery and aircraft, it delved into remote wooded and mountainous terrain, relying upon local fascists and the element of surprise. The *Jagdkommando* was in fact the progenitor of the division itself. The fate of Artur Phleps, its first commander (an ex-Imperial Austrian and Rumanian soldier), is obscure; at the war's end it was led by Major General August Schmidhuber. Still 25,785 men strong in March of 1945, major elements of the unit fought on after the 8 May armistice. The division had been dispatched to Slovenia by Löhr who wished to use it in conjunction with Rösener's forces and the White Guard in order to facilitate the Wehrmacht's withdrawal from Istria, but the Germans there (Ludwig Kübler's Ninety Seventh Corps) gave up first. The bulk of its members were finally tricked into surrendering on 15 May between Kranj (Krainburg) and Radovljica (Radmannsdorf), many of them being slaughtered shortly thereafter near Celje. Certain of those who made it to Austria were later extradited by the British. They included Schmidhuber who was tried and executed for war crimes (as was Kübler). Bender, Vol. 3 (1973), pp. 8–17 (includes the order of battle); Djilas, 423; Deakin, 29–33; Duprat, 163; Hnil čka, 137–9; Paul Hausser, *Waffen SS im Einsatz* (Göttingen: Plesse Verlag K.W. Schutz, 1953), pp. 193–4; Otto Kumm, *'Vorwärts Prinz Eugen': Geschichte der 7. SS Freiwilligen-Gebirgs-Division "Prinz Eugen"* (Osnabrück: Munin-Verlag GmbH, 1978), p. 377ff; and Gerald Reitlinger, *The SS: Alibi of a Nation, 1922–1945* (New York: Viking Press, 1968), p. 200. For the quislings, see note 162.

144. The fifty thousand odd soldiers of the ROA were commanded by the ex-Soviet Lieutenant General Andrei Vlassov. Altogther almost a million Soviet citizens fought for the Nazis. The Serbian Volunteer Corps was set up by Dimitrije Ljotic (a sort of Orthodox counterpart to the Croatian Catholic extremist, Pavelic), served on the German side from the very beginning, and had been evacuated to the Ljubljana Gap in October of 1944. The retreating Serbian collaborationists (2400 men) apparently also included a few vestiges of Milan Nedić' German satellite State Guards and Border Guards who had been transferred to Vienna but had returned to Yugoslavia in order to fight the the SNLA alongside the *Ljotici*. Who the Chetniks were is not clear. At least three Mihailović units were in Slovenia at the time. The contingents commanded by Momčilo Djujić and Miodrag Damjanović had been fighting the SNLA in Istria and Primorje under the command of HSSuPF Globocnik. There were even a few surviving Slovene Chetniks (note 162). The bulk of the Chetniks and the Serbian Volunteer Corps managed to save their skins by surrendering to to the Second

New Zealand Division west of the Isonzo river. Since 27 March 1945 all Serbian and Slovene quislings were, in a sense, Chetniks and Royal Yugoslav troops since they had been placed under the nominal command of Mihailović. This appears to have been window dressing for the Western Allies, who, so many of the collaborationists naively believed, would turn against Tito and thus have need of them. Hans Werner Neulen, *An deutscher Seite: internationale Freiwillige von Wehrmacht und Waffen SS* (Munich: Universitas Verlag, 1985), pp. 226-9; and Jožo Tomasevich, *The Chetniks: War and Revolution in Yugoslavia, 1941-1945* (Stanford, Cal.: Stanford University Press, 1975), 440-453.

145. Strle, 201-211, 220-2 (esp. note on p. 205); Prušnik-Gašper, 286-9; Pust, 179-184, 187-193; Rausch, 80-1; Milan Basta, *Rat je završen 7 dana kašnije*, 2nd. ed. (Zagreb: Globus, 1977), pp. 327-330; PRO WO 170/4337 (War Diary of the Sixth Armored Division); PRO WO 170/4631 (War Diary of the First Derbyshire Yeomanry, R.A.C.); and PRO WO 202/309, p. 103. Although not much is known about the topic, yet other Slovenia-based Nazi and quisling forces also refused to surrender to the partisans and punched their way through after the armistice via the Seeberg pass and Eisenkappel; there were similar instances inside Yugolavia. Cf. Walzl, passim. The failure to destroy the Hollenburg bridge was conceivably due to overconfidence evoked by the proximity of the British or, conversely, to the lack of a skilled demolitions team. Certainly the whole business bespeaks very poor SNLA intelligence and central direction. Rösener's peregrinations in the seven days after Rupnik's fall (5 May) are not easy to reconstruct. Walzl's last mention of him (p. 140) confirms Special Force Six's information (Appendix H, 187) that he made a special trip to Klagenfurt in order to stiffen Rainer's back (albeit on 6, not 5 May). It follows from the text and the interrogation report reproduced in Appendix I (193-194) that the HSSPF returned for several days to his post in Slovenia as "Commanding General of Rearward Army Group E" and arranged for the retreat of the *Korpsgruppe* initially bearing his, not von Seeler's name. (The original, physically impossible task of the *Korpsgruppe* had been to push through to Rijeka (Fiume) in order to relieve General Ludwig Kübler's Ninety Seventh Corps which had fallen back from Trieste and was under attack by the Yugoslav Fourth Army that had advanced up the Dalmatian coast; Walzl, 116.)

146. General Keightley reported to the Eighth Army commander, Lieutenant General Richard McCreery, on May 13 that, in a long discussion with the "Kommissar of Hq Fourth Army" (Hočevar), he explained to his Yugoslav interlocutor that "I believed he had not the correct facts about DRAVA river scrap and that we had come to his help at the first possible opportunity". As the conversation ended on cordial terms and Hočevar did not raise the matter again, Keightley would seem to have made his point successfully. PRO WO 204/1358 and WO 204/6870; and Hočevar in discussion. The common view of the Carinthian Slovenes and their neo-Nazi foes is based solely upon hearsay evidence. A careful reading of the Derbyshire Yeomanry's War Diary (note 144) provides not the slightest hint of collusion.

147. The contemporary formulation "All surrendered personnel of established Jugoslav nationality who were serving in German forces should be disarmed and handed over to local Jugoslav forces" (AFHQ Emergency OPD 14 May 1945 to 15th Army Group, PRO WO 204/6870) is imprecise and was first taken by the

present writer to refer only to non-Germans who formally belonged to the Waffen SS and other regular Wehrmacht contingents. It means, however, not just them but autonomous quisling formations (thought on the day in question to be mainly Croatian). For Morgan's visit, see Cowgill et al, 77. For the Banat Swabian manned Waffen SS Divsion "Prince Eugene", see note 142. Another infamous unit, one regiment of which ended up in Carinthia, was the Waffen SS Volunteer Mountain Division "Handžar" No. 13. (Croatian No. 1). Officered by fez-outfitted Reich, Austro-, and ethnic Germans, the rank and file apart from the NCO's were Muhammadan Bosniaks, whose savagery beggars description. However, the Muslims were released from service in the autumn of 1944 because they were regarded as useful only on their own turf. Some fought on independently while the vestiges of the division were turned into a non-Slavic "battle group". Its survivors were sent back to Yugoslavia and slaughtered outside Maribor. Bender, Vol. 3, p. 151; Davidson, 244 – 7; Duprat, 353 – 5; Hausser, 103; and Neulen, 216 – 218. It is not clear how many SS troops – Waffen SS or police – surrendered in Carinthia. While the document previously cited (note 131) lists a lump sum of 5200 SS, it is conceivable that only Reich and Austro-German cadre personnel are meant and that the 43,000 Yugoslavs it also mentions include the rank and file of various SS formations. The total number of repatriated quislings – "evacuated Yugoslav personnel" – was 26339. War Diary 44, 46th Infantry Division, PRO 170/4353. As indicated (note 142), Tito did insist upon the return of some Reich and Austro-German officers and non-coms for trial.

148. Djilas, op. cit., 338.

149. See Carnier, 139 ff; Walzl, 45 – 8, 104 – 5, 234 (who seems unduely sympathetic towards the Cossacks and Caucasians); and Cowgill et al, passim. The shared Nazi-British fear that the Slovene and Italian partisans would form a political alliance and link up militarily, though not entirely groundless, represented only a remote eventuality. There were sharp differences between the radical, indeed ruthlessly homicidal "Garibaldini" of Carnia and the more conservative "Osoppo Division". Indeed even among Italian Communists, as with their Carinthian German comrades, there was distrust of the Slovenes on patriotic grounds and a reluctance to cede national territory. For this subject, see note 13; Carnier, 120 – 2; as well as Walzl, 66 and 124.

150. The chief proponents of the skullduggery thesis – who are as much concerned with the Yugoslav quislings as with the Cossacks – are Nora Beloff and Nikolai Tolstoy. Beloff's volume, *Tito's Flawed Legacy: Yugoslavia and the West* (London: Victor Gollancz, 1986), although written in readable English, is marred by various misstatements such as the assertion (p. 127) that Deakin kept his knowledge of the partisans' murderous treatment of collaborationists to himself. (The WO file cited below clearly demonstrates the opposite.) Tolstoy's rambling, anecdotal work, *The Minister and the Massacres* (London: Century Hutchinson, 1986), is a mishmash of undocumented assumptions and overly facile inferences, insinuations, (whether deliberate or unintentional), distortions, and plain factual error. One especially egregious example of distortion are references (pp. 78, 121, 422) to Macmillan's reports to the Foreign Office of 13 and 14 May, which make a mountain out of a molehill: the fact that the Minister Resident did not immediately **mention** his side-visit to Klagenfurt is of minimal significance. (It is true that he neglected to report his recommendation on the Cossack handover

when he did send a longer message; however, this was a matter of established cabinet policy.) Instances of factual inaccuracy are putting the Yugoslavs into Klagenfurt before the British (p. 11), turning the Predil pass into a border crossing between Yugoslavia and Austria (p.15); making Villiers a close personal friend of Tito (p. 47); and renaming Wilkinson "Williams" (p. 392). The account of developments in Slovenia is hopelessly slanted; there is no mention at all of Rösener's role unless the reference to a "General Reissler" (p. 18) may be taken as such. The text is also shot through with inconsistencies and contradictions which cannot be discussed here. For this, see the documentation of his running press battle with his first major critic, Dr. Robert Knight: "Harold Macmillan: Was There a Klagenfurt Conspiracy?", *Intelligence and National Security*, 1 (1986), pp. 234–254, and the summer 1986 issues of the *Times Literary Supplement*. The debilitated, nonagenarian Macmillan refused to comment on the affair before his recent death. However, Lord Aldington has undertaken a libel action against Mr. Nigel Watts and Tolstoy (who is said to have caused Macmillan much suffering as his life ebbed away). Tolstoy wrote a brochure published anonymously by Watts – at outs with Aldington over a accident claim made to the latter's insurance firm – that was distributed to the parents and old boys of Winchester College, of which Aldington was then the Warden. It was suggested that Aldington, as Macmillan's alleged accomplice, was in effect a war criminal and unfit to serve the College. The case, now a cause celèbre, is scheduled to be heard on 2 October 1989. The *Interim Report* of Cowgill et al (note 124) and Jackson's study (note 110; see esp. p. 347) have put the quietus to Tolstoy's charge, at least for the great majority of historical scholars, that the former prime minister and British officers behaved iniquitously, alas too late in the former instance. See also Christopher Booker, "The Conspiracy that Never Was", *The Spectator*, 24 September, 1988, pp. 9–12 (reply by Tolstoy, "Death Without Glory", ibid., 29 October 1988, pp. 15–18); Alistair Horne, "Klagenfurt Calumnies", ibid, 8 October 1988, pp. 16–17; and John Keegan, "Honour is Restored at the End of an Ugly Affair", *The Daily Telegraph*, 24 September 1988, p. 10. For Djilas's view of the repatriation tragedy, see his interview in *Encounter*, December, 1979, pp. 40–2. See also note 184. For the exchange of messages and discussion that led to the recommendation of early April, see PRO WO/1357.

151. Horne, loc. cit.; see also the first volume of his biography, *Macmillan 1894–1956* (London: Macmillan, 1988). Stephen K. Pavlowitch, in a careful critique of the *Minister and the Massacres* (*English Historical Review*, Vol. 104 [January 1989], pp. 274–276), believes that, in one sense at least, there was a British-Yugoslav deal. (Tolstoy does not, opting merely for a conspiracy!) He describes it as "a rough-and-ready, *implicit* [this writer's italics], quid pro quo" and specifies the political factors that were inextricably linked to the worry over a clash of arms: Churchill and Stalin's basic bargain of October 1944; British "anxiety to save Austria (and Italy) from Communism and something of the 'fifty-fifty arrangement' in Yugoslavia". Conversely, Tito was afraid that the Anglo-Americans might employ the collaborationists against him themselves. There were also deep-seated psychological factors within the Western camp. For both "Beehive" and Nicolson, see note 138.

152. That numerous *domobranci* – the proportions will certainly never be known – were war criminals seems beyond dispute. As Peter Moore reported

already in late August 1944, "..... the White Guard[s] are by their actions declared enemies of the Allies; their existence deprives the Partisans of much needed manpower and immeasurably eases the task of the Germans; any attempt to get [them] to desert becomes increasingly difficult as [they] become implicated in further atrocities." PRO FO 371/44263, R14117/8/92. See also Appendixes, p. ? Frank and moving discussions of the atmosphere – and pyschology – of atrocities, which of course were mutually reinforcing, will be found in Djilas, op. cit., 94, 283 – 5, 336 – 8, and Deakin, op. cit., 22 ff; see also Paul H. Hehn, *The German Struggle Against Yugoslav Guerrillas in World War II: German Counter-Insurgency in Yugoslavia, 1941 – 1943* (New York: East Europe an Quarterly and Columbia University Press, 1979), pp. 133, 137 – 8, 169 – 7 (for Nazi atrocities). For the *domobranci*, see PRO FO 371/48825, R2044/6/92. The handover of all remaining Yugoslav collaborationist prisoners acording to the agreements of 19 and 20 May took place for the most part between May 24 and May 29 and was definitively terminated on June 4 as the result of the intervention of the Red Cross official, John Bigge, with the Eighth Army commander, General Sir Richard McCreery. By that time just under two thirds of them had been sent to what was in most instances their death. PRO WO 202/3/9, pp. 43 – 4, and Knight, loc. cit., 250 – 251. The Slovene civilians were not repatriated. For the repellant details of the extermination of the White Guard, see *La Tragedia del pueblo esloveno;* Kolman, Ludvik, *The Viktring Tragedy* (Cleveland: Historian [sic] Committee of the American Slovenian Anti-Communist War Veterans Association, 1970); Pust, 206 ff; *Zveza društev slovenskih protikomunističnih borcev Tabor, Matica Mrvih: podatki o Slovencih pomorjenih po zložinski Osvobodilni Fronti, 1941 – 1945*, 4 vols. (Cleveland: ZDSPB Tabor, 1968 – 70); and ZDSPB Tabor, *Bela Knjiga slovenskega protikomunističnega upora, 1941 – 1945* (Cleveland: ZDSPB Tabor, 1970). The Yugoslav historian, Tone Ferenc, who knows the SNLA source materials well, disputes the commonly cited figure of 11,000 killed. He suspects that 6000 – 7000 is a more likely total and observes that there are still many surviving White Guardsmen in Slovenia today. For Villiers' possible, albeit at best marginal involvement in the return of the quislings, see note 183 .

153. William Deakin, "Vdaja nemške vojske na Balkanu (april – maj 1945)" in Biber, *Konec*, 805.

154. Cf. T. Barker, 203 ff.

155. For this subject, see *Allied Airmen and Prisoners of War Rescued by the Slovene Partisans* (Lubljana: Research Institute, 1946). Compiled from the records of SNLA headquarters, it lists a total of 303 rescued U.S. fliers. Three aircraft crashed on Austro-Carinthian territory, a number more close to the pre-1941 border including one in the Meža valley. (Peter Kuchar recalls helping the crew of one bomber get away.) See also Edi Šelhaus and Janez Žerovc, *Zbogom, Liberty Bell!* (Ljubljana, 1988). The émigré assertion (Kolman, p.12) that the partisans murdered some downed fliers is contradicted by all the evidence although it may be true that White Guardsmen also saved a few of them as did the Chetniks in Serbia. The author is much indebted to his friend John Rucigay, who had to ditch his B-24 over Istria and was most hospitably received by the SNLA, for a thorough discussion of this issue. Rucigay, a copilot, recalls that the partisans were quick to scavenge in the wreck of his plane and made good use of the salvageable twin machine-guns.

156. Cf. Rausch, 82-5.
157. Nicolson, loc. cit. ("sitrep" of 9 May). British prisoners on the other hand were extremely well-treated, perhaps a case of Carinthian German foresight. Walzl, p. 90 discusses this issue and points out that there was a whole gamut of individual situations. Farmworkers were best-off and sometimes treated virtually as family members. See also note 34.
158. "From the spring of 1944 [Churchill] was constantly haunted by fear of Soviet domination of all South-East Europe, which he wanted to prevent, not purely to serve British interests, but also, it seems fair to say, to save small independent states from extinction.... The activities which the British actually carried out in the area, through support of resistance forces and contacts with opposition groups in the satellite countries, helped to a limited extent to defeat Germany. But they left Britain virtually powerless – except in Greece – to exercise any influence on the post-war settlement." E. Barker, 125.
159. Cf. Maurice Matloff, "Allied Strategy in Europe, 1939-1945" in 1945", in Paret, op. cit., 677-702. The British began to study the tactics of guerrilla warfare as early as 1938, albeit on a rather minor scale. Gubbins, then a lower-ranking staff officer, undertook a thorough analysis of the subject in the late spring of 1939. Later on, under his guidance, the SOE produced a series of handbooks on partisan operations in both English and foreign languages including Slovene. Although the Clowder Mission did not distribute any of this material (Wilkinson), the similarities between Gubbins' crisp prescriptions and the fighting in Carinthia are striking. Foot, 11-15, and Howarth, 6-8. One can only assume that the Spanish Civil War background of leaders like Rozman-Stane was as significant in northwestern Yugoslavia and adjacent Slovenophone regions as it was elsewhere in the country.
160. In the preface to *Gamsi na plazu* (German editions).
161. The reference is to the report of the International Commission of Historians established by the Austrian Foreign Ministry to investigate the flood of allegations against Waldheim and published in German as a supplement to the 15 February 1988 issue (no. 7) of the Austrian periodical *Profil*. If, as one may assume, the object of Waldheim and his right-wing supporters was exoneration, the scheme backfired disastrously. Written largely, it seems, by a West German civil servant who is the best qualified scholar for the subject, Professor Manfred Messerschmidt (*Militärgeschichtliches Forschungsamt Freiburg im Breisgau*), it largely and independently parallels the impressive work of Herzstein (note 120). The latter author refers to Waldheim as a "facilitator" in the commission of war crimes. (The Austrian government apparently has not announced plans, at least not yet, to publish the commission's report, whether in German or English, as it did an exculpatory "white book" in 1987. The hesitation is understandable since the evaluation of Waldheim's wartime career is tantamount to moral condemnation with the clear implication of a degree of legal culpability).
162. "White Guard" was a catch-all term dating from 1942 for the anti-Communist militias that sprouted in Italian-occupied, central Slovenia from 1941 onward. The so-called "village guards" (*vaške straže*) were a force which represented a partly spontaneous but probably more Italian-instigated response of staunchly Catholic peasants to partisan visitations. The rustics, who took up arms in the late spring and early summer of 1942, provided a nucleus for the ultimately 4500-5000 man-strong *Milizia Voluntaria Anticommunista* (M.V.A.C.). Fostered by the

Italians in every part of Yugoslavia under their control, it emerged in Slovenia in August of the same year under the aegis of Ljubljana's bishop, Gregorij Rožman. The former Habsburg and Royal Yugoslav officer, Leon Rupnik, who became the city's mayor, did not play a role at this juncture. Other components, close to the Slovene People's Party (which by 1942 had assimilated two other small bourgeois factions, the Sokol and the Liberals, under the label "Slovene Alliance"), were the three "Slovene Legions", associated with the name of Marko Natlačen. They began to appear in the autumn of 1941 but did not engage in combat for almost a year. The so-called "Styrian Battalion" evolved into the "Legion of Death". Yet another, organizationally distinct group was Major Karel Novak's Slovene Chetniks, who came on stage in March of 1943 and were also called the "Blue Guard". Although they supported Draža Mihailović (who wanted to create a Greater Slovenia), they should not be confused with the non-Slovene Chetniks operating in Slovenia at the end of the war (see note 143). Perhaps 300-400 White Guardsmen (both Chetniks and M.V.A.C.) were massacred by the partisans after surrendering at the siege of Count Auersperg's castle at Turjak in September of 1943 and elsewhere. Several hundred others were tried: those not acquitted were executed or put into labor battalions. The contingents that escaped the SNLA were reorganized, reequipped, and greatly augmented as the *Slovensko domobranstvo* (Slovene Home Guard) by Rupnik after the establishment of the Nazis' "Operational Zone Adriatic Littoral". Rösener authorized the process on 24 September 1943, and the troops, who were allowed to use the Slovene flag with the Carniolan eagle, were formally sworn in on 24 April 1944 at a ceremony also attended by Rösener and Rožman (There were smaller, analogous collaborationist bands in the Littoral, Gorenjsko, and Lower Styria [*vermanšaft, brambovci*].) Gauleiter Rainer's plans (see p. 14) to set up a Nazi satellite state allegedly served to secure the loyalty of Rupnik and his ultra right-wing followers. Carnier, passim; Neulen, 220-2; *Narodoosvobodilna vojna*, 321-330; Tomasevich, passim; and Walzl, 120-1. Although Alexander expressly warned them to desist from aiding the Germans via radio broadcasts and leaflet drops and threatened to punish them as war criminals (cipher message of 2 September 1944, PRO WO 202/419), the quislings sought to justify their actions with the argument that international law permitted them to use force in order protect themselves from disorderly elements. *La tragedia del pueblo esloveno*, 176. Kolman (p.8) alleges that the SNLA sometimes deliberately provoked reprisals against anti-Communist peasants both to get rid of known opponents (false denunciations served the same purpose) and to secure recruits. In any case, there is perhaps a rough parallel between the White Guard and Revolutionary Era American colonists who found themselves caught between the British and the Tories on the one hand and the rebels on the other. Some of them, as, for example, in South Carolina (which Professor John Shy is studying), ended up *nolens-volens* as Tory militiamen. Admittedly, their postwar fate was a bit milder than that of the *domobranci*.

163. Cf. p. 18.

164. This document does not appear to have been deposited in or was removed from the PRO; it may or may not be preserved in the inaccessible SOE archives.

165. See note 166.

166. The "Mongols" were the Turkmeni and Azerbaydzhani rank-and-file of the 162 Division.

167. Cf.

168. Lindsay's observer at the raid, Sgt. Edward Welles, was highly critical of partisan tactics during the action, and the bridge had to be finished off a month later by RAF Beaufighters. The Germans also proved adept at quickly repairing the damage inflicted upon their communications during "Operation Ratweek" (a BAF bombing campaign). Information from Lindsay and Moore. Cf. note 100.

169. This was almost certainly true at the time. For the Koralpen partisans, see note 110.

170. Yugoslav deviousness may well have been due to continuing fear of an Allied landing in Istria. Cf. p. 36.

171. Force 399 was another Bari-based, Central Europe-oriented SOE operation led by Major General E. Stawell. Foot, 204.

172. A Force was an MI6 "disinformation" enterprise. West, p. 315.

173. Special Force One was an SOE body that dealt mainly with the Italian partisans. Foot, 230.

174. The "Rankin" categories derived from the official SOE "Instructions Governing Employment of Special Operations Personnel in Occupied Countries under Conditions of Enemy Withdawal or Collapse" (not available).

175. The Clowder Mission had sought to penetrate Austria all the way from the Plöcken (Gail valley) to the Brenner passes. The Carnic Alps mission near Forni Avoltri was recalled in October of 1944, the conditions being as inclement as in the Karawanken. Wilkinson.

176. Among the very few Clowder Mission people still with the SNLA at this time was Captain Alex Ramsey ("Knudsen"), one of the men destined to reinforce Hesketh-Prichard. PRO WO 202/420 and Wilkinson. According to Patrick Martin-Smith, Ramsey may have arrived in Klagenfurt even earlier than Wilkinson (cf. p. 60).

177. Later events showed that the Macmis evaluation of the material provided by the informant (Dr. Václav Pišot) was generally sound. Even his claim that the Whites had killed Allied aviators, which contrasts sharply with the quislings' previous behavior (note 155), is probably correct since they were subject to very heavy air attack toward the end of the war. The reference to the *domobranstvo*'s poor morale should also be understood in light of the date in question and also reflects a change from the collaborationists' more sanguine outlook a few months earlier. The statement that captured Whites would be treated according to their deserts was not absolutely wrong in so far as some 4–5000 of the 11,000 "repatriates" from Carinthia were sorted out and escaped being massacred. (Cf. note 152)

178. The Slovenes did not make the historiographic case they could have in the interwar period; this has been done only since 1945. Cf. T. Barker, passim.

179. The Slovene-sponsored branch of the ÖFF and the two battalions in question proved too politically unreliable to be used for the purpose Deakin foresaw. Cf. note 113. The Saualpen party does not appear to have included any Austro-Germans.

180. Deakin's carefully balanced, judicious memorandum is a superb example of the utility of a professionally trained historian in the gathering of political intelligence.

181. The soldiers of the Fifth Corps successfully carried out Keightley's instructions notwithstanding Alexander's inability to reach agreement with Tito. A careful

reading of the three divisional war dairies and of their constituent units makes it clear that they handled their extremely difficult assignment with remarkable aplomb and, on the whole, effectively parried the Yugoslavs, in Friulia as well as in Carinthia. However, the disgust of many of the men who were required to assist in the return of the collaborationists – a task that required both dissimulation and, on occasion, the application of force – is not reflected in these sources.

182. The original document is printed, not typed and mimeographed as in the other instances. W.H.B. Mack was a Foreign Office representative in Caserta, to whom information was sent by Jack Nicholls, political adviser to the Fifth Corps and hence the link with Number Six Special Force. Cf. Cowgill et al, 83.

183. For Piesch, see page 61 and note 119.

184. The historiographically grounded political intelligence work of Sixth Special Force is hardly less impressive, given the momentary conditions, than Deakin's. The prescience revealed in discussing a possible, later Pan-German or neo-Nazi revival is especially notable even if the actual circumstances were destined to be related not to an economic depression but rather to enduring ethnic-political conflict. Moreover, the document records certain details not otherwise available, especially the role of the Church in the Nazi régime's handover of power to the "democratic" politicians. However, a few corrections are in order. There were at least some Protestant German nationalists of indigenous Carinthian origin; they were converts who left the Catholic Church because of its Imperial Austrian or pro-Habsburg orientation (*Los-von-Rom-Bewegung*). The timing of the movements and actions of Rainer, who left Trieste (where he was evidently awaiting an Allied landing in the hope of making common cause against the Communists) only on 28 April and returned Klagenfurt on 3 May after consulting Kesselring in Berchtesgaden, is only approximate. The purblind Gauleiter's speeches were more equivocal and rambling than defiant; what he was apparently aiming for was British occupation with acceptance of a German security force that would continue the struggle against Communism and the partisans. The role of Kraßnig, who apparently underwent an especially thorough British interrogation (which began immediately on 8 May) and may have served as the source of much of the data reported, was not as crucial as the text seems to suggest. (Villiers finds it hard to recall the details of this period of his military career.) Whether the partisans contacted Stossier of their own accord or vice versa is not clear; the two sides had been communicating sporadically since the end of 1944; Walzl, 127. For the surrender mission to Salzburg, cf. Walzl (p.147), who speaks of a mysterious, highly unlikely "British colonel from the Hotel Moser-Verdino". For Rösener, see note 145. The evolution of the original, evidently self-styled "action commitee" contacted by Natmeßnig into an "executive committee" and finally into a "provisional provincial government" has not been fully clarified even by the quintessentially fact-oriented Walzl (p. 138 ff). What he has succeeded in elucidating, however, are the fissures within the Austrian Communist Party both in May of 1945 and earlier over the annexation of southern Carinthia by Yugoslavia. He has also determined that the KPÖ, which included many disappointed former Social Democrats, was thoroughly infiltrated by the Gestapo and riven by personal rivaries; the heavy losses it suffered were due to the Nazi double-agents rather than to any treachery by party members (pp. 59–63, 142–3).

185. The document has been transcribed from the handwritten original.

Notwithstanding a categorical denial in a letter sent by Villiers to one of Tolstoy's stalking horses (op. cit., p. 390-7), the Russian-descended author clearly wishes to leave his readers the impression that Sixth Special Force Staff Section was the chief mechanism for the return of the Serbian quislings and the *domobranci* to the SNLA, in which connection it supposedly acted disreputably (op. cit., pp 390-7). A published account by Branislav Todorovic, a partisan defector, is the shaky basis for Tolstoy's assertion. (Lockhead's name is sometimes erroneously given in this and other sources as "Lakhed" or "Lockheed".) Villiers himself wishes to say nothing further about the matter (letter to the present writer of 16 February 1989), presumably because of Lord Aldington's pending lawsuit against Tolstoy and and Watts (note 150). In all events Document H and I, taken together, leave little doubt that SSFSS concentrated upon collecting political intelligence in May of 1945. Nonetheless, Villiers' insistence, as conveyed to Tolstoy, that he **knew** absolutely nothing of the repatriations is most puzzling. He was, after all, on the spot, and his military role required him to keep informed of local events. His subordinate Lockhead, was directly, if marginally involved in the business. Thousands of Carinthian civilians, quite apart from British troops, witnessed or heard first-hand about what was happening as the writer learned himself when he first visited Carinthia in 1953. For the rambunctious Popski and his marauders, see note 122.

186. The report is in file WR 3433 (PRO FO 371/51243) which contains further correspondence and commentary on the subject. The upshot was a telegram from Ambassador Stevenson in Belgrade: "I do not think any purpose would be served by the enquiry suggested in letter of 9th November from Vienna to German Department. Moreover, intervention by His Majesty's Government on behalf of the Austrians, many of whom are known to be Nazis, would certainly be misunderstood here". Certain of the names on the list appear to be those of Slovenophone Carinthians. A few are specifically denoted as being German citizens, especially persons from the *Luftgeräte Werke, G.m.b.H.*, at Ferlach.

Supplementary Bibliography

(Dušan Biber has provided the Serbo-Croatian references.)

Banac, Ivo, *With Stalin Against Tito: Cominformist Splits in Yugoslav Communism* (Ithaca, N.Y.: Cornell University Press, 1988). Traces inter alia the growing tension between Moscow and Belgrade in the last year of the war.

Biber, Dušan, "La position internationale de la Yougoslavie au cours la dernière année de la deuxième guerre mondiale" in *Revue internationale d'histoire militaire*, 64 (1986), pp. 441-466. Biber has researched the period in question extensively for several decades and published a series of articles based upon PRO sources in the Zagreb weekly *Vjesnik u Srijedu* as early as 1973 (see esp. numbers: 1119, [17 October]; and 1120 [24 October]).

Ivanović, Doko (Djoko), "Rad pozadine 3. armije u završnim operacijma" in: *Završne operacije za oslobodjenje Jugoslavije*, Vol. 9, Naučni skup 23. i. 24 april 1985 (Belgrade: Vojnoizdavački i Novinski Centar, 1986). An account of the role of Third Yugoslav Army at end of the war by the now retired lieutenant general who, along with Hočevar, negotiated the details of the collaborationists' return. The latter subject is mentioned only in passing.

Kuchar, Helena, *Jelka* (Ljubljana: Delavska Enotnost, 1988). Slovene edition of the late "Jelka's" recollections. Contains new family biographical data.

MacDonald, Callum, *The Killing of SS Obergruppenführer Reinhard Heydrich* (New York: Free Press, 1989). One major theme is the involvement of the SOE.

Nicolson, Nigel, "The Great Betrayal" ("Tito's Victims: The Allies' Shame"), *The Independent Magazine* (London), 22 April 1989, pp. 22-27. Subjective, journalistic reminiscences of the Fifth Corps intelligence officer who contradicted his superiors' repatriation policy and now regrets his decision to recant.

Šelhaus, Edi, *Stotinka sreče* (Ljubljana: Založba Borec, 1980) A detailed study by an ex-partisan journalist-photographer of all "one percent lucky" Allied fliers saved by the SNLA.

Tito, Josip Broz, *Sabrana djela*, Vol. 28 (Belgrade: Komunist, 1988). Reproduces the Yugoslav leader's 14 May 1945 order that forbade killing quisling prisoners and prescribed trials for suspected war criminals. The reversal of this policy during the last week of May was most likely related to the continuing Trieste crisis and the fear that, even disarmed, the repatriates could become a fifth column manipulated by their escaped colleagues in northern Italy, some of whom were already working for Allied intelligence. The Yugoslav Army went on full alert on 24 May. *Zbornik dokumentata i podataka o narodnooslobodilačkom ratu narode Jugoslavije*, Vol XI, Part 3 (Belgrade: Vojnoistorijski Institut, 1976). Document No. 137 (pp. 563-4), which should bear the date 19 May rather than 10 May, states that Ivanović, accompanied by one or (if necessary) more brigades, was "especially authorized by this Headquarters to proceed to the Allied Command for Carinthia in order to take over [former Nazi-held] POWs, [other] Yugoslav citizens as well as to carry on negotiations regarding the handover of Ustashi and Chetniks who have surrendered to Allied troops" and that the task of the units in question was to "escort the prisoners to Ljubljana or some other place".

INDEX

(For subjects, see also capitalized and italicised headings in the Documentary Appendixes; Carinthian place names are given bilingually where appropriate.)

A Force, 136, 140, 228
Abductions by partisans, 24, 67, 76, 195 f, 218f. See also Assassinations and Executions.
Abwehrkampf, Carinthian, see Self-Defense Struggle.
Addis, J.M., 52
Administrative sectors, SS, 13
Adriatic Coastland (Operational Zone Adriatic Littoral), 14, 227. See also Primorje, and Venezia Giulia.
AFHQ, see Allied Forces Headquarters.
Agents, secret, infiltration of: by Allies, 28, 119, 130ff, 216; by Yugoslavs, 197f. See also "Austrians".
Agitprop, 10, 102f
Agreement, British-Yugoslav, over evacuation and repatriation, 67-70, 22ff, 225. See also Massacres.
Air Force, Ninth U.S., 66
Air Forces, Balkan and Royal, see Balkan Air Force and Royal Air Force.
Aidussina, see Ajdovščina.
Airdrops, see Sorties.
Airmen, Allied, downed, 78, 131f, 152, 211, 225, 228
Airstrips, 135
Ajdovec, 148
Ajdovščina, 106, 149
Aldington, Lord, 69, 74, 215, 224
Alexander, Harold, 34, 54, 56, 63ff, 68, 74f, 76, 175ff, 183, 212, 216, 227f
Allied Forces Headquarters, 28, 32, 36, 38, 68, 73f, 210, 217 142, 181, 188. See also Alexander.

Allied Military Government: in Carinthia, 61, 196, 198; in Italy, 175
Alpenfestung, 57, 175, 213
Alpenland, 13
Alpenvorland, see Administrative sectors, SS.
Alpine-Adriatic regional scheme, 14
Ambushes, 17, 33, 39f, 44, 52, 139. See also Tactics, guerrilla.
American Austrian Mission, see OSS.
Anders, Wladysław, 213
Anschluß, 8f, 165, 179f, 188f. See also "Greater Carinthia".
Antisemitism, 79. See also Globocnik
Apulia, 5
Arbuthnot, Robert K., 174, 215
Armaments, see Logistics and Weaponry.
Armies, Yugoslav: Third, 56, 65, 69; Fourth, 58, 60, 65, 69, 71, 219, 222
Armistice, 8 May 1945, 59
Army, British, Eighth, 56, 62, 64, 68, 216. See also McCreery, Richard.
Army, Imperial and Royal, (Austro-Hungarian), 55, 227
Army, Slovene National Liberation, see Slovene National Liberation Army.
Army, U.S., Third, 66
Army, Yugoslav, see Yugoslav Army.
Army, Yugoslav National Liberation, see Yugoslav National Liberation Army.
Army Group, Allied, Fifteenth, 75
Army Groups, Nazi: "E", 28, 55; Southeast, 28, 55, 55; Southwest, 56, 216. See also Löhr.
Arnoldstein/Podklošter, 7

Artillery, 125, 148. See also Weaponry.
Assassinations, see Executions, by partisans.
Atrocities, by Nazis and White Guard, 40f, 45f, 159, 163, 210, 220f; by partisans, 157. See also Executions, Massacres, Reprisals, and War Crimes.
Aussiedlung, 8f, 23, 49,176
"Austria" and "Austrians": defined, xii; as Allied agents, 32, 36, 60, 208; as Hitler's victims, 79; as Nazi soldiers, 55, 58f, 221, 223; deficient patriotism, 180, 202; national characteristics, 184. See also Battalions, SNLA, Austrian; Gaiswinkler; Globocnik; *Kampfgruppe "Avantgarde" Steiermark*; Leoben-Donawitz; Löhr; Moscow Declaration; Rainer; Resistance; and Waldheim.
Austria, Republic of: prewar, 170, 179f; postwar, 5, 79; restoration of, 37, 54. See also Anschluß and Renner.
Austrian Socialist Party (SPÖ): prewar (Social Democrats), 21, 179f, 185, 217, 220; postwar, 71. See also Wedenig.
AVNOJ, 115

B-17 and B-24, see Flying Fortress and Liberator.
Baker Street, 29. See also SOE.
Balkan Air Force (BAF), 37, 44, 53, 74, 208, 210, 228.
Banat (Danube) Swabians, 220
Bandits, partisans viewed as, 0
Bari, 32, 37, 53
Barracks police, 14
Battalion, "German", 57, 70, 220
Battalions, SNLA: Austrian, 53, 57, 150, 172f, 228; Cankar, 17; Carinthian, 22-6; First or Kranjc, 17;
Battalions, Wehrmacht, 127f
Battalions, White Guard, mobile, (*pokretne*), 51ff
Bärenschlucht, 50
BBC, 35, 84, 103

Bebler, Alex, 87, 116, 133, 170
Bela pec, 23
Bela Krajina, 40, 96, 114
Belgrade, 8, 53f, 68, 154, 165
Belin Jože, 34
Belluno, 191
Beloff, Nora, 223
Berger, Gottlob, 221
Bevk, France, 116
Biber, Dušan, 210, 212, 219
Bieffke, see Germans, Reich.
Bigge, John, 131
Bismarck, Otto von, 75
Bistra valley, 23
"Black, Dick", 32
Blaich, Major, 187
Blatnik, John, 211
Blažič-Melchior, Peter, 22
Bled, 129
Bleiburg/Pliberk, 68, 204, 219, 191, 197f
Blue Guards, see Chetniks, Slovene.
Bočna, 123
"Body count", see Casualties.
Bogomolov, Colonel, 134f, 151, 153, 157
Bohinj, 5
Border guards, 15, 71, 129
Borders, see Frontiers
Borghese, Prince Livio
Boris, Captain, 157
Bosnia and Bosniaks, 5, 223,
Bračič, Mirko, 91, 114
Brambovci, see *Wehrmannschaft*.
Brecelj, Marjan, 116
Bren light machine guns, 125, 137, 208
Brežice, 129
Brice, Roland, 167
"Brigade tendencies", 43
Brigades, shock, SNLA and YNLA: defined, 89; Dalmatian, 37; First (Tomšič), 113, 120; Second (Šercer), 113, 120; Fourth (Gubčeva), 113; Fifth (Cankar), 113; Sixth (Šlander), 120; Eleventh (Zidanšek), 25, 62, 120, 217; Thirteenth (Bračič), 70f, 120
Brigades, British: First Guards, 75, 191;

Thirty Eighth Irish, 68, 69f, 219f;
Sixty First Infantry (Derbyshire), 72, 216, 222
Brigata Garibaldi, see Partisans, Italian.
Brimelow, Lord Thomas, 217
Brindisi, 137
Broad, Philip, 37f, 209
Brody, battle of, 213
Brown, Captain, 192
Bruck an der Mur, 28
Bulgarians, 55, 65
Burgenland, 77
Bush, Gordon, 122, 136, 136
Butt, 145
"Buxton, Major", see Villiers, Charles.

Cadet School, Klagenfurt, see Waffen SS.
"Cahusac, Major", see Hesketh-Prichard.
Camp followers, 73. See also Refugees.
Canadians, Slavic, 206. See also Jones, William.
Canale valley, 7ff, 59ff, 181
Canaro, 14
Carinthia: bilingual (Slovene-speaking), 7f; invasion by geographic demarcation, 7; socioeconomic conditions, 179f; support for partisans, 11f; violation of minority rights, 169f. See also Allied Military Government, "Greater Carinthia", Nationalism (German), Economy, Naziism, Resistance, Trade unions, and Wedenig.
Carinthia, Yugoslav, see Meža valley.
Carinthian Germans, see Germans, Carinthian.
Carinthian Provincial Archives, 8, 38
Carnia and Carnic Alps, 8, 28, 141, 145, 181, 223, 228
Caserta, see Allied Forces Headquarters.
Casualties, Nazi and Slovene, 78
Catholic Church, Roman, in Carinthia and Styria: 183; Slovene members, 23, 185. See also Clergy.
Caucasians, see Legionaries.

Celje, 221
Celje-Dravograd railway, 116
Celje-Ljubljana highway, 122f, 140
Celje-Maribor railway, 116
Cerkno, 5, 19, 91, 206
Chambrun, Count Louis Charles de, 167
Chetniks: politically-motivated alteration of meaning, 272 ; Serbian (Mihailović), 14, 71, 73, 206, 221; Slovene (Blue Guard), 105, 221, 227. See also Damjanović, Djujić, Ljotić, Nedić, and Serbian Volunteer Corps
Četa (small SNLA unit), 120
Črmošnjice (as Slovene headquarters), 5, 27, 40, 147, 155
Črna: 129; battle of, 33f, 40, 70
Črnomelj, 40, 96, 146ff, 150, 152, 172.
Christian Social Party, Austrian, 179f, 185. See also Clerical fascism and *Heimwehr*.
Churchill, Winston, 53f, 55, 64f, 72, 74, 107, 212, 226
Ciphers and deciphering, see Codes and ULTRA.
Clausewitz, Carl von, 75, 111
Clemanceau, Georges, 166
Clerical fascism, 21, 70. See also. See also *Heimwehr*.
Clergy: Carinthian German, 186f, 189; Carinthian Slovene, 10
Clowder Mission: conceived, 10; operations in Slovenia and Carinthia, 12, 27-39, 44f, 191-5. See also Hesketh-Prichard, Saualpe, Resistance, Number Six Special Force Staff Section, Stafford, Wilkinson, and Villiers.
Codes, 47, 50, 101f. See also Radios and ULTRA.
Col, 149
Collaborationists, see Quislings.
Command and control system (SNLA), 31, 33, 40, 48, 96f, 123f, 139, 144f, 222
Commissars, see Command and control system.
Communications, military, see

Index

Couriers, Highways, Lines of communication, Radios, and Railways.
Communist Party, Austrian (KPÖ), 12, 18, 21, 28, 35, 52, 201f, 205, 208, 229
Communist Party, Slovene (KPS): attitude of leaders, 209; controls Liberation Front, 10ff, 171, 133, 154; eager for postwar sinecures, 10f, 157f; operatives in Carinthia, 20; sociopolitical program, 23, 161, 164, 181f, 185
Company, Carinthian (SNLA), 18, 21f
Conspiracy, alleged, to return "Cossacks and Yugoslav quislings, 74f, 223
Coolidge, Archibald Carey, and Coolidge Commission, 165, 168
Corps, British: Fifth, 56, 65, 67, 69f, 72f, 74ff, 76, 174-7, 191, 215f, 219, 229; Thirteenth, 56
Corps, Italian, Twenty Second, 166
Corps, Nazi, Ninety Seventh, 221f
Corps, SNLA: Seventh, 5, 88f, 137, 145fg, 150, 159f; Ninth. 5, 28, 30, 39, 52, 88f, 91, 101, 149f, 153, 175, 206, 216
Corvinus, King Matthew, 21
"Cossacks": as autonomous quisling formation in northeast-Italy, 73f, 76; as Fifteenth SS Volunteer Cavalry Corps, 73; Kuban, 74. See also Legionaries, Caucasian.
Counterinsurgency, 28. See also Hunt-and-kill, Fleckner, and Police Regiments.
Couriers, partisan, 5, 31, 40, 48, 78, 96f. See also Command and control.
Courts-martial, 22
Crawley, J.C., 193
Crayon Mission, 206, 216
Croatia and Croats, see Burgenland and Ustashi
Customs guards, see Border guards.
Cvijić, Jovan, 167
Czechoslovakia, 5, 28, 196
Czernin, Manfred, 36

Dachau, 35

Dakota (DC-3), 5f, 44
Dalmatia, 56
Damjanović, Miodrag,
Darewski, Neville, 202, 206
Davidson, Basil, 77
Davies, W.D., 196, 202
Deakin, Sir William, 45, 51, 52ff, 57, 68f, 74, 76, 221, 228
De Bono, General, 166
Death's Head (concentration camp) guards, 15
Defense circuits, 13
Defense works, see *Alpenfestung* and Fortifications.
Denazification, 196
Deserters, Wehrmacht, 20, 24f, 202
Demolitions, 51, 95, 117, 121f, 125f. See also Railways.
Deportation, see *Aussiedlung*,
Derbyshire Yeomanry, First, see Brigades, British, Sixty First Infantry.
Detachments, partisan, see *Odredi*.
Diex/Djekše, 50
Displaced persons, 65
Dillon Mission, see OSS.
Discipline, military, within SNLA, 6, 216. See also Looting.
Division, New Zealand, Second, 56, 221f
Division, SNLA, Fourteenth Shock, 3, 30, 43, 56, 65, 70, 120, 122, 143, 149
Divisions, British: Forty Sixth Infantry, 56, 220; Seventy Eighth Infantry, 56, 215; Sixth Armoured, 56, 59f, 75, 215
Divisions, Nazi: Brandenburg Special Use, 71, 121; 162nd Turkmeni-Azerbajdzhani, 106, 227; 438th Special Use, 58, 199. See also Waffen SS.
Djilas, Milovan, 11, 45, 73
Djujić, Momčilo, 221
Djurić, Ljudrag, 68
Dönitz, Karl, 181, 186
Dolan, I.H.P., 72
Dolenjsko (Dolenjska), 5, 25f, 88, 91, 106, 112ff, 179, 184, 188

Dolfuß, Engelbert, 179, 184, 188
Dominko, Captain, 191
Domobranstvo: Croatian, 129; Slovene, 15, 64, 71, 76, 129, 133, 162f, 205, 224f, 227f. See also Morale.
Domanov, Timofei, 74
Domžale, 129
Draft, military (Wehrmacht), and effect upon partisans, 4, 20f
Drau/Drava river, 7, 45f, 48, 71f, 164. See also Hydroelectric works.
Dravograd, 129, 165, 170
Dreta valley, 123
Drvar, 6
Dubajić, Sima, 191
Ducal Chair, 65

EAM, see Liberation Front, Greek.
Eberndorf/Dobrla vas, 198
Eberstein, 50
Ebriach/Obirsko, 20, 22, 40, 204
Economy, Carinthian, 23, 78, 179f, 185, 204, 206. See also Timber.
Eden, Anthony, 52
Eighth Army, see Army, British.
Einsatzstaffel, 221
Einsatz zones, 225
Einspieler family, 24
Einspieler, Valentin, 204. See also *Nemčurji*.
Eisenerz, 28
Eisenhower, Dwight D., 66, 112
Eisenkappel/Železna Kapla, 86, 20ff, 24f, 30, 39, 51, 57, 59, 222
Enns valley, 66
Ethnic traitors, see *Nemčurji*.
Executions: by partisans, 22ff, 48f, 76, 204; by Nazis, 44, 61, 208

Faakersee/Baško jezero, 39
Factory security guards, 15
Fajfar, Tone, 116
Fascists, Italian, 106, 119
Feldgendarmerie, 71
Feldkirchen, 166
Ferenc, Tone, 210, 212, 225
Ferlach/Borovlje: 7, 21, 44; 64, 70ff, 222
Ferlitsch, Hans, 109

Filipović, Sulejman, 116
First Society, Imperial Austrian, 204
Fisher, James, 137f
Fleckner, Hans, 5, 31, 40, 44
Floridsdorf, 132
Flotsam, Allied station, 19
Flying Fortress (B-17), 63
Foch, Ferdinand, 110
Force 399: 130, 136, 228
Foreign Office: against Wilkinson's plan to penetrate Carinthia, 38f. See also Broad, Harrison, Macmillan, and Stafford.
Forni Avoltri, 228
Fortifications: 15f, 40. See See also *Alpenfestung*.
Fourteenth Division, see Division, SNLA.
Fourth Operational Zone (SNLA), 22, 25f, 33, 39f, 46, 50, 118-40, 143, 149
Franta, Šever, 30
Freibach/Borovnica, 165
Freischar, see *Landwacht*
Freedom Front, see Liberation Front.
Free zones, see Liberated zones.
Freyberg Sir Bernard, 56
Friulia, 12ff, 216. See also Carnia and Carnic Alps
Frol, Franc, 116
Frontiers, postwar and British attitude toward, 29, 36ff, 163-73. See also Irredentism.

Gailberg pass, 74
Gail/Zila (Zilja) river and valley, 8, 39
Gaiswinkler, Albrecht, 208
Galbraith, James, 192
Gamekeepers and gamewardens, see Hunting.
Garibaldini, see Partisans, Italian.
Garibaldi-Natisone Divis on, see Partisans, Italian.
Gebirgsjäger, see Mounta n Infantry, Light.
Gemona, 216
Gendarmerie, 13, 58, 71
General SS, 15
General Staff, Slovene, 5, 19, 25

Germans: Carinthian, 9, 11; ethnic, 9; Reich, 12
Gestapo, 2, 10, 13, 21f, 35, 45, 59, 131, 180, 186, 204, 208, 210, 218, 22.
Glamočko polje, 5
Globocnik, Odilo, 11f, 61, 216, 221
G-men, 13
Goodwin, James M., 51, 122, 137, 211
Gorenjsko (Gorenje, Gorenjska), 7, 11, 14, 17f, 78, 89, 101, 105f, 108, 112f, 123, 206
Gorizia, 14, 111
Gorni Grad, 123
Gornik-Iztok, Gajko, 47
Gothic Line, 36
Goya, Francisco, 77
Graben, 20
Grat-Kijev, Ladislav, 34, 47, 201
Graz, 60, 70, 132, 165f
"Greater Carinthia", 12
"Greater Styria", 7. See also Styria.
Greece, 64, 156. See also Liberation Front, Greece.
Green Cadres, 8, 20, 77
"Greens", see Police Regiments.
Grenadier Guards, 191
Grenzwacht, see Border guards.
Griblje, 152
Großauer, Hermann, 187, 189, 215
Grosuplje, 148
Gruber, Hermann, 189
Gubbins, Sir Colin McVean, 39, 67, 226
Guerrilla warfare, nature of, 24, 77f, 110. See also Tactics, guerrilla.
Gunsmiths, xii, 21, 44
Gurk, diocese of, 189

Hagenegg castle, 9, 25
Hajka, see Hunt-and-kill.
Halifax bomber, 137, 139, 153
Hanni Josef, 189
Hanau, Julius, 8, 203
Handžar division, see Waffen SS
Harding, Lord John, 56, 63
Harmel, Heinz, 61, 216
Harrison, Geoffrey W., 37, 209
Hayden, Captain, 197f
Headquarters, Croatia, see Otočac.

Headquarters, Slovenia, see Črmošnjice.
Hedgehog garrisons, 106, 114
Hefter, Adam, 189
Heimatblock, 165, 179
Heimatdienst (Heimatbund), Kärntner, *23, 168, 207*
Heimatschutz, Kärntner, 179
Heimwehr, 129
Henderson, Neville, 188
Herke, Hans, 187, 189, 215
Hermagor/Šmorje, 8
Hesketh-Prichard, Alfgar C.G., 5f, 27, 31-6, 43, 46, 50, 60, 76, 83, 131, 143, 145, 211, 220
High command, Slovene, see Črmošnjice and General staff
Heydrich, Reinhard, 5
Highways: to Loibl and Seeberg passes, 44. See also Loibl and Seeberg passes.
Himmler, Heinrich, 12, 30
Hintergupf/Zavrh, 58
Hitler Youth, 15
Hočevar, France, 69, 73, 75, 219, 222
Höhere SS-und Polizei-Führer, 13. See also Globocnik and Rösener
Hofer, Andreas, 109
Hojnik family, 31
Hollenburg/Humberk, castle and bridge 71f, 222
Holocaust, see Globocnik
Honner, Franz, 53
Horne, Alistair, 75
Howarth, Patrick, 49
Hrastnik, 129
Hughes, George, 5
Hungarians, soldiers in Carinthia and Styria, 57, 81, 214
Hunt-and-kill commandos: defined, 31, 221; 17, 31, 39
Hunting, 9f, 21, 24, 47
Huntington, Colonel, 126
Hydroelectric power works, Drau river, 16, 78

Idrija, 105, 149
Informers, see Spies.

Innitzer, Stefan, 183
Innsbruck, 205
Intelligence collection, 99-102, 119, 130, 151, 161ff, 195f
Inter Services Liaison Department, 32, 132, 136, 139, 195. See also "Black, Dick".
Irredentism, Slovene, 28, 37f, 51,, 83f, 132, 134, 158, 162, 164-73,, 212; Western Allies' distrust because of, 173; post World War Two, 195f
ISLD, see Inter Services
Isonzo/Soča river, 56, 61, 63, 222
Istria, 6, 14, 19, 63, 88, 175, 221. See also Adriatic Coastland, Primorje, and Venezia Giulia.
Italy: Carinthian policy in 1919, 166ff; withdrawal from Axis side, 13, 91, 186. See also Partisans, Italian, and Provincia di Lubiana.
Ivanović, Doko (Djoko), 69, 73, 75
Izvršni odbor, see Odbori (Liberation Front, committees).

Jagdkommandos, see Hunt-and-kill.
Jajce, 5
Jambrišak, Milivoj, 116
JANL, see Yugoslav National Liberation Army.
Jauntal/Podjuna, 18, 21, 30
Jehovah's Witnesses, Carinthian, 205
Jelka, see Kuchhar, Helena.
Jelovec, 112
Jesenice, 128, 170
Jezersko, 7
Jones, William, 19, 27, 38, 51, 206f
Jovanović, Jovan, 167
Judenburg, 28
Julian Alps, 5
Jungfer generator plant, 18
Justifications, see Executions, by partisans.

Kadras, Josef, 186f, 189
Kärnten, see Carinthia.
Kärntner Partisanen, see Battalion, "German", and Österreichischer Freiheitsbund.
Kálmán, Imre, 214

Kamnik and Kamnik Aps, 120, 128f
Kampfgruppe "Avantgarde" Steiermark (Koralm partisans), 29, 34, 47, 51, 131, 180, 201f
Kampfgruppe Rösener and Kampfgruppe Werner von Seeler, see Rösener and Seeler.
Kapfenberg, 28
Karawanken mountains, 18, 38, 40
Kardelj, Edvard, 115f
Karstwehr, 14
Kasachi Stan, 74
Keightley, Sir Charles, 56, 599, 61ff, 67, 72ff, 174-77, 215, 222, 228
Kernmaier, Ferdinand, 188
Kesselring, Albert, 60, 217, 229
Kew, see Public Record Office.
Kidrič, Boris, 113, 116, 154f, 172
Klagenfurt/Celovec, 11, 25, 59ff, 62, 64, 166f, 172, 174ff, 187f, 224
Klagenfurt-Bruck an der Mur railway, 35
Kleinkrieg, see Tactics, guerrilla.
Knight, Robert, 224
Knittelfeld, 28, 166, 181
Kocbek, Edvard, 115f
Kömmelgupf/Vrh, 48
Kočevje: 76, 147f, 106, 113, 152, 157; "Pits of", 76
Konspiracija, see Security rules, partisan
Koprein Petzen/Pod Peco, 79
Kordun, 147
Koralpen (Koralm), see Kampfgruppe "Avantgarde" Steiermark.
Koroško (Koroška), see Carinthia and Meža valley (Yugoslav Carinthia).
KPÖ, see Communist Party, Austrian.
KPS, see Communist Party, Slovene.
Kraigher, Boris, 27, 87
Kranj, 221
Kranjska Gora, 60
Krasič, 153
Kraßnig, Franz, 187, 190, 229
Krener, Franc, 58, 71f, 75
Kripo, 13. See also Security services, Nazi.
Krka river, 149

Križnik, Anton, 116
Kuchar, Helena, xi, 4, 23, 44
Kuchar, Peter, xi, xiii, 51, 72, 211, 225
Kübler, Ludwig, 221f
Kühnsdorf/Sin a vas, 23
Kveder-Tomaž, Dušan, 154, 156
Lamm, 48
Lammie, J.C., 52
Landbund, 179f, 184f,188
Landesschutz regiments and *Landesschützen*, see Territorial Riflemen.
Landing grounds, see Airstrips.
Landwacht, 15
Lavanttal/Labotnica, 47
Lavamünd/Labot, 65
Lavrič, Alfred, 164f
Laze, 123, 127
Lecce, 5
Lawrence, T.E., 90, 102, 110
Lee, Sir Arthur,68
Lee-Enfield rifles, 208
Leer, Sylvester, 187, 189, 215
Legions, Slovene, 227
Legionaries: Caucasian, 73; Turkmeni and Azerbajdzhani, 106f
Legitimism, Habsburg, in Carinthia, 185, 205
Leitgeb brothers and family, 11, 23f, 204
Leoben-Donawitz partisan group, 28, 207f. See also *Österreichische Freiheitsfront*.
Leskošek-Luka, Franc, 37f, 46, 116, 170
Liaison officers, Allied, 50–4, 100
Liberated zones: defined, 212; mentioned, 5, 43f, 52, 57, 90, 110, 114, 120, 122f, 149
Liberation Front, Greek (EAM), 209
Liberation Front, Slovene (OF): defined, 6; local committees (cells), Carinthia, 10, 20, 23, 29, 61, 202; political program in Carinthia, 10, 12; 23; relationship to ÖFF, 171; role in postwar Carinthia, 70, 220; in Slovenia 133, 154. See also: Communist Party, Slovene; Slovene National Liberation Executive Committee; SNL Committee; and SNL Council.
Liberator (B-24) bomber, 44, 153, 206, 225
Lienz, 74
Lika, 206
Lindsay, Franklin A., 46, 51ff, 118–40, 209
Lines of communication, military, 55, 63, 65, 111, 120, 140, 174, 216, 220f
Lipinski, Alexander, 22
Lipje, 149
Liquidations, see Executions
Litija bridge, 51, 121f, 149, 211, 228
Littoral, see Adriatic Coastland, Istria, Primorje, Trieste and Venezia Giulia.
"Little war", see Guerrilla warfare and tactics, guerrilla.
Ljotić, Dimitrije, 221
"Livingston", 221
Ljotici, see Serbian Volunteer Corps.
Ljubljana, 58, 112, 138, 150, 155, 164, 166
Ljubljana Gap, plan for offensive through, 36, 228
Ljubljana-Kočevje road and railway, 91, 113, 148, 162
Ljubljana-Trieste railway, 51
Ljubljana-Novo Mesto road, 148, 151
Ljutomer, 164
Lobnik, 20
Lockhead, Finlay, 61, 191f
Löhr, Alexander, 55, 58f, 61, 79, 181, 186, 191, 194, 216f, 220f
Logar valley, 7, 32,
Logistics, British, 216. See also Lines of communication
Logistics: partisan, 23, 28, 49, 91, 123, 153; cutoff by British, 52, 158
Loibl/Ljubelj pass and tunnel, 7, 15, 58, 70, 130, 170, 206,
Long Range Desert Reconnaissance Group, see Peniakoff.
Looting, by partisans, 6, 62, 64, 67, 69, 218, 220. See also Discipline.
Lower Carniola, see Dolenjsko.

Low, A.R.W. "Toby", see Aldington, Lord.
Lož, 112
Lubej, France, 116
Lubno, 123
Luftwaffe, see Blaich, Major
Luka, see Leskošek.
Lukas, Julius, 187, 189
"Lute", see Pišot

Mack, W.H.B., 228
Maclean, Sir Fitzroy and Macmis, 5f, 19, 29, 51f, 68, 209, 222
Macmillan, Harold, 38, 52, 54, 62-5, 68, 74f, 126, 217, 219, 223f
Magovec, Božidar, 115
Mahnič-Boj, Franc, 34
Mannlicher rifles, 203
Mao Tse-Tung, 9
Marchland mentality, 178, 183f. See also Nationalism, German
Marenburg, 129
Maribor, 164, 198
Maribor-Klagenfurt railway, 122
Maria Elend/Pod gorje, 73
Maria Saal/Gospa Sveta, 65
Marlborough, duke of, 92
Martin-Smith, Patrick, 61, 228
Massacres: by Nazis, of Sadovnik family (at Peršman farm), 59; by Slovenes and other Yugo-Yugoslavs, of quisling prisoners (repatriates), 67, 73, 76, 2188, 225; Spitzbauer family, 48; at Turjak castle, 227. See also Atrocities, Reprisals, and War crimes.
Matthews, Major, 128, 136
Mayer, Hans, 58, 187
McCreery, Richard, 56, 62f, 68, 73, 76, 218, 225
McFarland, Lanning, 140
Medical facilities: Nazi, 210; partisan, 45, 99, 218
Meng, Colonel, 58, 187
Messerschmidt, Manfred, 226
Mesto (town command post), 120
Metlika, 96, 153
Meža valley (Koroško, Yugsoslav

Carinthia), 7, 9, 15, 18, 21ff, 25, 29, 32, 34, 40, 44, 65, 78, 165, 218
Mežica, 22, 25
MI5, xi
MI6, 29, 32, 217
Mießtal, see Meža valley
Mihailović, Draža, 53, 211, 221f, 227
Miklauzhof/Miklavčevo, xi, 22
Milač, Metod, 11
Miles, Sherman, and Miles Mission, 60, 115
Militiamen, see Landwacht, Milizia Voluntaria Anticommunista, Odbori (parttime militia), Reich Labor Service, Village Guards, Volkssturm, and Wehrmannschaft.
Milizia Voluntaria Anticommunista, 113, 226f
Milutinović, Ivan, 115
Mines, see Demolitions.
Mirko, see Ulčar.
Mislinja, 121, 129
Mivšek, Anton, 30, 34
Močevje, 147
Modras partisan group, 145
"Mongols", see Legionaries, Turkmeni-Azerbajdzhani.
Moore, Peter N.M., 19, 51ff, 224ff
Morale: Domobranstvo, 152, 155; German, 151f
Morgan, William, and Morgan Line, 63, 73, 75
Moritsch, Andreas, 207
Moscow Declaration, 12
Mountain infantry, light, 15, 39. See also Regiments, Naz..
Mozirje, 123
Mrhar, Stane, 20
Mürzzuschlag, 217
Murray, Horatius, 75, 174 215
Murau, 217
Mustang fighter, 145

Nadlesk, 152
Narodni svet, Istria and Primorje, 116, 117
National Committee, Yugoslavia, 115
National Liberation Committee and

Council, see Slovene National Liberation Front Committee and Council and Liberation Front, Slovene.
National liberation struggle, 9, 202
Nationalism, German, in Carinthia, 11, 78, 178f, 204,215. See also Marchland mentality and Naziism.
Nationalism (patriotism), Slovene, 11, 37, 203f. See also Irredentism.
Natlačen, Marko, 227.
Natmeßnig, Meinrad, 60, 186ff, 188, 190, 214, 229
Naumov, Lieutenant Colonel, 157
Naziism, Nazis and Nazi Party (NSDAP): terminological distinction, xii; occurence in Carinthia, 11f, 79, 85, 179f; in Styria, 185; revival of (also crypto-Naziism), 72, 182f, 229; role at end of war ("surrender faction"), 59f, 67, 180f. See also: Abductions; Denazification; Nationalism, German; Persecution; SA; SS; and Werwolf.
Nazi-Soviet Pact, 21
Nedić, Milan, 22
Nedici, see Serbian Volunteer Corps.
Nemčurji: defined, 10; 23, 67, 204
Newole Karl, 215
News media, partisan, 103
New Zealanders, see Division, New Zealand.
Nicholls, Jack, 228
Nicolson, Nigel, 75, 219
Niedere Tauern mountains, 181
Noedelchen, Ferdinand, 58, 60, 214
Noms de guerre, 21, 201. See also Ciril, Buxton, Cahusac, Jelka, Luka, and Mirko.
Notranjsko (Notranjska), 11, 199, 88, 91, 106, 113. See also Črnomelj and Crmošnjice.
NOV in POS, see Odredi and Slovene National Liberation Army and Yugoslav Army.
Novo Mesto, 106, 148
Novak, Karel, 227

NSDAP (Nationalsozialistische Deutsche Arbeiterpartei), see Naziism.
Number Six Special Force Staff Section, 60, 178-92, 229. See also Villiers and Viktring.

0.5, see Resistance, "Austrian"
Oath, partisan, 20
Občina, 148f
Oberkrain, see Gorenje
Obir, Little and High, peaks, 17, 39, 45
Occupation, by British Army, of Carinthia, 56-76, 182, 215, 219f. See also: Allied Military Government; and Carinthia, invasion.
Odbori, as parttime militiamen, 89f
Odbori, as Liberation Front committees (izvršni, okrozni, pokrajinski, rayonski, terenski), 92, 116. See also Liberation Front, local committees, Carinthian; and Slovene National Liberation Front Executive Committee, SNLF Committee, and SNLF Council.
Odredi (partisan detachments): defined, 6, 18, 89f; Carinthian (Koroško), 43, 45,, 57f, 65, 120, 131; Eastern (vzhodnokoroški) Carinthian, 20, 29f, 34, 40, 208f; Kamnik, 22, 120, 170; Kožje, 120; Kokra, 20ff,, 60, 65, 120; Lacko, 47, 101; Motorized, 60, 65, 71; Savinja valley, 21; Staff of the Carinthian Group of Odredi (ŠKGO), 30-3, 40, 43; Styrian Group of Odredi, 17; Upper Carniolan, 18; Western Carinthian (zahodno-or zapadnokoroški), 19f, 28, 30f, 39f, 123, 170, 208f
ÖFF, see Österreichische Freiheitsfront.
Österreichischer Freiheitsbund, 70
Österreichische Freheitsfront, 28, 35, 53, 57, 171ff,
OF, see Liberation Front.
Office of Strategic Services, U.S., 51, 130f, 136, 145, 187f, 211
Okanina, 128

Okrogar-Nestl, Anton, 40
Okrozni odbor, see Odbori (Liberation Front, committees)
OKW (Oberkommando der Wehrmacht), 57
Olševa plateau, 222
Operations, military: Beehive, 75, 219; Coldstream, 66, 75; Crossword, 56; Elsmere, 145; Grapeshot, 56, 216; and Ratweek, 228.
Orpo, 13. See also Security services, Nazi.
OSS, see Office of Strategic Services.
Osoppo Division, see Partisans, Italian.
Otočac, 5,
Otok, 152
Owen, Douglas, 128
OZNA (Odelek za zaščito naroda), see Security Services, Slovene Communist.

Padrnalchev, Colonel, 157
Paka, 152.
Pan German Party, 157
Pan Germanism, see Nationalism, German.
Pannwitz, Helmut von, 73
Panzerfäuste, 71. See also PIATS.
Parachutes and parachute drops, 110. See also Sorties.
Paris Peace Conference, 165f
Parker, L.H., 198
Particle board, see Timber.
Partisans, Austro-German, see Battalion, "German"; Gaiswinkler; Kampfgruppe Avantgarde" Steiermark; and Leo-ben-Donawitz partisan group. See also Battalions, Austrian.
Partisans, Italian, 14, 28, 38, 74, 176, 181, 223
Partisans, Slovene, see Odbori, (parttime militia), Odredi, and Slovene National Liberation Army.
Partizanke (female partisans), 4, 30f
Pasterk, Jurij, 20, 22
Pasterk-Lenart, Franc, 22
Paternion, 12

Patriotism, Slovene, see Irredentism, Slovene, and Nationalism, Slovene.
Pavelić, Ante, 56
Pawlikowsky, Bishop, 183
Peck, Sydney Capel, 167
Peniakoff, Vladimir, 192, 217
Perjés, Géza, 214
Persecution, Nazi, of Carinthian Slovenes, 8f. See also Aussiedlung.
Peršman farm, see Massacres.
Perunčić, Mile, 116
Petek, Franc, 31, 220
Petelinegg/Petelinjek heights, 167
Peter-Pirkham, Albert, 167
Petite guerre, see Guerrilla warfare and Tactics, guerrilla.
Petzen/Peca, Mount, 21
Philips-Valvo mica mine, 47f
Phillips, John, 211f
Phleps, Artur, 221. See also Regiments, Nazi.
PIATS, 125. See also Panzerfäuste.
Picadilly "Club" and Picadilly "Hope", see Airstrips.
Piesch, Hans, 61, 187
Pine Forest Conference, 23
Pirjevec-Ahac, Dušan, 20, 159, 220
Pišot, Václav, 228
Piskernik family, 24
Pitt, William, 92
Plešnik, 32
Plöcken pass, 74, 215, 228
Platoon, Carinthian (SNLA), 18
Plebiscite, Carinthian, 38, 84, 165-9
Plsarovina, 153
Po valley, 36
Počula Saddle, skirmish at, 39f
Pölling, 47
Pohorje hills, 22, 139, 123
Poland and Poles, 27, 36, 213. See also Anders, Darewski, Lip nski, POWs, and ULTRA.
Polčanje, 121
Polanšek, Valentin, 24
Polić, Zoran, 116
Police Regiments, SS: defined, 14f, 205; tactics, 31; Thirteenth, 14f, 30, 44, 47, 57f, 151; Fourteenth, 151;

Seventeenth, 71, 194; Nineteenth 44, 71, 194; Twenty Fifth, 71; unspecified, 27, 34, 46, 50, 59, 139, 223
Ponikve, 148
Popski, Major, see Peniakoff.
POWs: British and American, 78, 92, 131f; French, 78; Polish and Ukrainian, 20, 22, 78; Soviet, 47f; Yugoslav, 78; unspecified, 25, 206. See also "Austrians" as Allied agents and Surrendered enemy personnel.
Predil/Predel pass, 60, 224
Prevalje, 198
Pribicević, Rade, 116
Primeval anxiety, 24
Primorje (Primorsko, Primorska), 5, 11, 19, 56, 89, 91, 114, 221 See also Adriatic Coastland, Trieste, and Venezia-Giulia.
Primožič-Marko, Franc, 19f, 30f, 33, 220
Prince Eugene Division, see Waffen SS.
Propaganda, political: neo-Nazi, 24; SNLA, 43. See also: Agitprop; Communist Party, Slovene, sociopolitical program; and Liberation Front, political program in Carinthia.
Propustnica, 33
Protestantism in Carinthia and Styria, 183, 229. See also nation-alism, German.
Provincia di Lubiana, 14, 19, 27f, 137
Provisional Provincial Government, Carinthian, 60ff, 181, 186-9, 229
PRO, see Public Record Office.
Prušnik-Gašper, Karl, 4, 9, 20ff, 23, 29f, 34, 39ff, 43ff, 46, 48, 70f, 79, 220
Ptuj, 145
Public Record Office, xiii, 4, 6, 61, 227
Pula, 14, 63

Quislings, defined, xii, 11; 67f, 70, 75. See also Chetniks, Cossacks, *Domobranstvo*, Legions, Legionaries, *Milizia Voluntaria Anticommunista*, Serbian Volunteer Corps, *Schutzkorps Serbien*, Repatriation, Russian Liberation Army, Ustashi, Wariag (under Regiments, Nazi), White Guards, and Village Guards.

RAD, see Reich Labor Service.
Radios: 46f, 144 See also BBC BBC, Codes, Command and control, Couriers, and ULTRA.
Radovljica, 221
Railway lines, 118, 136; interdiction of, 25, 39, 52, 109, 138, 149f. See also Demolitions, Jones, Lines of communication, Litija, and ULTRA.
Rainer, Friedrich, 14, 18, 39f, 59f, 214, 180f, 186ff, 227, 229
Ramsey, Alex, 228
"Rankin" situations, 144, 209, 228
Rapine, see Looting.
Rapallo, Treaty of, 84
Rausch, Josef, 3f, 4
Rayonski odbor, see *Odbori* (Liberation Front, committees).
Realpolitik, 53, 75
Rečica, 135
Reconnaissance battalions, Second and Seventh, British, 59
Recruitment, partisan, 43, 92. See also Deserters, Draft, POWS, and Slave-workers.
Regiments, Nazi: Brandenburg Special Use, 129; Thirteenth SS "Artur Phleps", 71; 139th Light Mountain Infantry, 58; Wariag, 71. See also Police Regiments.
Reich Labor Service (*Reichsarbeitsdienst*), 15, 21,
Reichsgauen, Kärnten and *Steiermark*, see "Greater Carinthia" and "Greater Styria".
Refugees, civilian, Slovene,, 58, 71ff. See also Camp followers.
Renner, Karl, and Renner government, 165, 181f, 187
Renton, Edward, 61, 217
Repatriation, by British, of quislings, see Agreement, Conspiracy,

"Cossacks", and Massacres.
Replacement Army, 13, 15, 25, 50, 57f
Reprisals, Nazi, 108
Resistance, "Austrian": analyzed, 12, 201f; in Carinthia, 28, 35f, 49f, 59, 132, 142-5, 171f, 186ff, 215; in Styria, 205; in Vienna and Innsbruck ("O.5"), 205. See also: Battalion, "German"; Battalions, Austrian; Executions by Nazis; Gaiswinkler; Partisans, Austro-German; and *Österreichische Freiheitsfront*.
Reus, 141
Revolution, social, as partisan goal, see Communist Party, Slovene, sociopolitical program.
Revolutionary Socialist Party, see Wedenig.
Ribar, Ivan, 84, 115
Ribičič-Ciril, Mitja, 30f, 33f
Ribnica,
Ribnikar, Vladislav, 115
Ritscher, Franz, 189
ROA and ROF, see Russian Liberation Army and Front.
Roads, see Highways.
Robesch/Robež, 17f, 20, 22
Rösener, Erwin, 13f, 37, 40, 58, 71f, 187, 193f, 205, 222, 224, 227
Rogozhin, Anatoli, 71, 73
Rogla, 128
Rosenbach/Podrožica tunnel, 46, 73, 191f
Rosental/Rož, 18, 39, 46, 60, 206
Royal Air Force, 33, 37, 53, 135, 210. See also Airstrips, Balkan Air Force, and Sorties.
Rožič, Valentin, 169
Royal Fusiliers, 4
Rozman-Stane, Franc, 22, 207, 226
Rožman, Gregorij, 14, 151, 227
Rucigay, John, 225
Rupnik, Leon, 14, 27, 58, 214, 227. See also *Domobranstvo*, Slovene.
Rus, Josip, 116
Ruskii Korpus, see *Schutzkorps Serbien*.
Russian Liberation Army and Front. See also Vlassov, Andrei.

Ruthenes, see Waffen SS.
SA (*Sturmabteilungen*), 15
SACMED, 68. See also Alexander.
Sadovnik family, see Massacres.
"Safe houses", 28, 192
Saint-Germain-en-Laye, Treaty of, 169
Sankt Andrä, 476
Sankt Leonhart, 47f
Sankt Margareten im Rosental/ Šmarjetu v Rožu, 58
Sankt Oswald, 50
Sankt Stefan im Gailtal/Šent Štefan na Zili, 201
Santner, Julius, 189, 215
Sarakoumov, Major, 157
Sargent, Sir Orme, 52,63
SAS, 217
Sattnitz/Gure hills, 20, 30, 34, 39, 65
Saualpe/Svinja, 15, 25, 30, 35, 132, 180; campaign on, 43, 56-50, 210
Sava river, 7, 45,
Savina river and valley, 121, 123, 139, 149
Saxe, Maurice, Maréchal de, 110
Scharf-Wallner, Erwin, 35
Schatzmayer, Friedrich, 187, 189, 215
Schmeisser, 33, 125
Schmiedhuber, August, 221
Scholz, Major, 199
Schraeder, Lieutenant, 137
Schupo, 13. See also also Security services, Nazi.
Schuschnigg, Kurt Edler von, 11, 189
Schutzkorps Serbien , 71
Schwabegg/Švabek, 46
SD (*Sicherheitsdienst*), 13, 59. See also Security services, Nazi.
Secret agents, see Subversion.
Security, British governmental mania for, xif
Security guards, factory, 15
Security rules, partisan, 32, 102
Security services: Nazi, 13ff; Slovene Communist, 23, 67, 101, 154, 157
Seeberg/Jezersko pass, 8, 20, 222
Seeler, Werner von and *Korpsgruppe von Seeler*, 70ff, 194.

Self-Defense Struggle, Carinthian, 23, 164f, 201, 219
Semič, 96, 148
Serbia and Serbs, as quislings, 69. See also Chetniks, Ljotić, Nedić, Mihailović, and Serbian Volunteer Corps.
Serbian Volunteer Corps, 71f, 191, 221. See also Ljotic
Sernec, Dušan, 116
Šentvid, 129
Ševnice, 129
Šercer, Ljubo, 112
Šimončič-Gašper, Vinko, 30
ŠKGO, see *Odredi*.
Shkuro, Andrei, 74
Šoštanj, 128
Shock brigade, 18
Šubašić (Royal Yugoslav) government, Shy, John, 227
ŠKGO, see *Odredi*.
Štajersko, see Styria, Lower or Slovene.
Štampetov viaduct, 51
Švabi, 20
Siena, 217
Simič, Stane, 93
Sipo, 13. See also Security services, Nazi.
Sippenhaftung, 25
SIS, see M16.
Sixth Special Force, see Number Six Special Force
Slaveworkers, 2, 5, 47f, 78, 132, 206. See also POWs and Todt.
Slovene Alliance, 227
Slovene Catholic Party, Carinthian, 185. See also Clergy.
Slovene Crimes Commission, 155
Slovene headquarters, see Črmošnjice.
Slovene National Committee, 58
Slovene National Liberation Army (SNLA); defined, 3, 6, 56; differential attitudes toward its allies, 27, 33, 36ff; goals in last stage of war, 52f; relationship to Communist Party, 161; training, 93; value as wartime ally, 77f. See also: Carinthia, invasion; Carinthian Battalion; Carinthian Company; Carinthian Platoon; Command and control; Battalions; Brigades; *Četa*; Corps (Seventh and Ninth); Division (Fourteenth); Fourth Operational Zone; *Odbori* (parttime militia); *Odredi*;, Yugoslav National Liberation Army, and Yugoslav Army.
Slovene National Liberation Front Executive Committee, SNLF Committee (SNOO), and SNLF Council or Parliament (SNOS), 23, 154
Slovene Partisan Detachments (POS), see *Odredi*.
Slovene People's Party, 227
Slovenes, Carinthian: in ethnic sense, 9, 23, 77, 217; in linguistic sense, 9, 77, 169, 173, 217; socioeconomic conditions, 9, 22, 77. See also *Nemčurji*, *Tschusch'n*, and *Windische*.
Slovenes, émigré, xii
"Smith", Captain, 32
Smodlaka, Josip, 115
SNLA, see Slovene National Liberation Army.
SNOO (*Slovenski narodnoosvobodilni odbor*), see Slovene National Liberation Front Committee.
SNOS (*Slovenski narodnoosvobodilni svet*), see Slovene National Liberation Front Council.
Social Democratic Party, see Austrian Socialist Party.
Solčava, 7, 21, 44, 123, 170
Sorties, aerial, 28f, 33, 40, 44f, 49f, 126ff, 137, 139, 141f, 153, 210. See also Dakota, Halifax, Liberator and Parachutes.
South Tyrolese, 9, 165
Soviet Union, see U.S.S.R.,
SPAM, 22
Spanish Civil War, veterans of, 9, 22, 85, 226
Special Force One, 139, 228
Special Operations Executive: Cairo

branch, 19, 92; established as subversion agency, 6; mentioned, 6, 12. See also Clowder Mission and Sixth Special Force Staff Section.
Special Operations Mediterranean, 32
Spies and informers, 13. See also Gestapo.
Spittal, 66, 193f
Spitzbauer, see Massacres,
Split, 153
SS, unspecified, 22, 181, 187. See also Administrative sectors, Death's Head, General SS, Himmler, Heydrich, *Höhere SS und Polizei Führer*, *Karstwehr*, Security services (Nazi), Police Regiments, and Waffen SS.
Stafford, David, 38
Staghound armored cars, 59
Stalin, Joseph, 68f, 75, 224
Stari Log, 149
Stawell, E., 228
Steiermark, see Styria, Austro-German and "Greater Styria".
Sten guns, 33, 47, 148, 208. See also Weaponry.
Sterntal, 198
Stettinius, Edward R., 212
Stevenson, Ralph C. Skrine, 68f, 230
Stična, 137
Stossier, Josef, 58, 60f, 186, 189, 220, 229
Strategy: British, grand, 79, 110; Slovene-Yugoslav, military, 56, 212
Strengths, troop, 160, 213
Strle, Franci, 3f
Styria: Austro-German, 7, 28, 178-85, 201f; Lower or Slovene, 7, 11, 18f, 22f, 25f, 43f, 51, 65, 89, 113, 118-40 (esp.128) 213. See also "Greater Styria" and *Reichsgauen: Steiermark*.
Subversion: Clowder Mission plan to incite, 28; Slovene-Yugoslav scheme to destabilize Carinthia after war, 195f.
Suha Krajina, 11
Surrender faction, see, Naziism.
Surrender mission, Carinthian German, 181, 187f

Surrendered enemy personnel, See also Quislings.
Supreme Allied Commander, Mediterranean, see Alexander.

Tactics, military: guerrilla, 22, 29 226; regular army, 72. See also Hunt-and-kill, Fleckner, Police Regiments, and Spanish Civil War.
Tagliamento river, 150
Tanks, Honey or Stuart, 71, 214
Tarnovo plateau, 149
Tarvisio, 59, 60, 180, 188. See also Canale valley.
Tauschitz, Stefan, 60, 187ff
Terenski odbor, see *Odbori Liberation Front*, committees).
Territorial claims, Yugoslavia, post-1945, 61, 77f. See also Irredentism.
Territorial Riflemen, 15, 57, 128f
Thornley, Roger, 209
Thurn-Valssassina-Como-Vercelli, counts of, 9f, 204
TIGR, 8
Timber industry, Carinthian, 23, 204. See also Leitgeb and Particle board.
Tito, Josip Broz, 5, 33, 37f, 55f, 57, 63f, 68f, 73, 75, 84, 109, 115, 132, 171, 173, 175ff, 182, 211f, 217, 222, 224, 228
Todorović, Branislav, 191f
Todt, Organization, Nazi, slave-labor, 121
Tolbukhin, Fyodor Ivanovich, 219
Tolmezzo, 36
Tolstoy, Nikolai, 215, 223f
Topusko, 153
Trade unions, Carinthian, 184
Trebnje, 140
Trebovje, 129
Tremerje, 121, 122
Trieste: as object of contention with Yugoslvia, 56f, 59, 63, 69, 73, 150, 158, 162, 229; mentioned, 14, 96ff, 22. See also Venez a Giulia.
"Trigger", 49. See also Saualpen.
Tryon-Wilson, Teddy, 217
Truman, Harry S., 64f

Tschofenig, Albin, 189
Tschurtschenthaler, Hans 187, 190
Tschusch'n, 10
Turjak, see Massacres.
Udine, 175
Ukrainians, see POWs and Waffen SS.
Ulčar-Mirko, Jože, 20, 46ff, 50, 145
ULTRA (ultrasecret "Enigma" decrypt system), 216f
Uniforms, partisan, 25, 94, 124
Union of Soviet Socialist Republics: seeks to employ partisan group in own interest, 201f; Slovene attitude toward, 85f, 134ff, 156; mentioned, 54. See also "Cossacks", *Österreichische Freiheitsfront*, POWs, and Stalin.
United States of America, policy over Trieste conflict, see Truman.
United States Army, see Operation Coldstream.
United States Army Air Force (USAAF), 36. See also Airmen, Allied, and Rucigay, John.
Unterdrauburg, see Dravograd.
Unterluggauer, Johann, 186, 189
Untersteiermark, see Styria, Lower.
Upper Carniola, see Gorenjsko.
Urbas, Hugo, 203f. See also Hunting.
Ustashi, 55, 64f, 68f, 71, 152, 205, 219

Vaterländische Front, 188. See also Dollfuß and Clerical fascism.
Venezia Giulia, 54, 62ff, 166, 170, 195. See also Adriatic Coastland, Primorje, and Trieste.
Venice, 191
Verdnik-Tomaž, Matija, 18, 30
Vermanšaft, see *Wehrmannschaft*.
Vesnić, Milenko, 166
Victims of Zell, 22f
Victory, Allied, partisan contribution to, 77f
Vidmar, Josip, 27, 113, 155
Vienna, 36, 58
Vilfan, Jože, 116
Viettinghof, Heinrich von, 180, 216f
Viktring/Vetrinje: as quisling encampment, 72; as Villiers' headquarters, 191
Villach/Beljak, 8, 54, 150, 174ff
Village Guards, 226
Villiers, Charles: role in Clowder Mission, 12, 19, 30–6, 38, 50, 205, 209, 224, 229; possible role in return of quislings, 61, 230
Violence, socially legitimized, 78f
Vipava (Vipaccio) and Vipava valley, 149
Vivoda family, 31
Vis, 171, 212
Vivodina, 147
Vlassov, Andrei, 221
Vlassovci, see Russian Liberation Army.
Völkermarkt/Velikovec, 30, 65f, 165, 198
Voivodina, 77
Vojna, 152f
Volkssturm, 15, 50, 71
VDV (*Vojska državne varnosti*), see Security services, Slovene.
VOS (*Varnostno obveščevalna služba*), see Security services, Slovene.
Vuchinich, Alexander and Wayne, 211
Vuchinich, George, 137, 211
Vujazinović, Todor, 116
Vzhodnokoroški odred, see *Odredi*, Eastern Carinthian.

Wadl, Wilhelm, 215f
Waffen SS: Cadet School, Klagenfurt, 15; Fifteenth Cavalry Corps, 73; "Galicia" (Ukrainian or Ruthenian) Division, 57, 213; "Handžar" Division, 223; "Prince Eugene", 14, 71, 220f; Sixteenth Panzer Grenadier Division, 72; unspecified, 223. See also Regiments, Nazi.
Waldheim, Kurt, 79, 226
Walzl, August, 3f, 61, 215f
War crimes and war criminals, 75, 159-63, 221, 224f, 227. See also Fleckner, Globocnik, Kübler, Löhr, Rainer, Rösener, Schmiedhuber, and Waldheim,

Index

Watts, Nigel, 224
Wars, types of, 78
Weaponry, 125f. See also Bren, Lee-Enfield, Mannlicher, *Panzerfäuste*, PIATS, *Schmeisser*, and Sten.
Weather conditions, adverse winter, 20f, 38f, 50, 127, 141, 143, 145, 157, 228. See also Sorties.
Wedenig, Ferdinand, 35, 61, 189, 205, 220
Wehrmacht, see Army Groups, Nazi; Divisions, Nazi; Corps, Nazi; Defense Circuits; Draft, Mountain Infantry; Regiments, Nazi; Replacement Army; Territorial Riflemen; and Waffen SS.
Wehrmänner, Wehrmannschaft, 15, 92, 108, 123, 128, 227 See also Militiamen.
Weimar republic, 14
Weir, C.E., 174, 220
Welles, Edward, 122, 136, 139, 228
Werwolf organization, 181
Wheeler, Mark, 205
White's Club, 49
White Guard, defined, xii, 226f; 11, 52, 69, 137ff, 150ff, 155. See also: Atrocities; Battalions, mobile; *Domobranstvo*, Slovene; Chetniks, Slovene; Legions, Slovene; *Milizia Voluntaria Anticommunista*, and Village Guards.
"White Russians", 73f. See also "Cossacks".
"Wild West", defined, 18; 25, 30f, 33, 45
Wilkinson, Maria Theresa, née Villiers, 205
Wilkinson, Sir Peter, 4ff, 12, 19, 27ff, 32ff, 44, 49f, 51, 59f, 67, 72, 79, 202, 205, 207ff, 216f, 224
Wilson, Woodrow, 165f, 168
Winchester College, 224. See also Aldington, Lord.
Windische, see Sloveres, Carinthian, linguistic; and *Tschusch'n*
Wolff, Karl, 217
Women, as partisans, see *Partizanke*.
Wounded, care of, see Medical.
Wurzen/Koren pass, 50
Wylie, Lieutenant, 152

Yalta Repatriation Agreement, 73, 217
Yugoslav Army, 55ff, 61, 63, 71, 219. See also Yugoslav National Liberation Army.
Yugoslav National Council, 164
Yugoslav National Liberation Army, 6

Zadar (Zara), 14, 147, 153
Zagorje, 129, 120
Zagreb-Karlovac road, 91, 153
Zagreb-Zidani most railway, 122f, 127
Zahodno- or *Zapadnokoroški odred*, see *Odredi*, Western Carinthian.
Zavoronkov, Major, 157
Zell/Sele, 8, 21, 24, 39, 58; "Republic of", 45. See also Victims of Zell.
Zeltweg, 181, 217
Žaučer-Matjaž, Pavle. 21, 79
Žečević, Vlada, 115
Žnider Hanzi, see Županc-Johan.
Žumberak, 153
Županc family, 22
Županc-Johan, Ivan, 20, 23
Žužemberk, 148f
Zidani Most and Zidani Most railway, 121ff, 126, 129, 153
Zollfeld/Gosposvetsko polje, 65
Zolla, see Col.
Zujović, Sreten, 116

1. THE DISMEMBERMENT OF YUGOSLAVIA, 1941

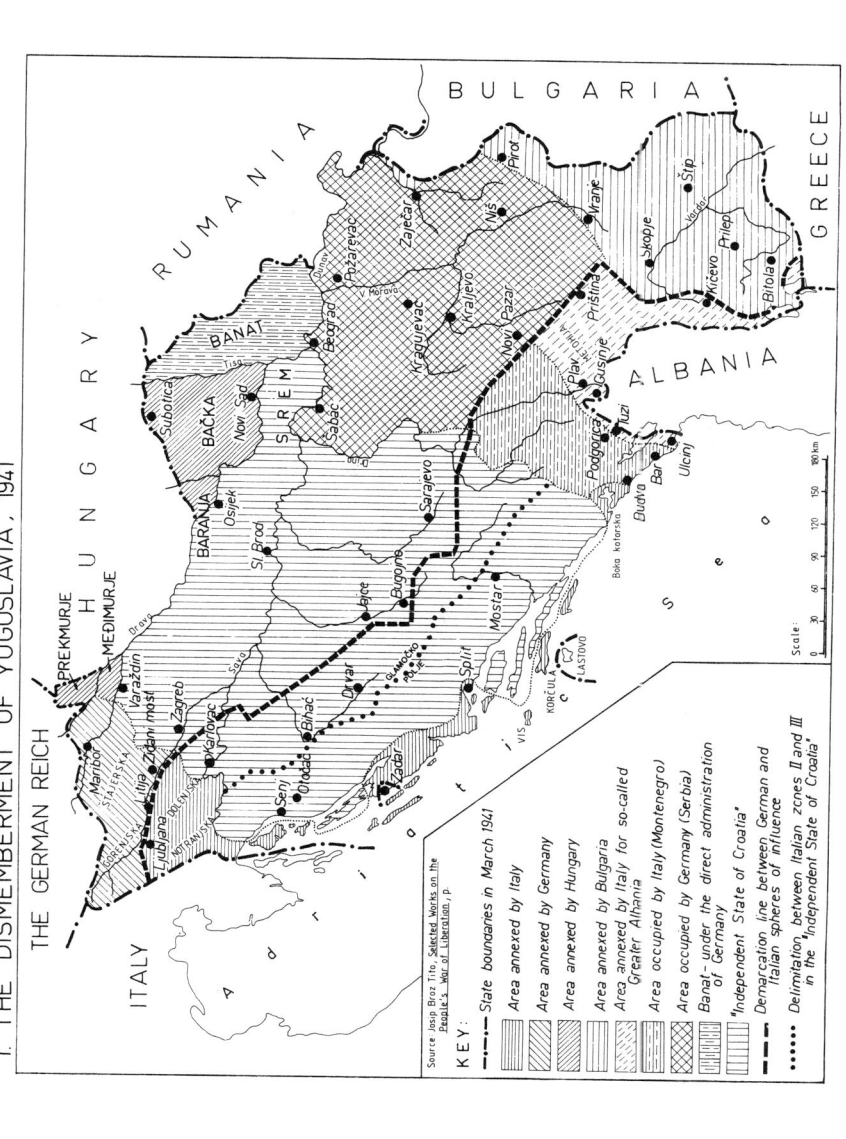

2. THE PARTITION OF SLOVENIA, 1941

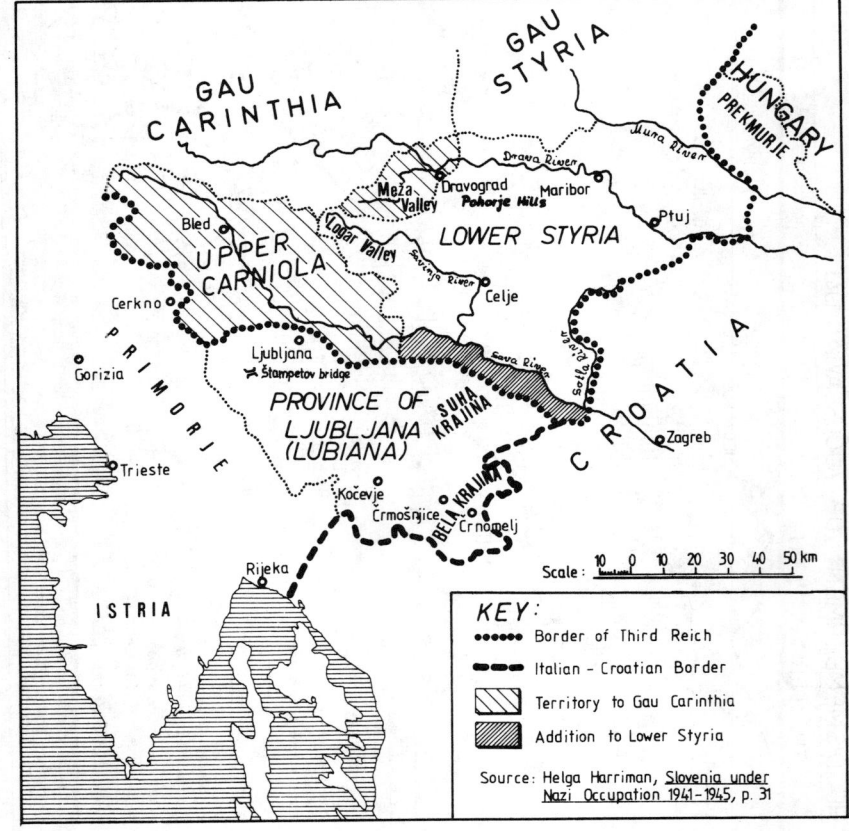

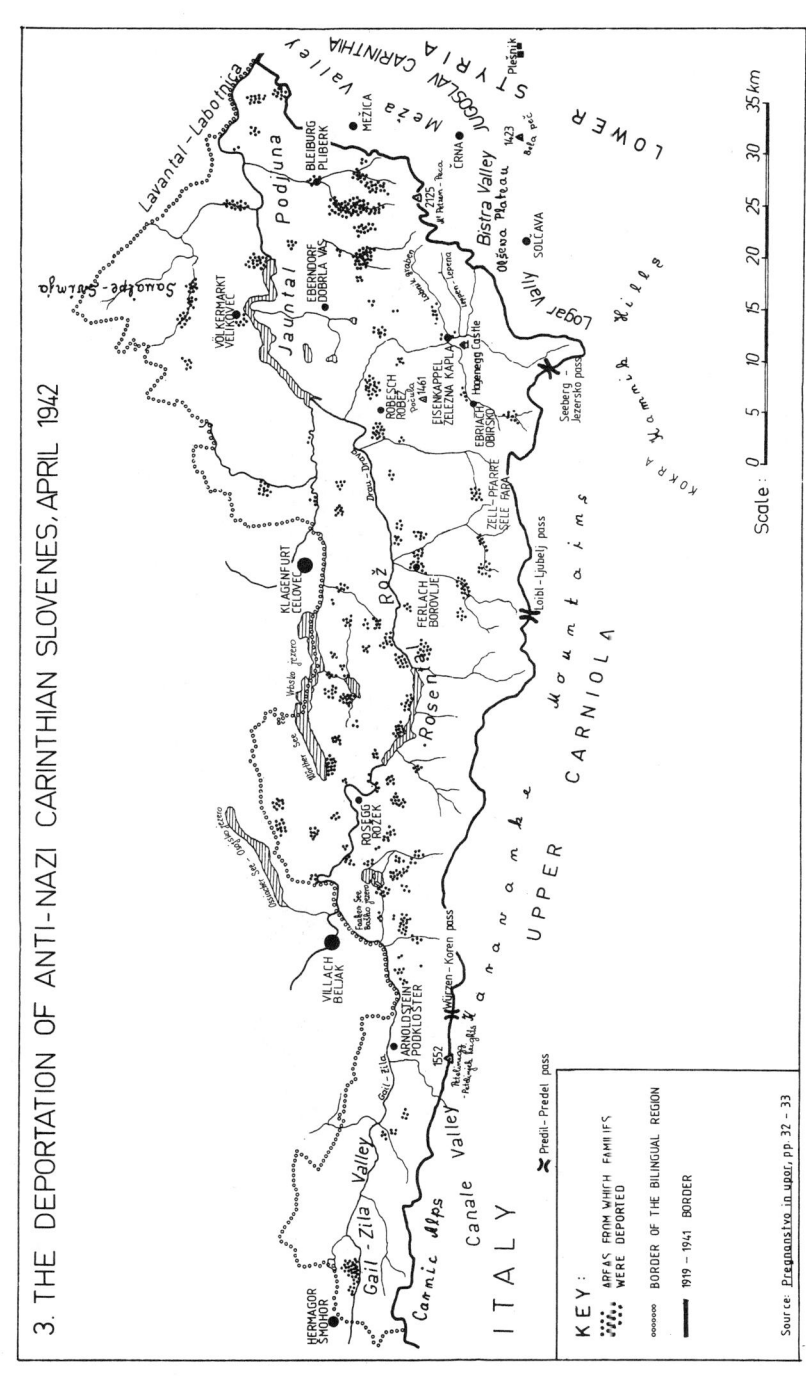

3. THE DEPORTATION OF ANTI-NAZI CARINTHIAN SLOVENES, APRIL 1942

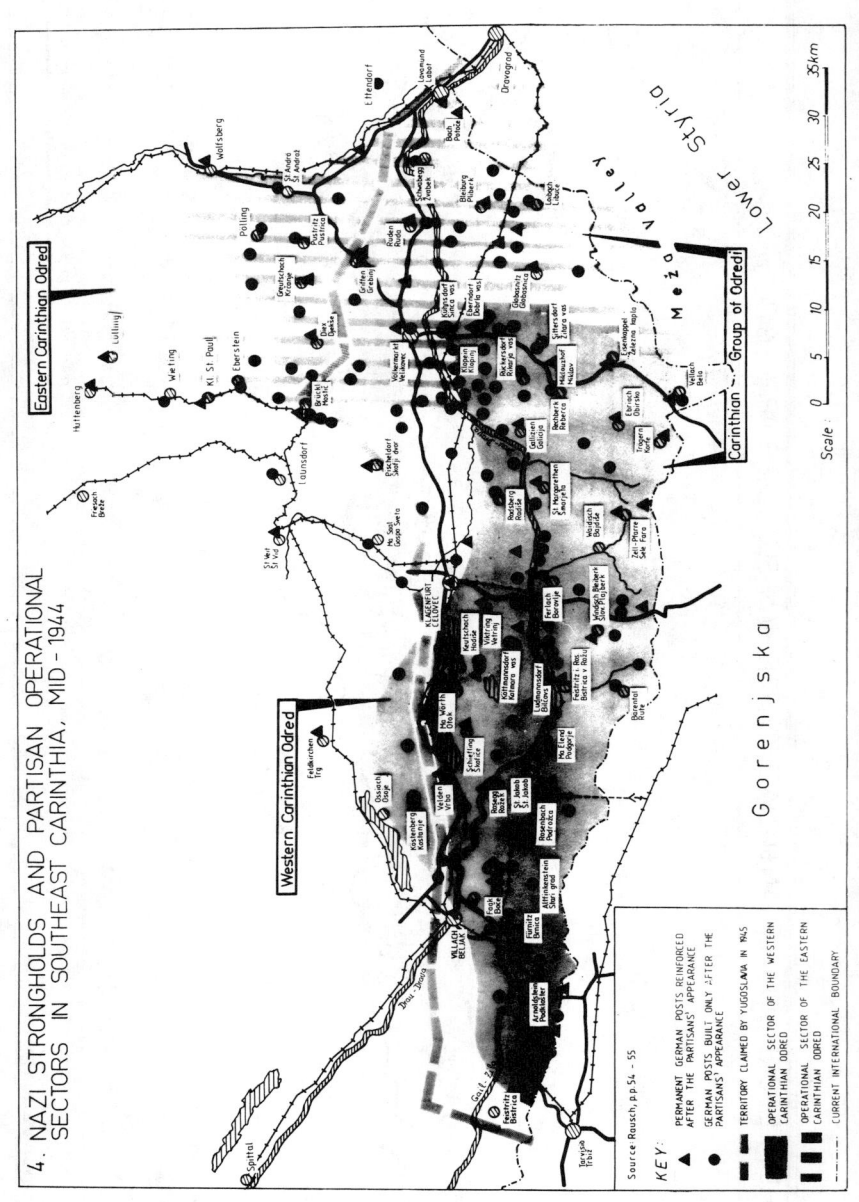

5. SABOTAGE ACTIVITY OF THE EASTERN CARINTHIAN ODRED

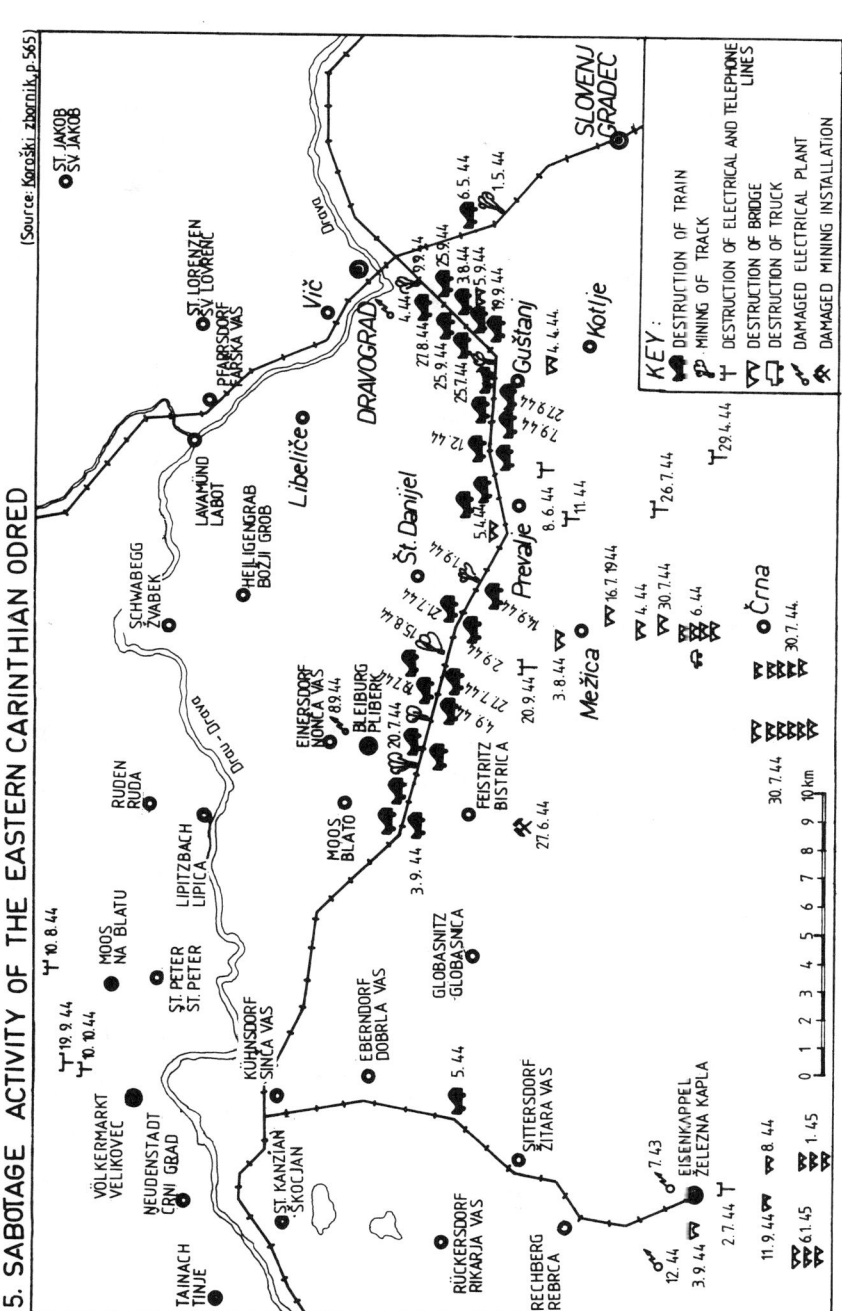

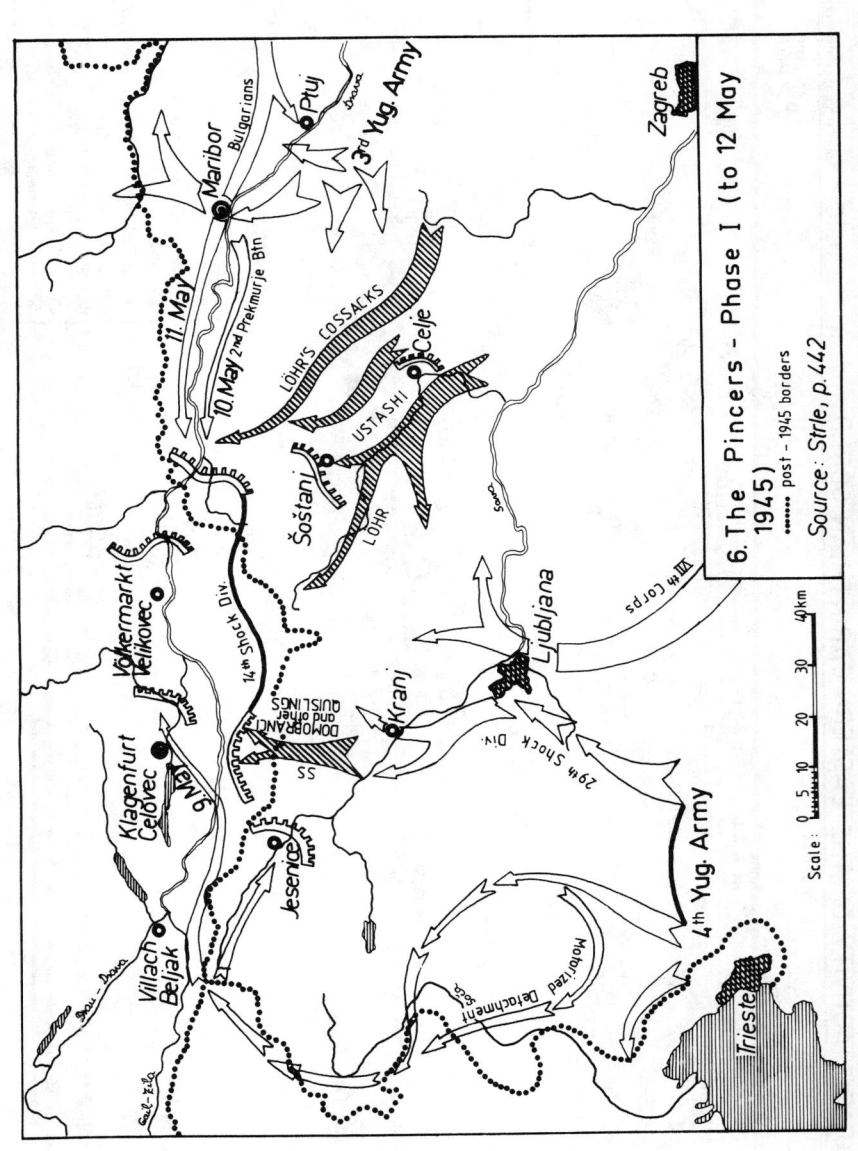

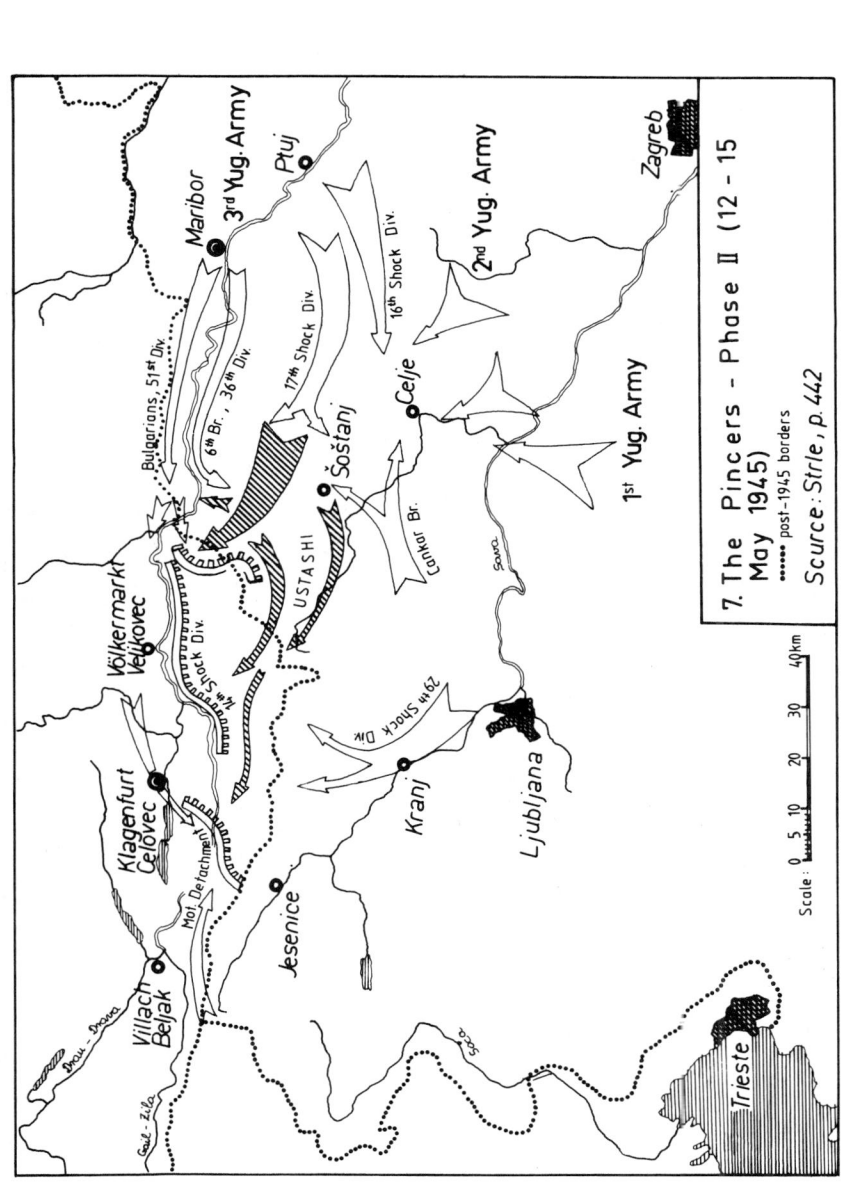

7. The Pincers - Phase II (12 - 15 May 1945)

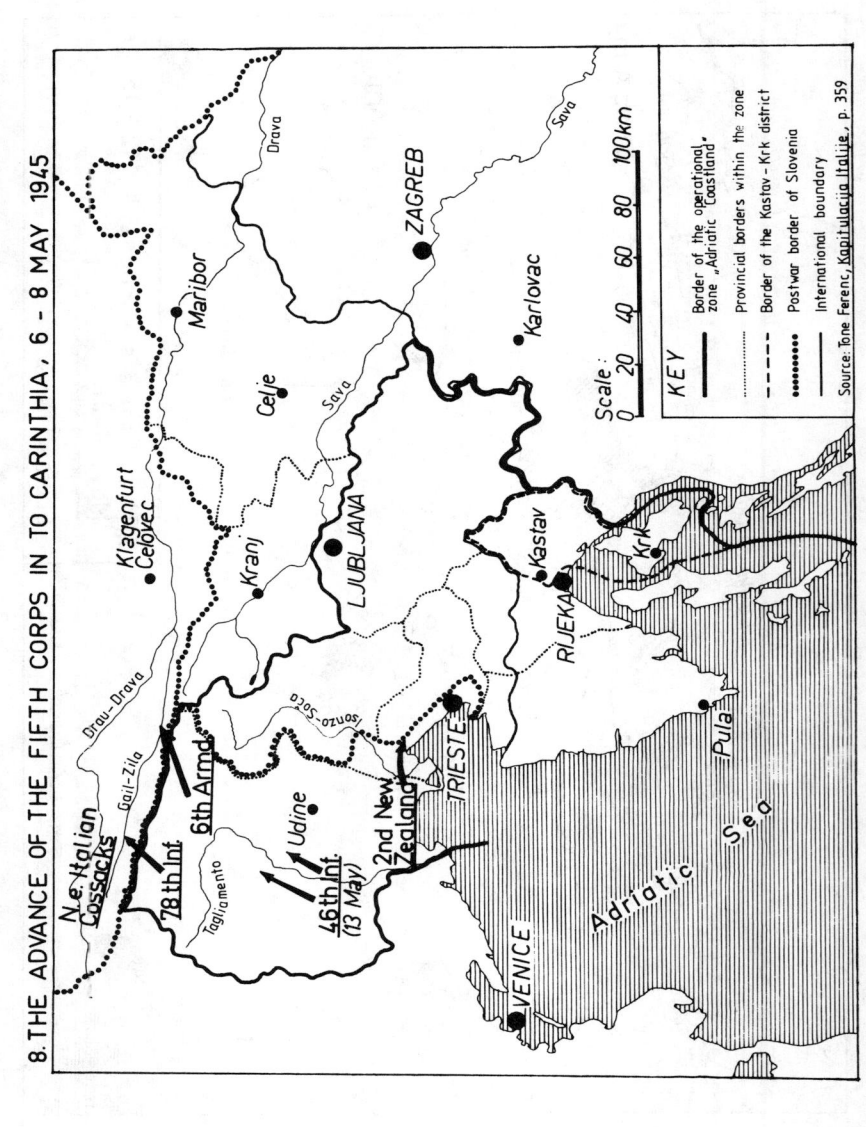

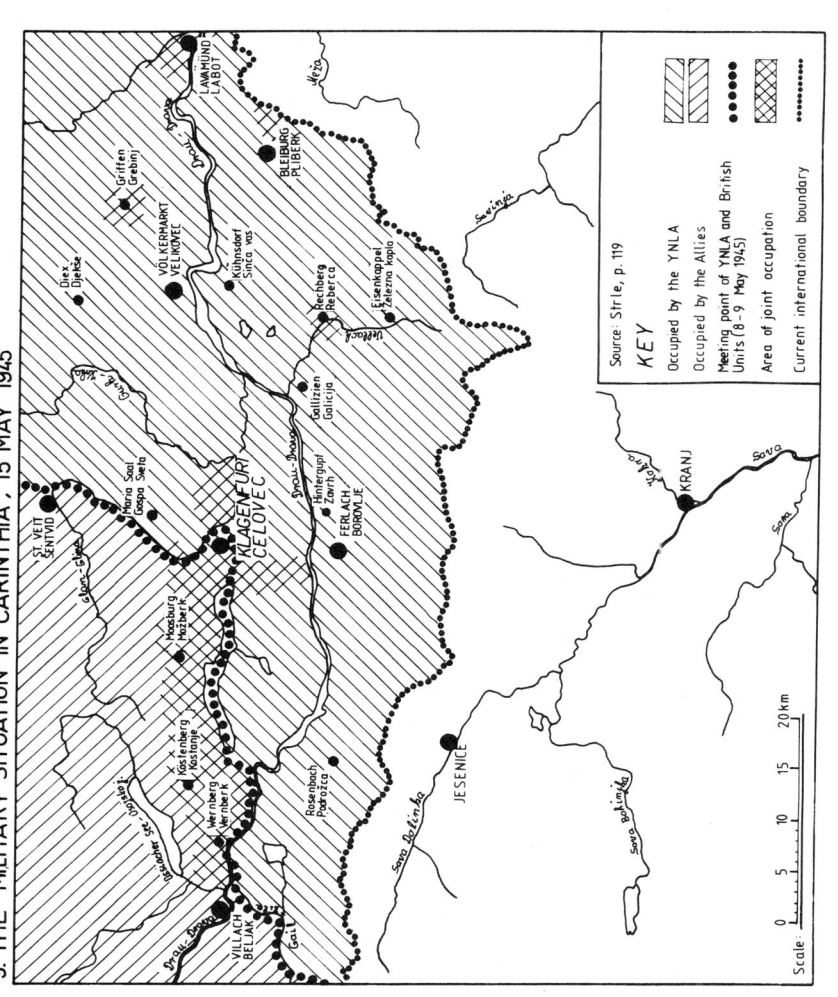

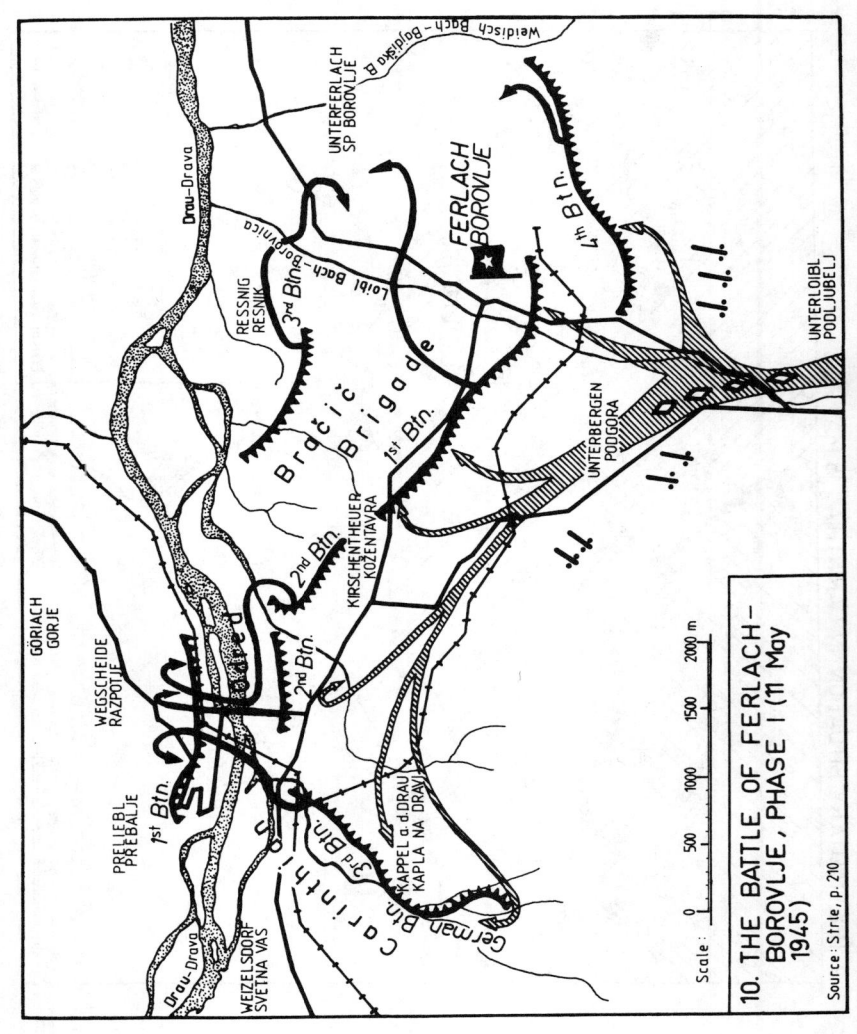

10. THE BATTLE OF FERLACH–BOROVLJE, PHASE I (11 May 1945)

Source: Strle, p. 210

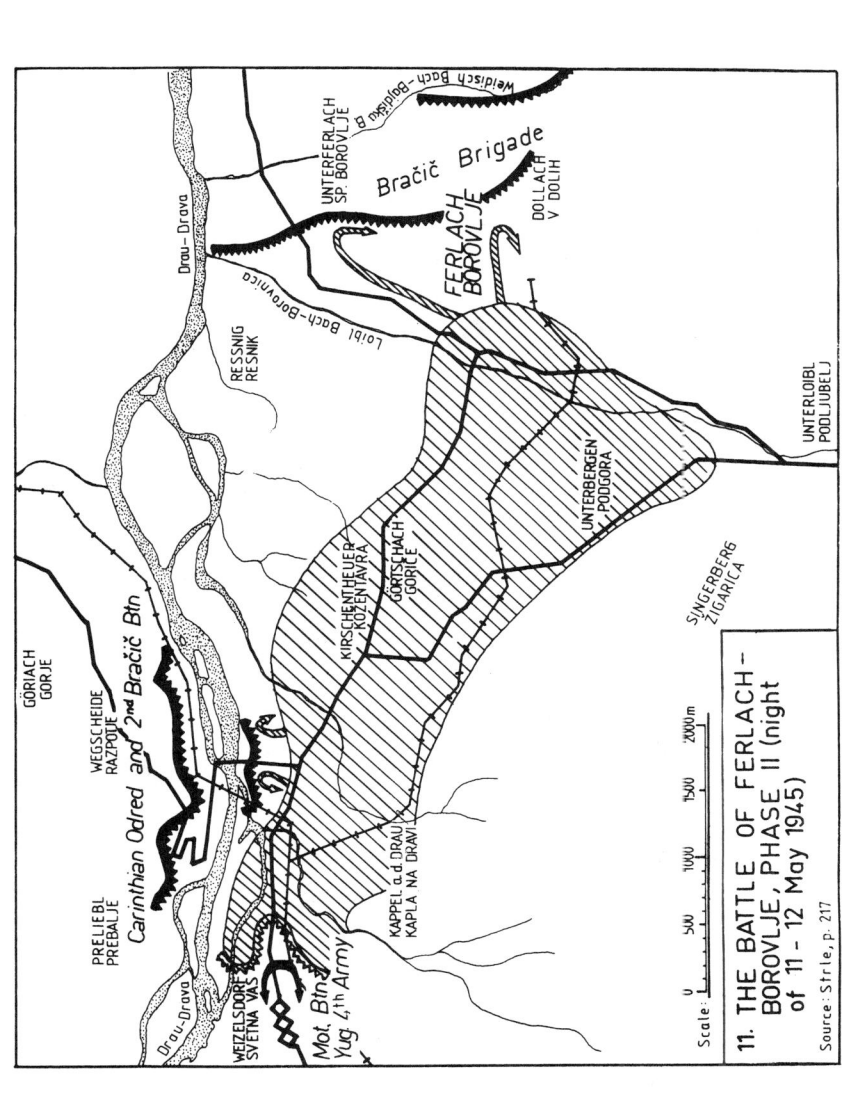

11. THE BATTLE OF FERLACH–BOROVLJE, PHASE II (night of 11–12 May 1945)

Source: Strle, p. 217

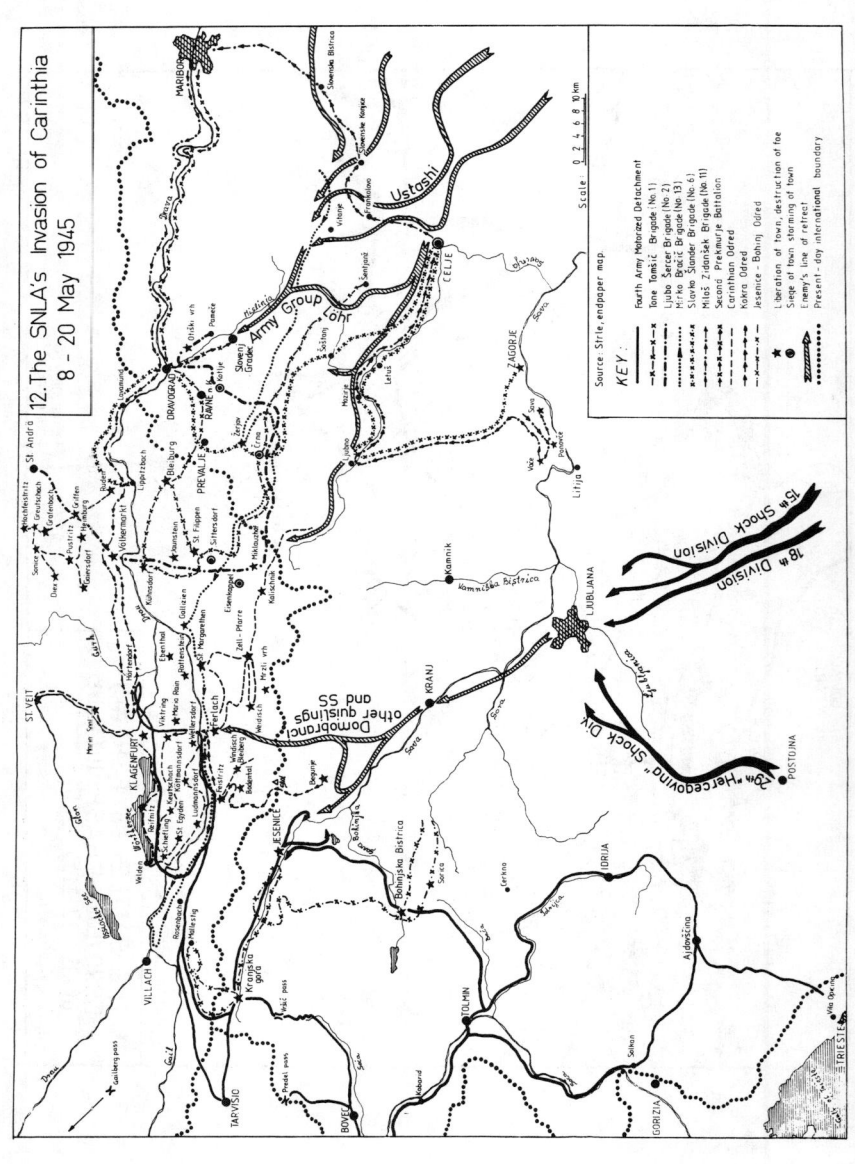

Karel Prušnik-Gašper (1944)

Franc Pasterk-Lenart (as a Wehrmacht soldier)

Reich Labor Service Militiamen (in the Miklauzhof-Miklavčevo area; note bunker on ridge)

"Jelka" With Her Own Four and Two Foster Children (April 1944; Jelka front center; Peter rear center; all three boys joined the partisans)

The Staff of the Fifth Courier Relay Sector (October 1944; Peter rear center holding Italian carbine; weapon on right is Lee-Enfield)

Charles Villiers and Peter Wilkinson (October 1944; on a training exercise in Wales 1944)

Sgt-Major Hughes and Hesketh-Prichard Hitch a Ride (on the way to the SNLA after visting Tito)

Hesketh-Prichard Gets a Partisan Haircut (note sentry's Sten gun)

Partisans During Skirmish with SS Police (January 1944; near Cerkno; Hesketh-Prichard carrying rucksack and Captain Davies wearing beret)

Wilkinson's Party Crosses the Reich Border (7 February 1944; near Škofja Loka)

Anton Okrogar-Nestl (in captured German garb and cradling a *Schmeisser*)

Hesketh-Prichard and the Saualpe Partisans (Hesketh-Prichard on far right wearing fleece-lined, leather flying jacket)